Natsuki Hokami

While I was drawing, I remembered
something: I really like those jelly
drinks that you have to shake. There
was a vending machine at the high
school I went that sold a mango gelatin
in the summer, and I bought a ton of
them. I suppose those gelatins are
probably gone by now.

Natsuki Hokami's first serialized manga,
Hell Warden Higuma, was published in
Weekly Shonen Jump in 2018.

Demon Slayer: Kimetsu Academy

VOLUME 2
SHONEN JUMP EDITION

STORY AND ART BY
NATSUKI HOKAMI

Translation / John Werry
Touch-Up Art & Lettering / E.K. Weaver
Design / Yukiko Whitley
Editor / Andrew Kuhre Bartosh

KIMETSU GAKUEN! © 2021 by Koyoharu Gotouge, Natsuki Hokami
All rights reserved.
First published in Japan in 2021 by SHUEISHA Inc., Tokyo.
English translation rights arranged by SHUEISHA Inc.

The stories, characters, and incidents mentioned in
this publication are entirely fictional.

Printed in the U.S.A.

Published by VIZ Media, LLC
P.O. Box 77010
San Francisco, CA 94107

10 9 8 7 6 5 4 3 2 1
First printing, April 2024

viz.com

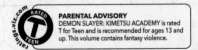

PARENTAL ADVISORY
DEMON SLAYER: KIMETSU ACADEMY is rated
T for Teen and is recommended for ages 13 and
up. This volume contains fantasy violence.

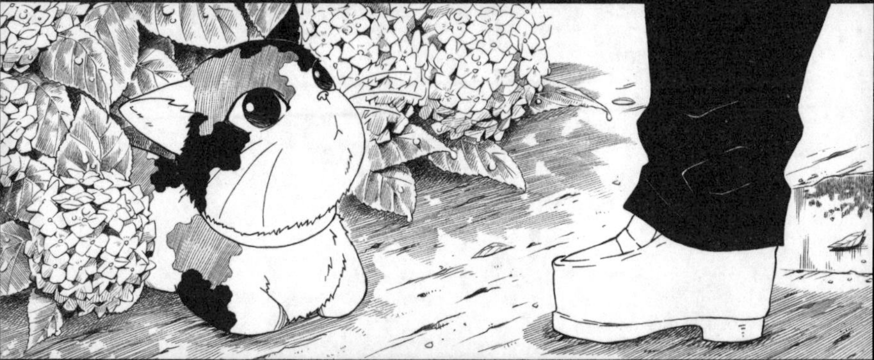

Story and Art by

Natsuki Hokami

Based on Koyoharu Gotouge's
Demon Slayer: Kimetsu no Yaiba

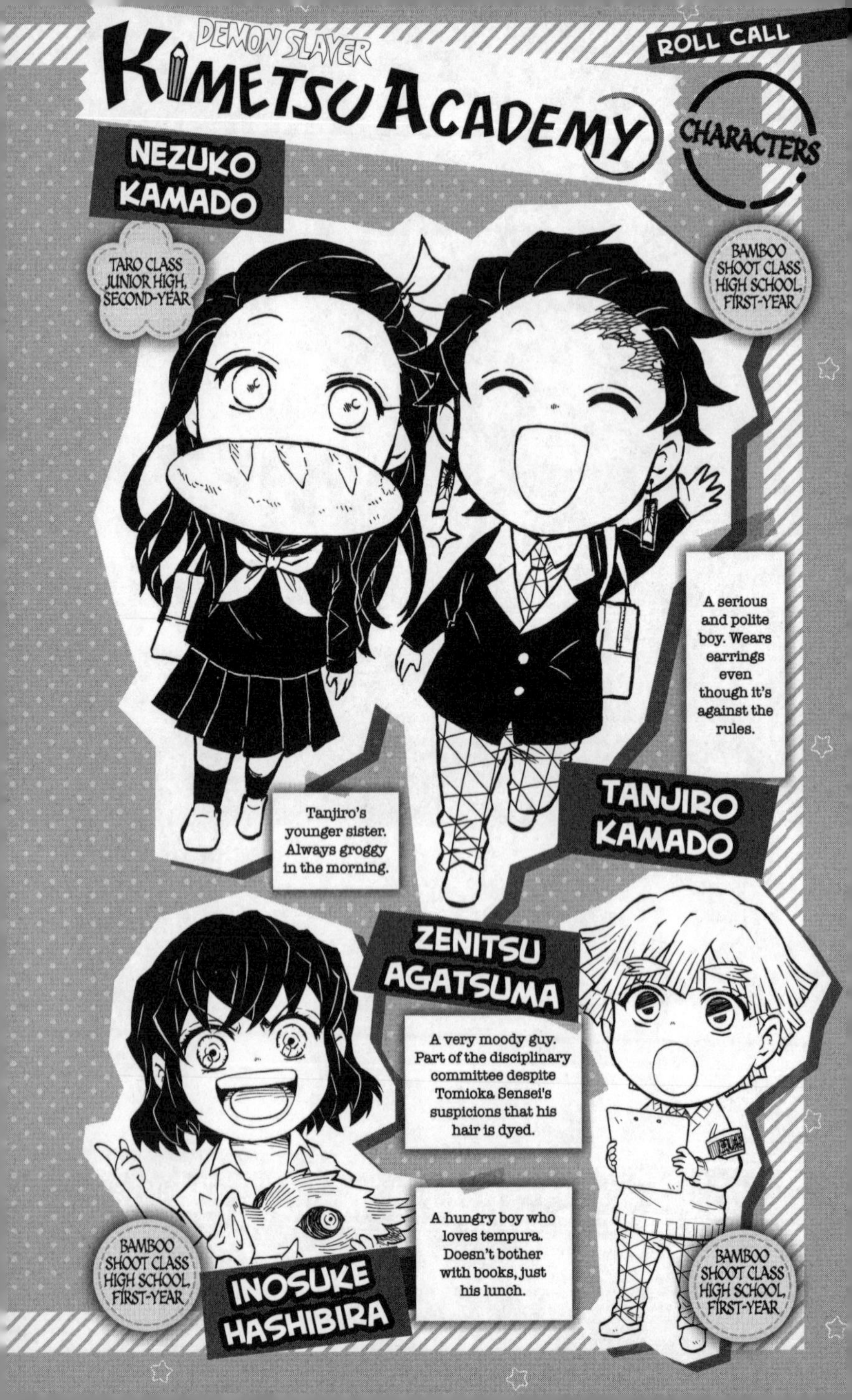
DEMON SLAYER
KIMETSU ACADEMY
ROLL CALL
CHARACTERS
NEZUKO KAMADO
TARO CLASS JUNIOR HIGH, SECOND-YEAR
Tanjiro's younger sister. Always groggy in the morning.
TANJIRO KAMADO
BAMBOO SHOOT CLASS HIGH SCHOOL, FIRST-YEAR
A serious and polite boy. Wears earrings even though it's against the rules.
ZENITSU AGATSUMA
A very moody guy. Part of the disciplinary committee despite Tomioka Sensei's suspicions that his hair is dyed.
BAMBOO SHOOT CLASS HIGH SCHOOL, FIRST-YEAR
INOSUKE HASHIBIRA
A hungry boy who loves tempura. Doesn't bother with books, just his lunch.
BAMBOO SHOOT CLASS HIGH SCHOOL, FIRST-YEAR

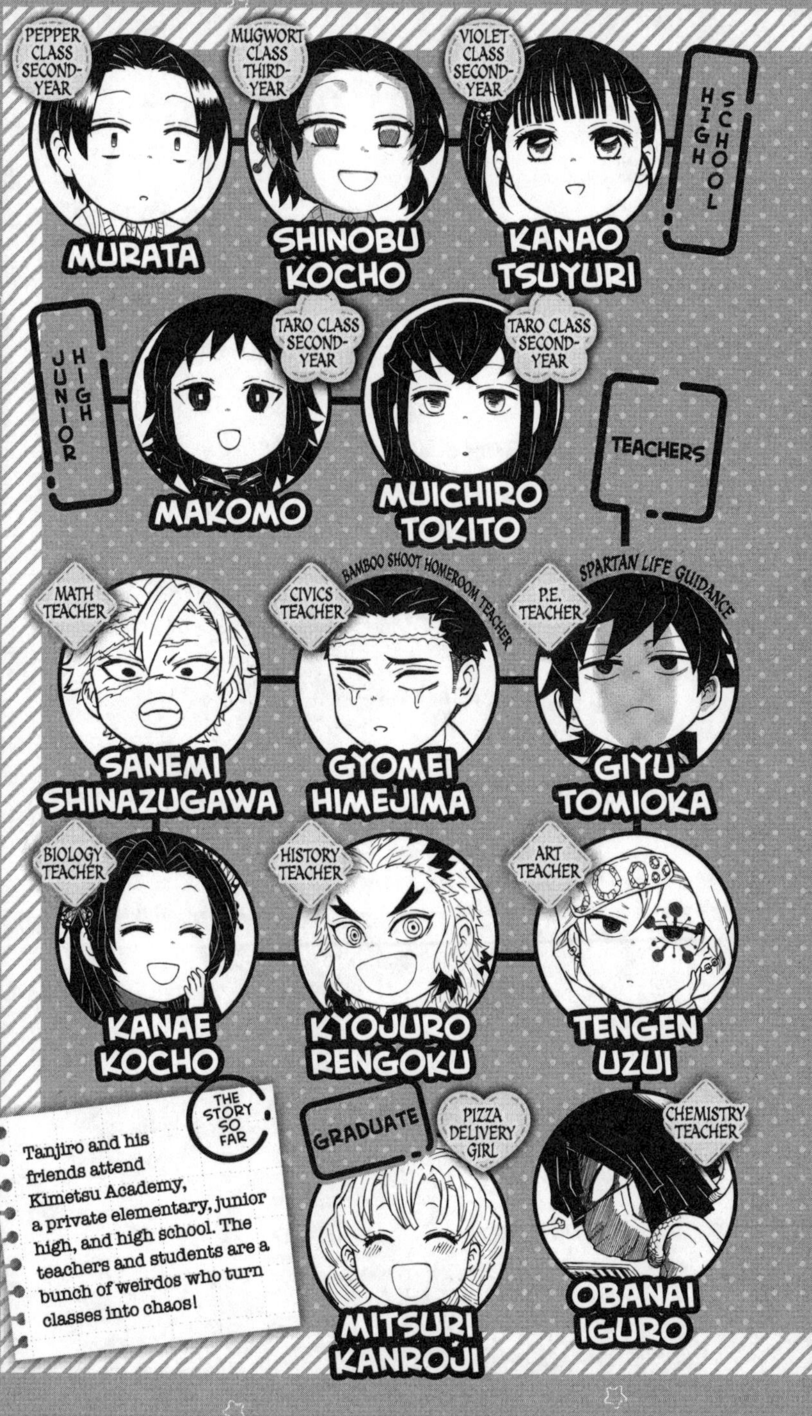
PEPPER CLASS SECOND-YEAR
MURATA
MUGWORT CLASS THIRD-YEAR
SHINOBU KOCHO
VIOLET CLASS SECOND-YEAR
KANAO TSUYURI
HIGH SCHOOL
JUNIOR HIGH
TARO CLASS SECOND-YEAR
MAKOMO
TARO CLASS SECOND-YEAR
MUICHIRO TOKITO
TEACHERS
MATH TEACHER
SANEMI SHINAZUGAWA
CIVICS TEACHER
BAMBOO SHOOT HOMEROOM TEACHER
GYOMEI HIMEJIMA
P.E. TEACHER
SPARTAN LIFE GUIDANCE
GIYU TOMIOKA
BIOLOGY TEACHER
KANAE KOCHO
HISTORY TEACHER
KYOJURO RENGOKU
ART TEACHER
TENGEN UZUI
GRADUATE
PIZZA DELIVERY GIRL
MITSURI KANROJI
CHEMISTRY TEACHER
OBANAI IGURO

THE STORY SO FAR

Tanjiro and his friends attend Kimetsu Academy, a private elementary, junior high, and high school. The teachers and students are a bunch of weirdos who turn classes into chaos!

CONTENTS

2 The Kimetsu Academy Night Tour

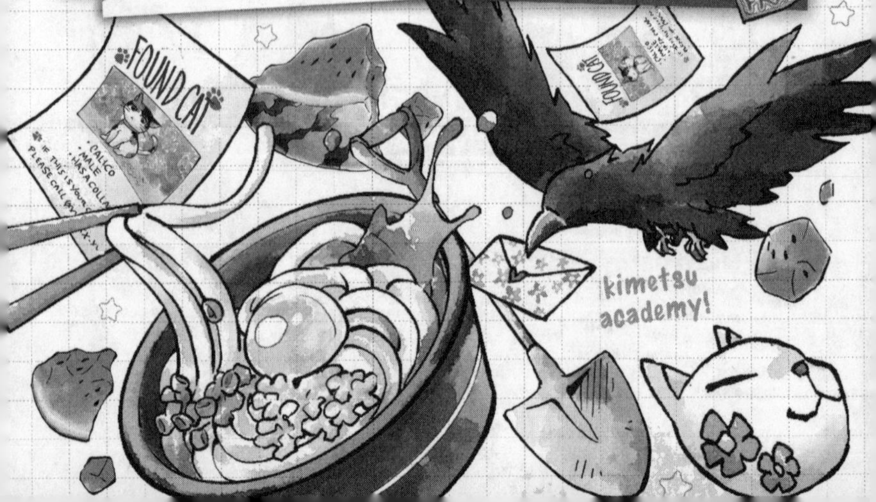

FOUND CAT
FOUND CAT
kimetsu academy!

CHAPTER 6: CATNIP FOR KITTIES, KITTIES FOR HIMEJIMA

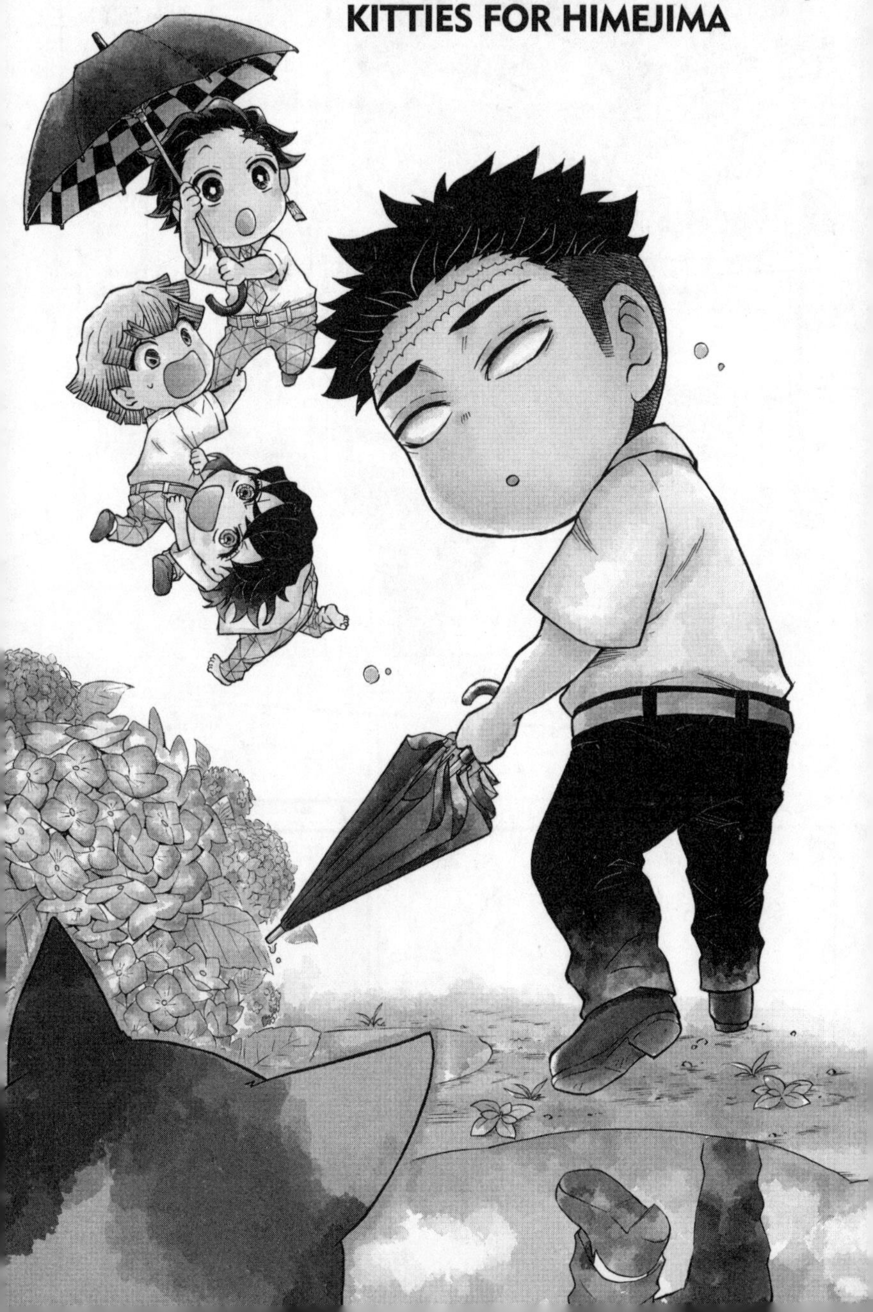

KIMETSU ACADEMY'S HIGH SCHOOL

GYOMEI HIMEJIMA
BAMBOO SHOOT CLASS HOMEROOM TEACHER

HOBBY: PLAYING THE SHAKUHACHI FLUTE

Kyah! Uzui Sensei!

HUH? WHY NOT USE THE SCHOOL KIOSK?

GYOMEI HAS A SECRET.

TO GET A DRINK FROM THE CONVENIENCE STORE.

WHERE'RE YA GOIN', HIMEJIMA SENSEI?

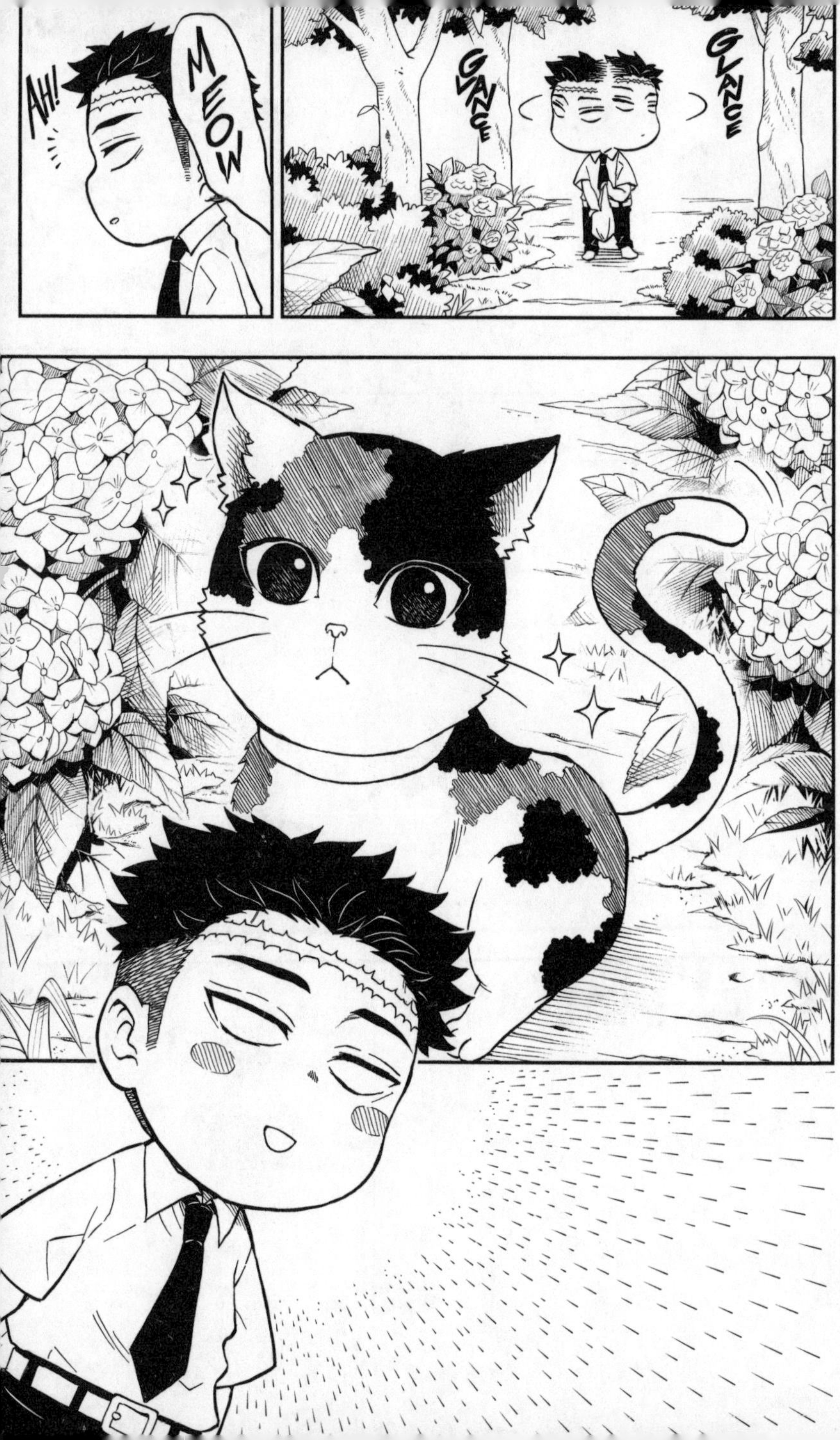
GLANCE
GLANCE
MEOW
AH!

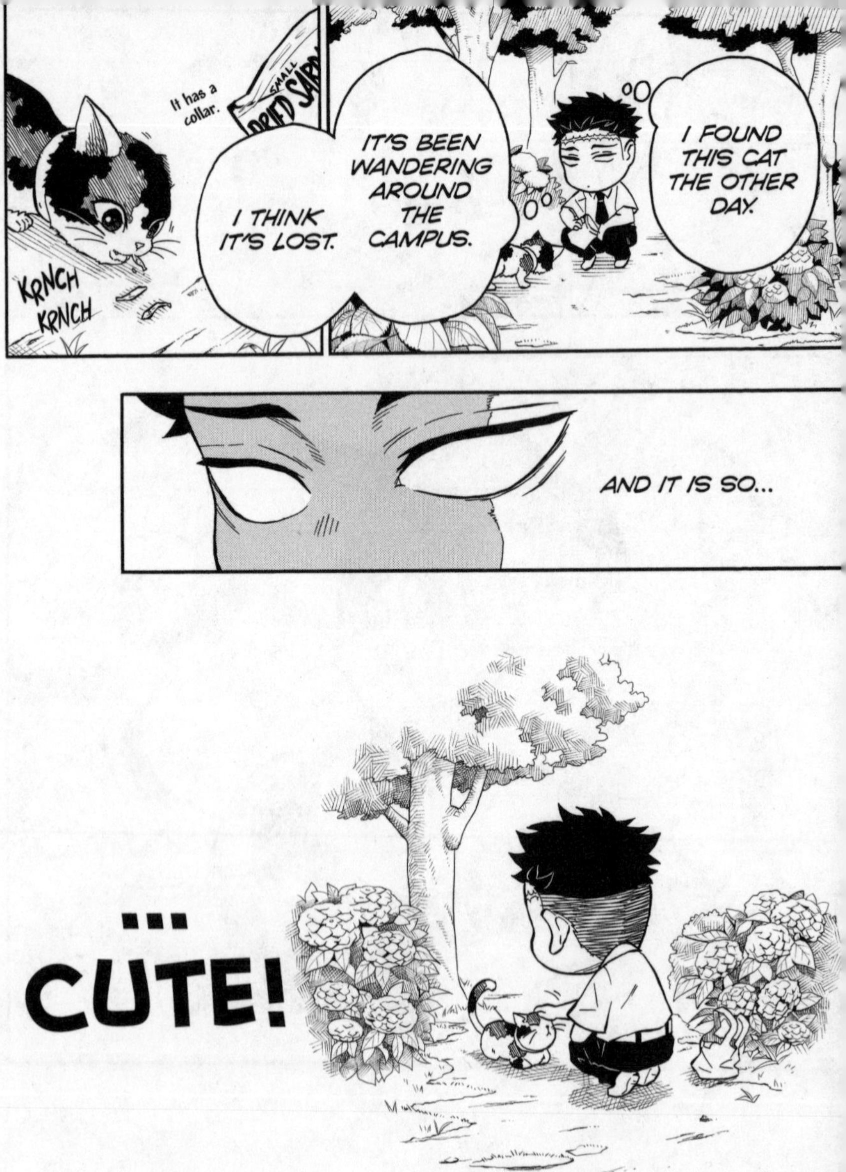
I FOUND THIS CAT THE OTHER DAY.
IT'S BEEN WANDERING AROUND THE CAMPUS.
I THINK IT'S LOST.
It has a collar.
KRNCH KRNCH
AND IT IS SO...
...CUTE!

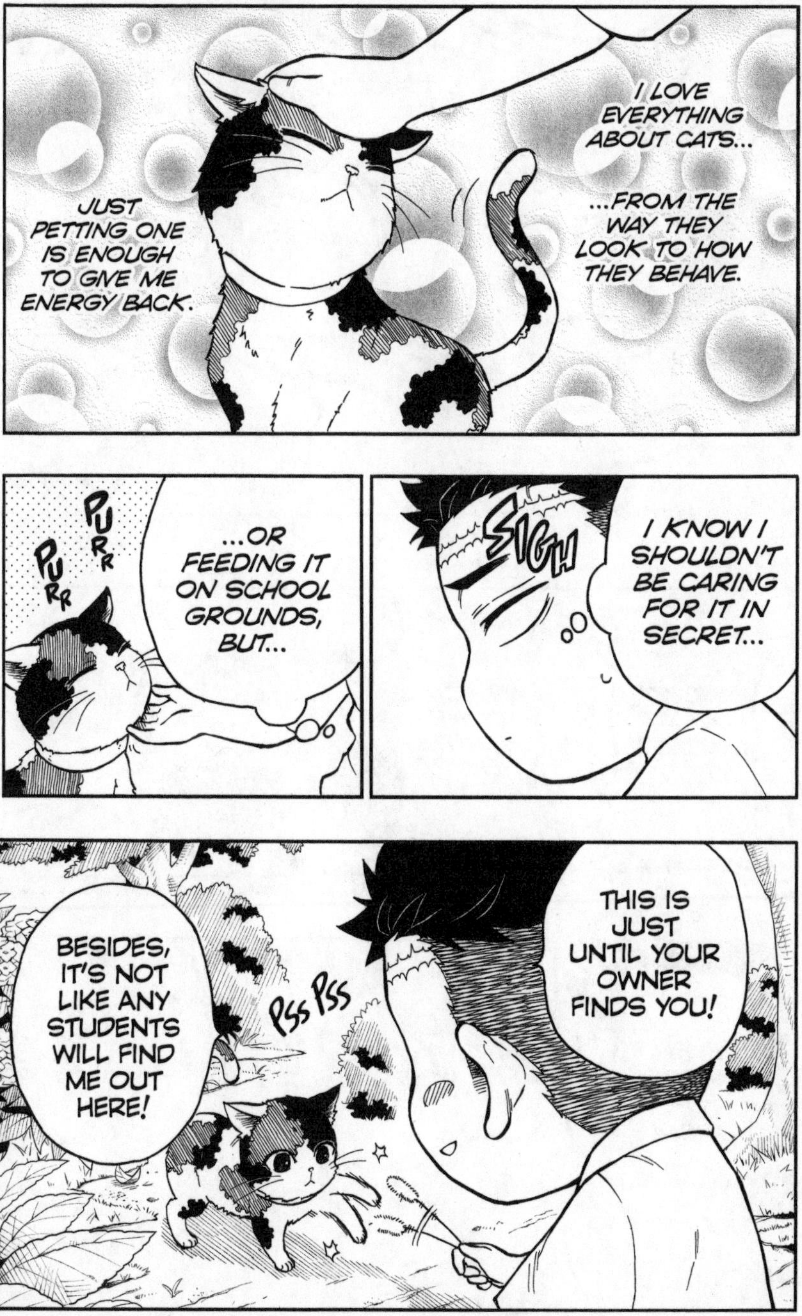
I LOVE EVERYTHING ABOUT CATS...
...FROM THE WAY THEY LOOK TO HOW THEY BEHAVE.
JUST PETTING ONE IS ENOUGH TO GIVE ME ENERGY BACK.
SIGH
I KNOW I SHOULDN'T BE CARING FOR IT IN SECRET...
...OR FEEDING IT ON SCHOOL GROUNDS, BUT...
PURR
PURR
THIS IS JUST UNTIL YOUR OWNER FINDS YOU!
PSS PSS
BESIDES, IT'S NOT LIKE ANY STUDENTS WILL FIND ME OUT HERE!

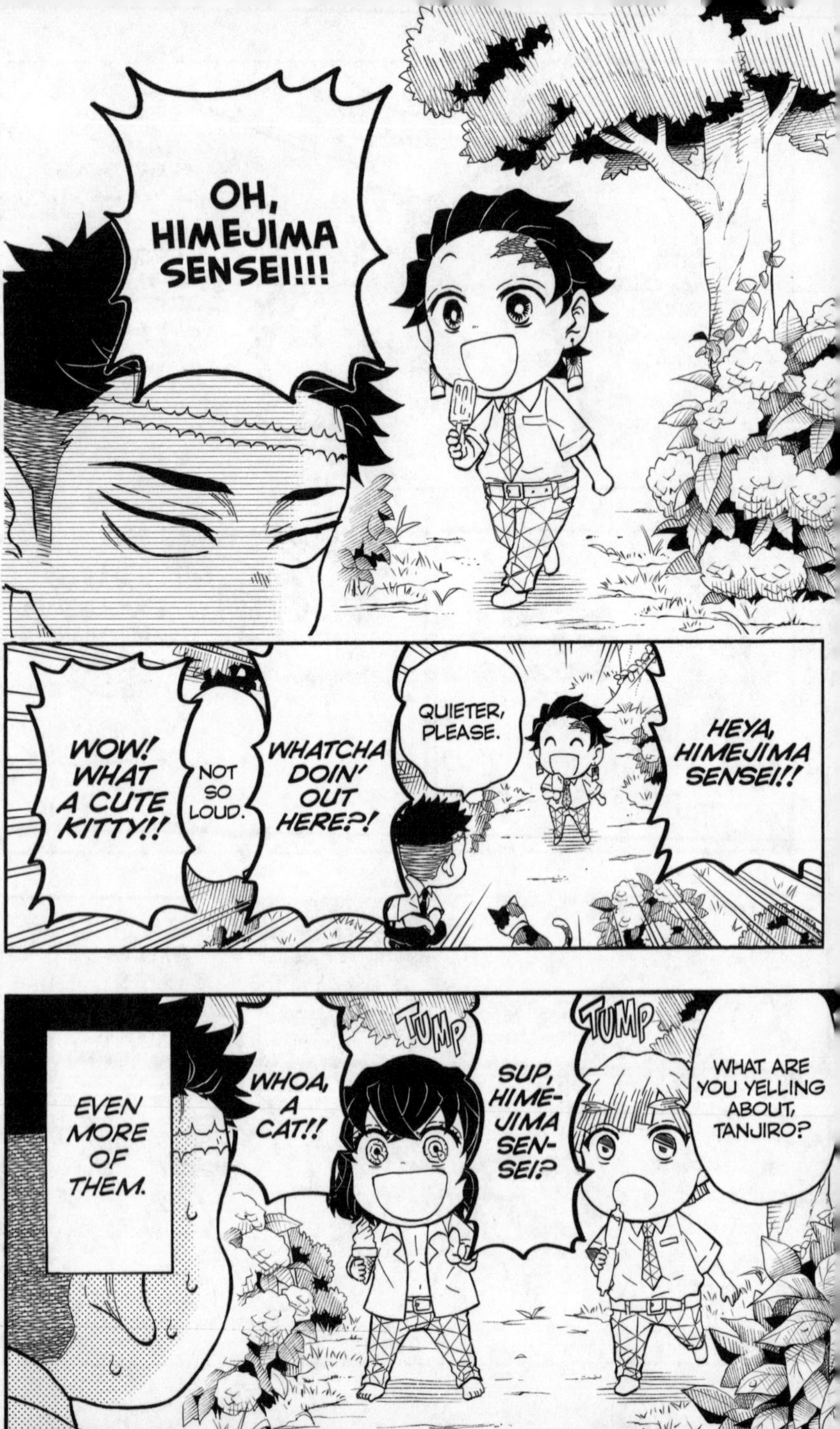
OH, HIMEJIMA SENSEI!!!!
HEYA, HIMEJIMA SENSEI!!
QUIETER, PLEASE.
WHATCHA DOIN' OUT HERE?!
NOT SO LOUD.
WOW! WHAT A CUTE KITTY!!
WHAT ARE YOU YELLING ABOUT, TANJIRO?
TUMP
SUP, HIME-JIMA SEN-SEI?
TUMP
WHOA, A CAT!!
EVEN MORE OF THEM.

IS IT LOST?

ITS OWNER MUST BE WORRIED.

YEAH...

TANJIRO KAMADO
BAMBOO SHOOT CLASS
FIRST-YEAR

YEAH! THE WHOLE CLASS COULD HELP!

INOSUKE HASHIBIRA
BAMBOO SHOOT CLASS
FIRST-YEAR

YOU SHOULDN'T KEEP SOMETHING LIKE THIS TO YOURSELF!

ZENITSU AGATSUMA
BAMBOO SHOOT CLASS
FIRST-YEAR

BESIDES ...

WELL, SOME STUDENTS MIGHT BE ALLERGIC.

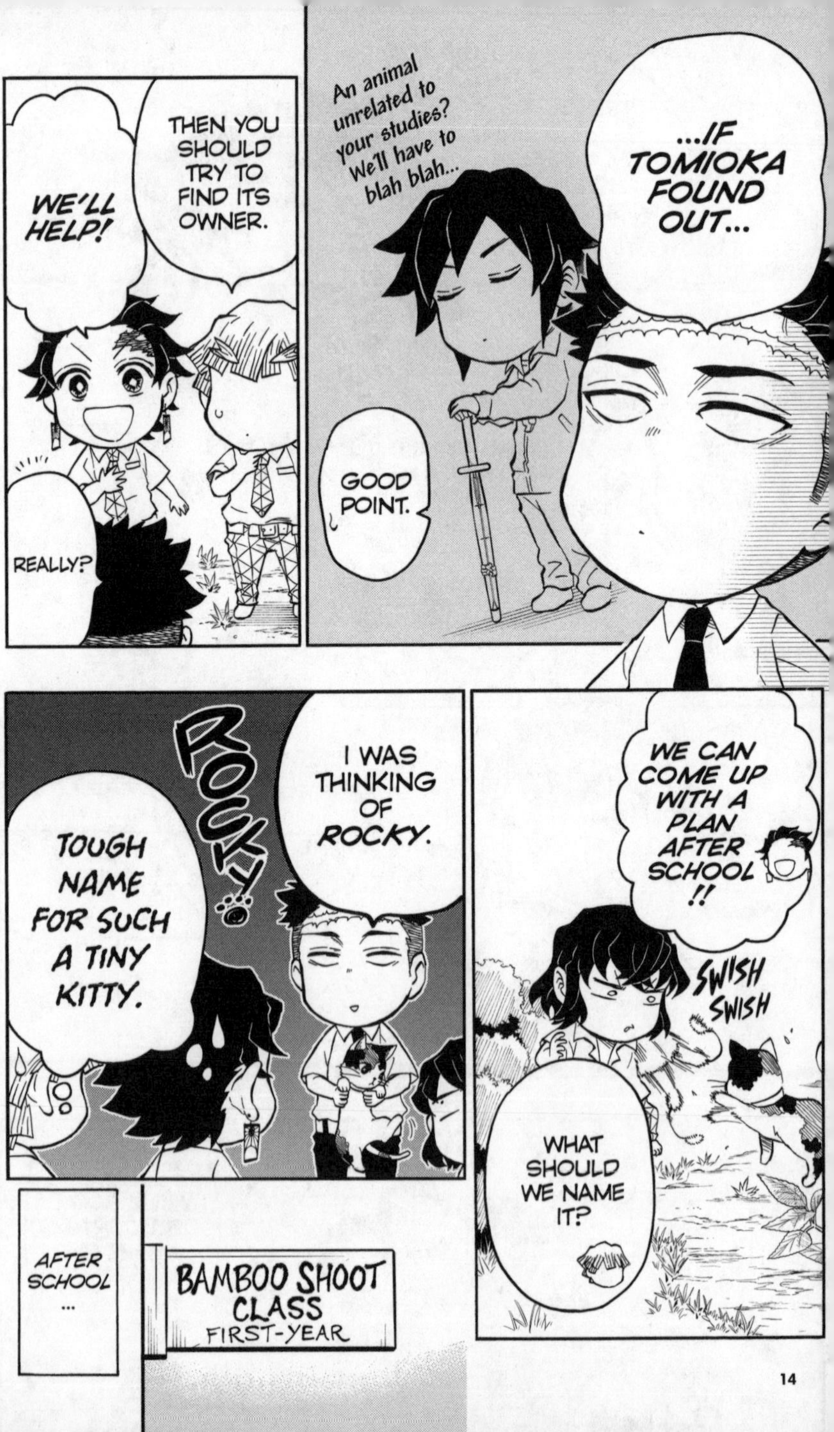
...IF TOMIOKA FOUND OUT...
An animal unrelated to your studies? We'll have to blah blah...
GOOD POINT.
THEN YOU SHOULD TRY TO FIND ITS OWNER.
WE'LL HELP!
REALLY?
WE CAN COME UP WITH A PLAN AFTER SCHOOL!!
SWISH SWISH
WHAT SHOULD WE NAME IT?
I WAS THINKING OF ROCKY.
ROCKY!
TOUGH NAME FOR SUCH A TINY KITTY.
BAMBOO SHOOT CLASS FIRST-YEAR
AFTER SCHOOL ...

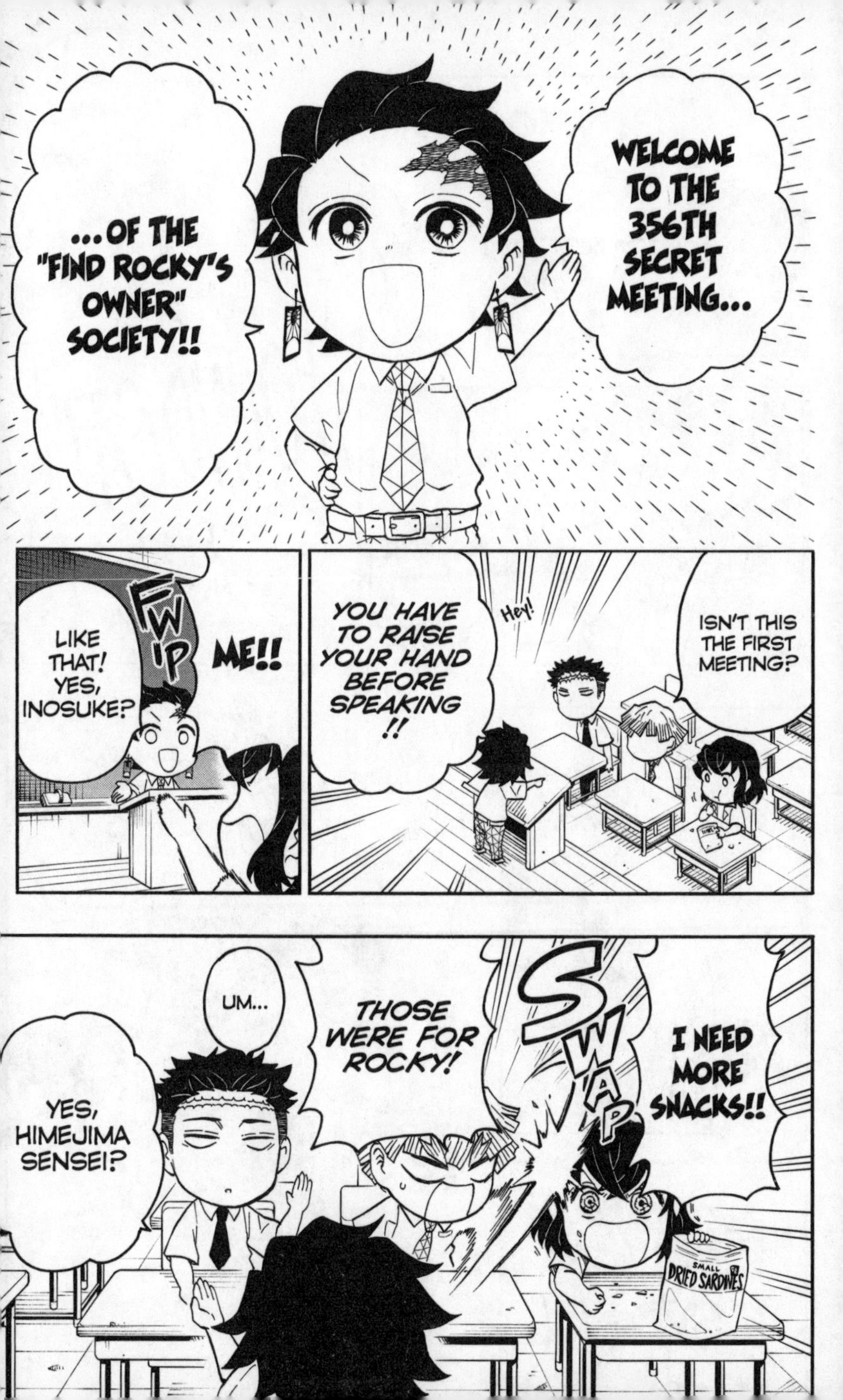
WELCOME TO THE 356TH SECRET MEETING...
...OF THE "FIND ROCKY'S OWNER" SOCIETY!!
ISN'T THIS THE FIRST MEETING?
Hey!
YOU HAVE TO RAISE YOUR HAND BEFORE SPEAKING !!
ME!!
FWIP
LIKE THAT! YES, INOSUKE?
I NEED MORE SNACKS!!
SWAP
THOSE WERE FOR ROCKY!
UM...
YES, HIMEJIMA SENSEI?
SMALL DRIED SARDINES

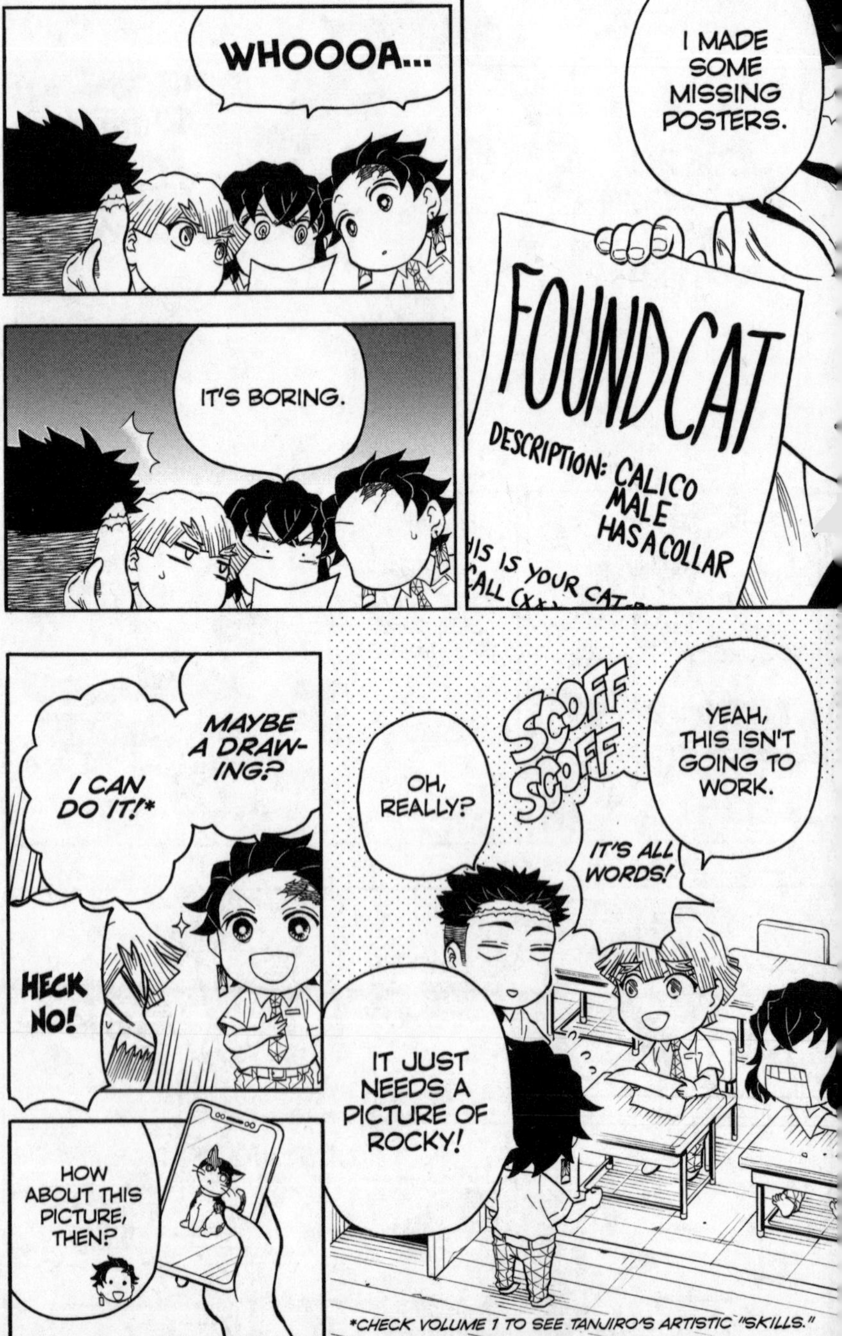
I MADE SOME MISSING POSTERS.
FOUNDCAT
DESCRIPTION: CALICO
MALE
HAS A COLLAR
WHOOOA...
IT'S BORING.
YEAH, THIS ISN'T GOING TO WORK.
SCOFF SCOFF
IT'S ALL WORDS!
OH, REALLY?
IT JUST NEEDS A PICTURE OF ROCKY!
MAYBE A DRAW-ING?
I CAN DO IT!*
HECK NO!
HOW ABOUT THIS PICTURE, THEN?

*CHECK VOLUME 1 TO SEE TANJIRO'S ARTISTIC "SKILLS."

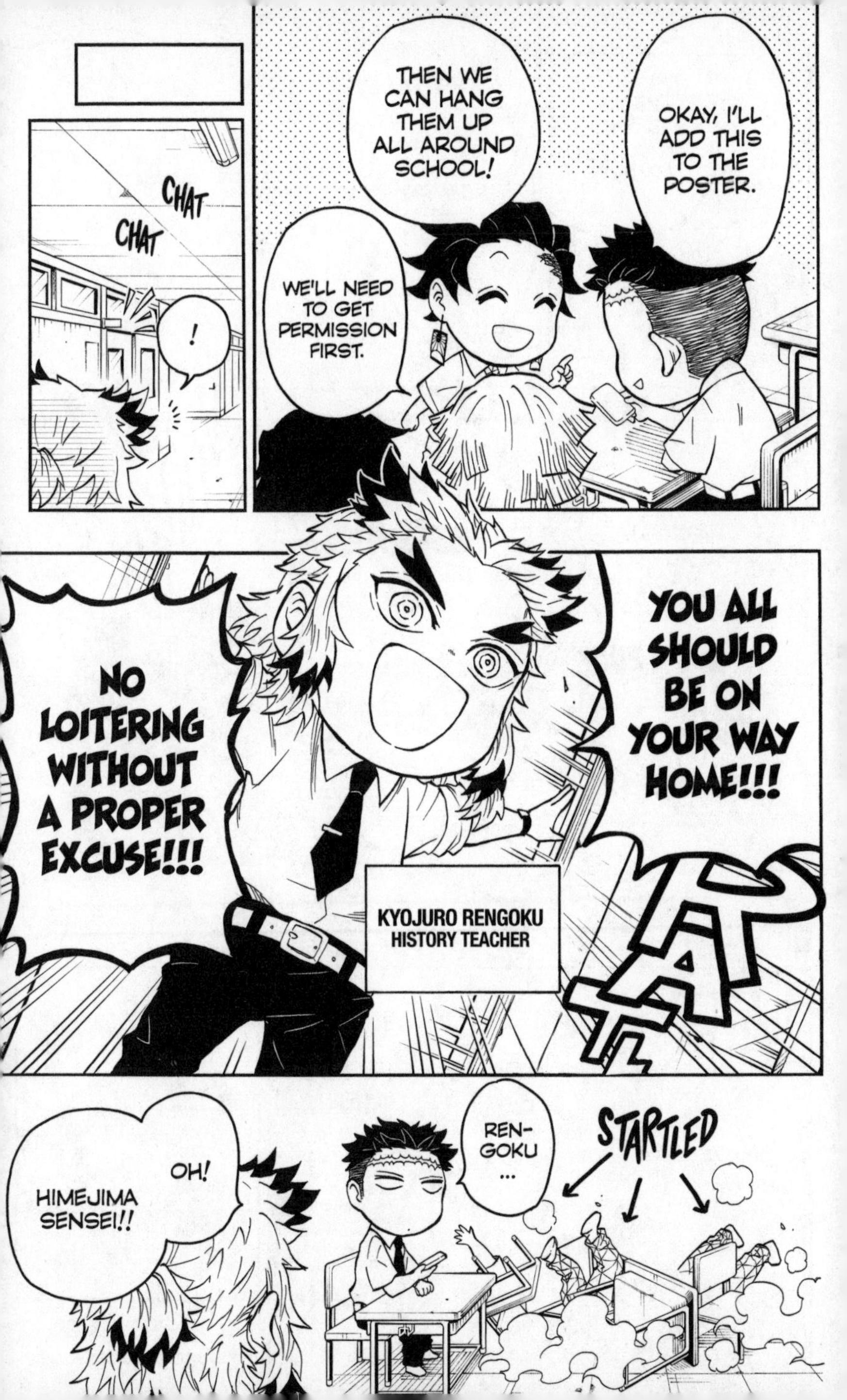

OKAY, I'LL ADD THIS TO THE POSTER.
THEN WE CAN HANG THEM UP ALL AROUND SCHOOL!
WE'LL NEED TO GET PERMISSION FIRST.
CHAT
CHAT
!
YOU ALL SHOULD BE ON YOUR WAY HOME!!!
NO LOITERING WITHOUT A PROPER EXCUSE!!!
PAT
KYOJURO RENGOKU HISTORY TEACHER
STARTLED
REN-GOKU ...
OH! HIMEJIMA SENSEI!!

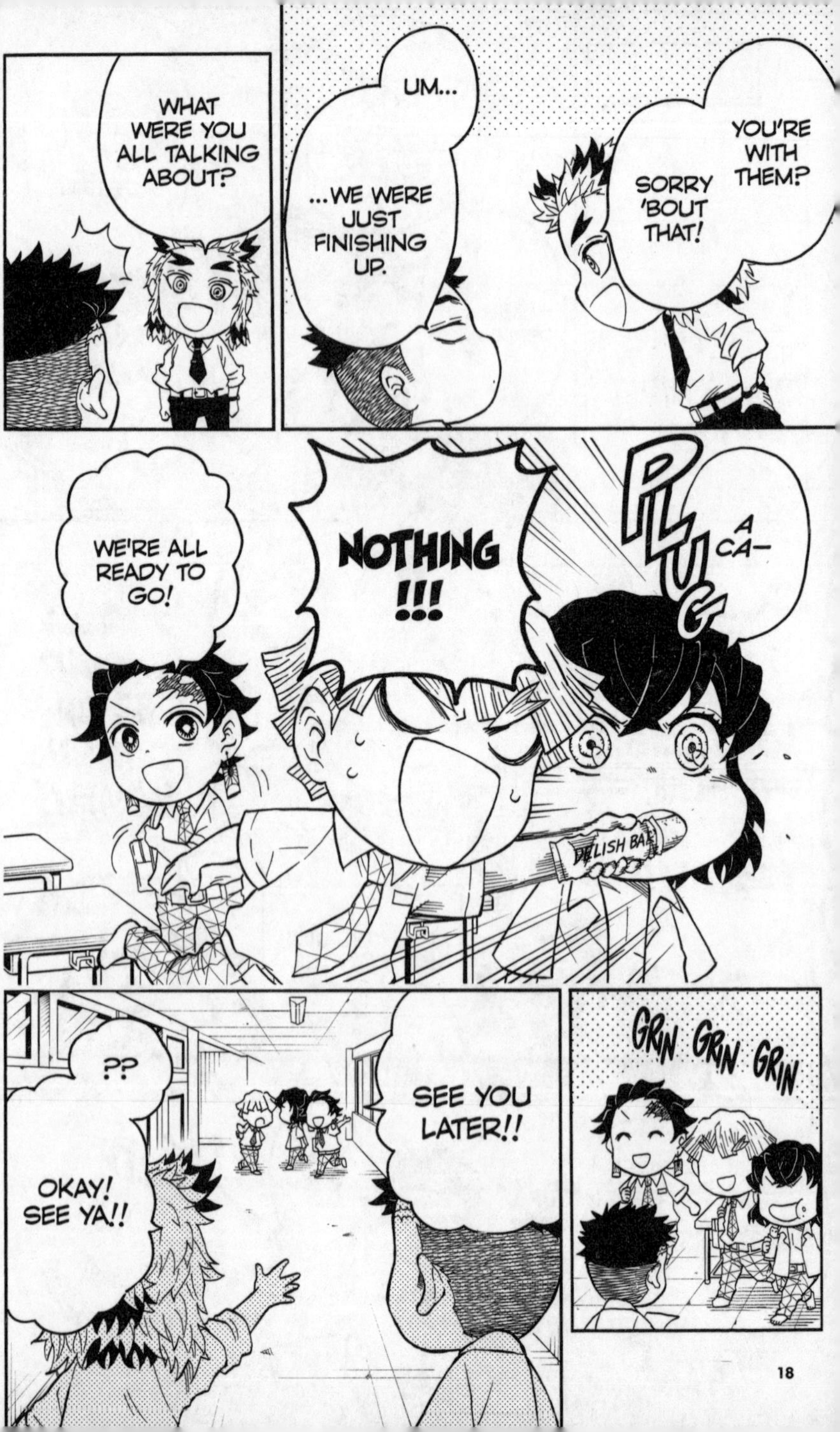
YOU'RE WITH THEM?
SORRY 'BOUT THAT!
UM...
...WE WERE JUST FINISHING UP.
WHAT WERE YOU ALL TALKING ABOUT?
A CA—
PLUG
NOTHING!!!
DELISH BA
WE'RE ALL READY TO GO!
GRIN GRIN GRIN
SEE YOU LATER!!
??
OKAY! SEE YA!!

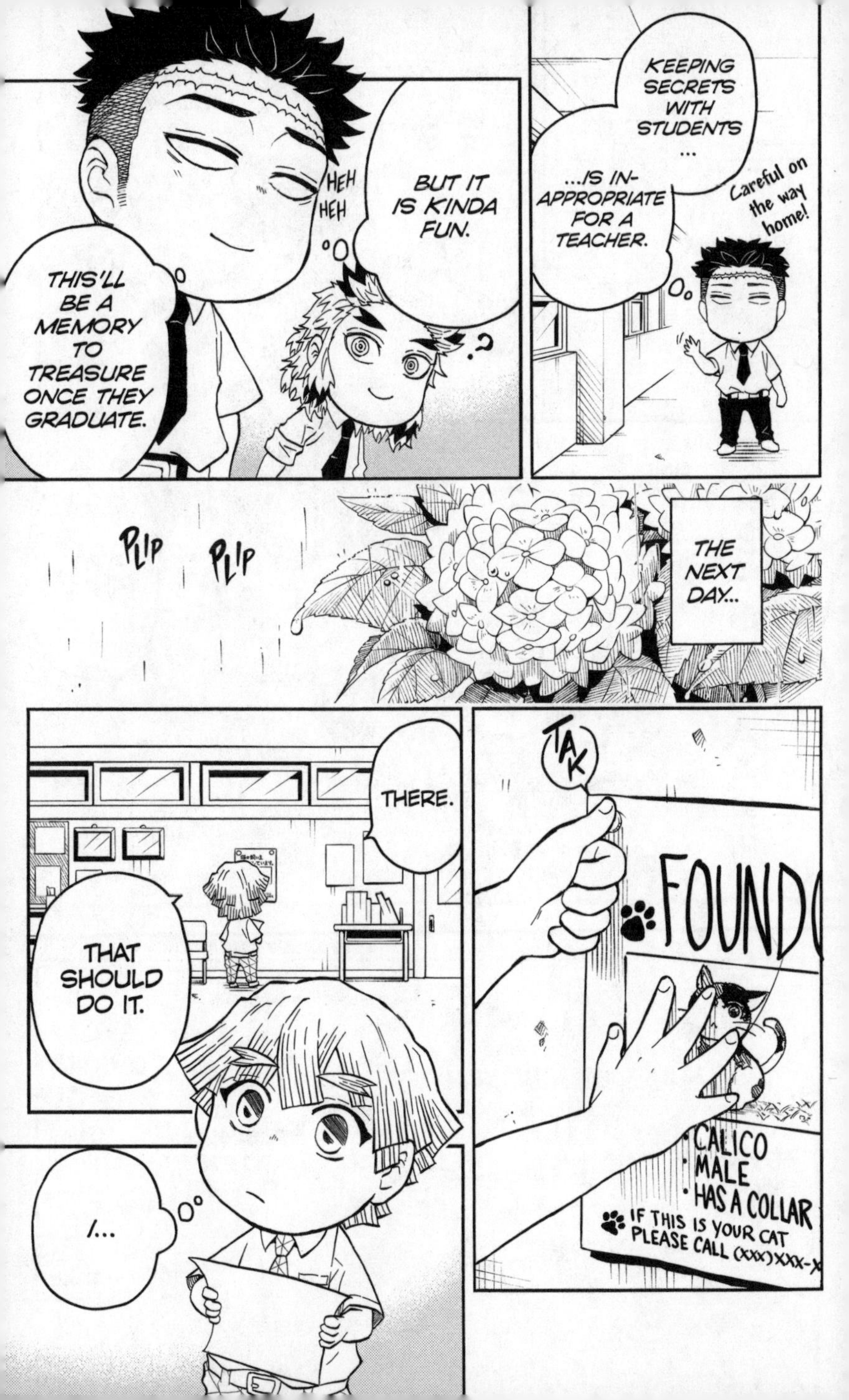
KEEPING SECRETS WITH STUDENTS ...
...IS IN-APPROPRIATE FOR A TEACHER.
Careful on the way home!
HEH HEH
BUT IT IS KINDA FUN.
THIS'LL BE A MEMORY TO TREASURE ONCE THEY GRADUATE.
THE NEXT DAY...
PLIP
PLIP
TAK
FOUND
• CALICO
• MALE
• HAS A COLLAR
IF THIS IS YOUR CAT PLEASE CALL (XXX)XXX-X
THERE.
THAT SHOULD DO IT.
I...

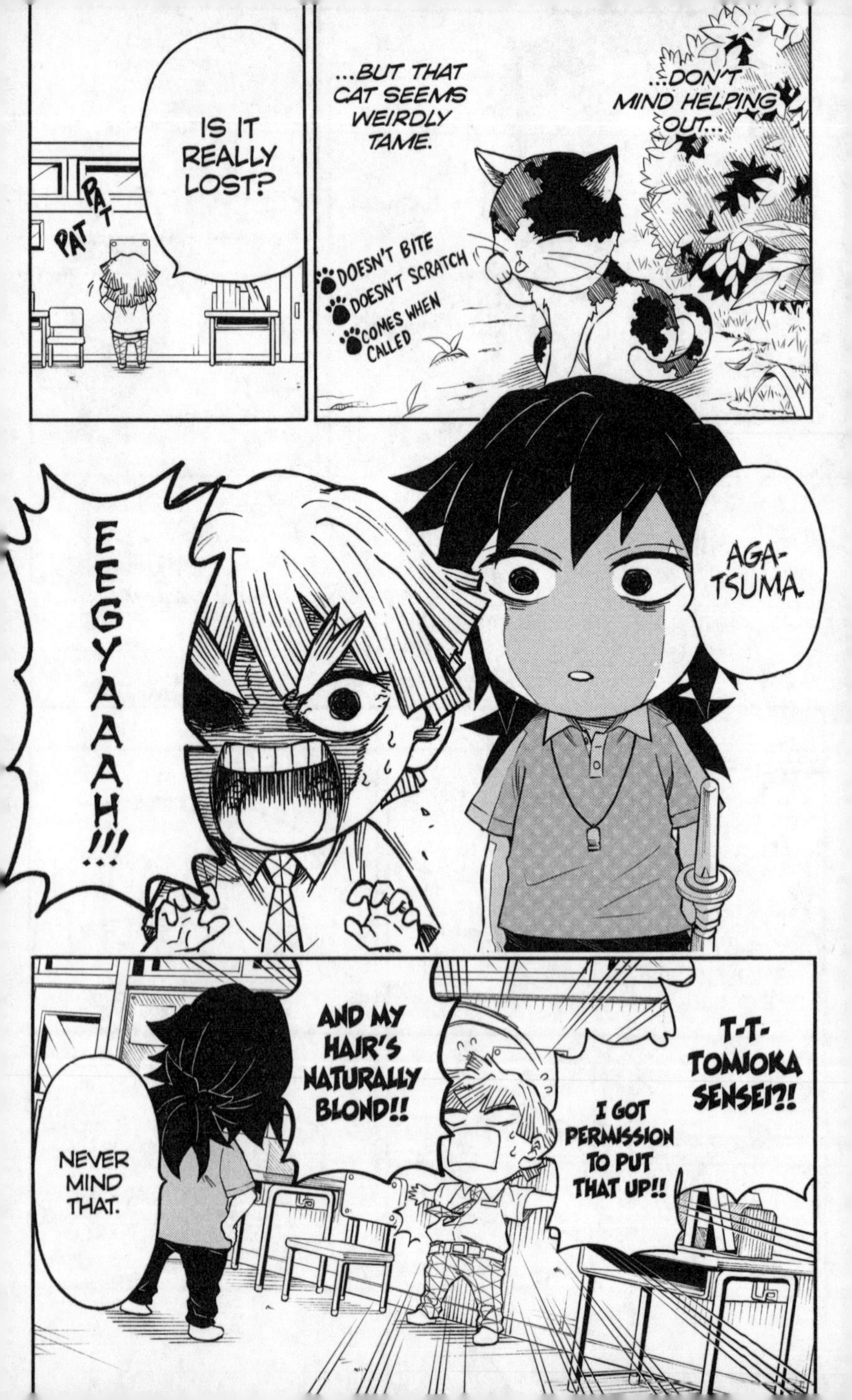
...DON'T MIND HELPING OUT...
...BUT THAT CAT SEEMS WEIRDLY TAME.
DOESN'T BITE
DOESN'T SCRATCH
COMES WHEN CALLED
IS IT REALLY LOST?
PAT PAT
AGA-TSUMA.
EEGYAAAAH!!!
T-T-TOMIOKA SENSEI?!
I GOT PERMISSION TO PUT THAT UP!!
AND MY HAIR'S NATURALLY BLOND!!
NEVER MIND THAT.

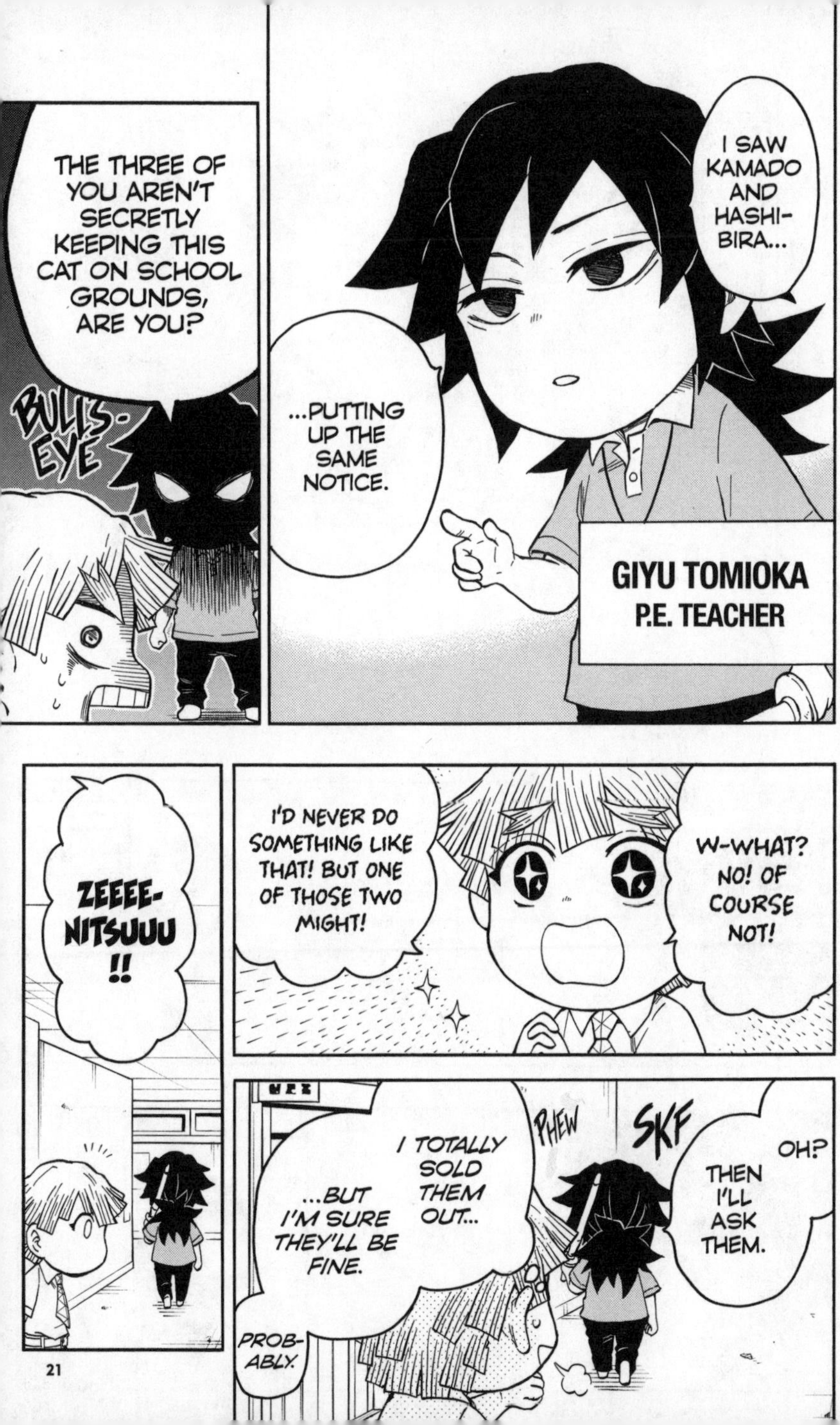
I SAW KAMADO AND HASHIBIRA...
...PUTTING UP THE SAME NOTICE.
GIYU TOMIOKA
P.E. TEACHER
THE THREE OF YOU AREN'T SECRETLY KEEPING THIS CAT ON SCHOOL GROUNDS, ARE YOU?
BULLS-EYE
W-WHAT? NO! OF COURSE NOT!
I'D NEVER DO SOMETHING LIKE THAT! BUT ONE OF THOSE TWO MIGHT!
SKF
OH? THEN I'LL ASK THEM.
PHEW
I TOTALLY SOLD THEM OUT...
...BUT I'M SURE THEY'LL BE FINE.
PROBABLY.
ZEEEE-NITSUUU!!

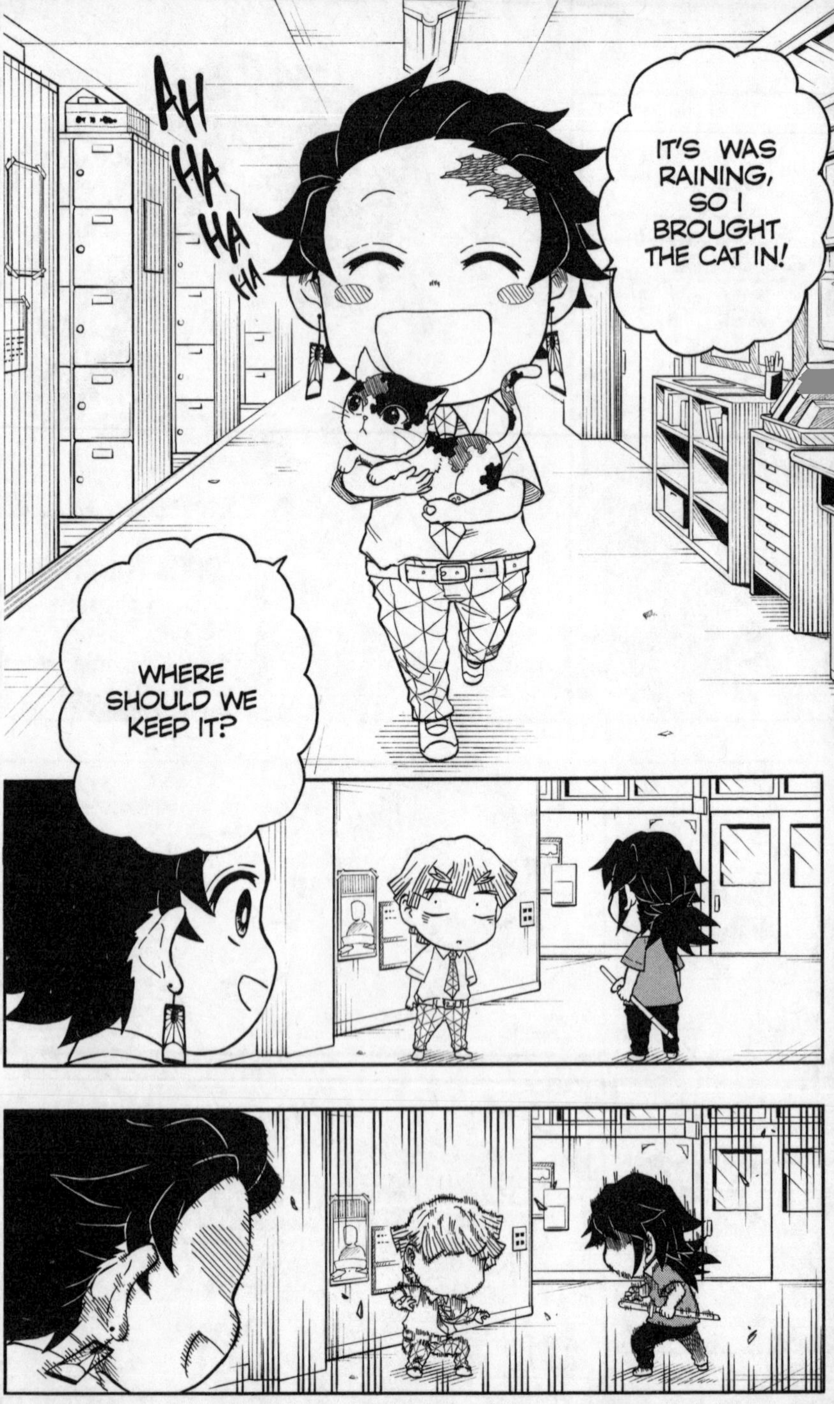
IT'S WAS RAINING, SO I BROUGHT THE CAT IN!
AH HA HA HA
WHERE SHOULD WE KEEP IT?

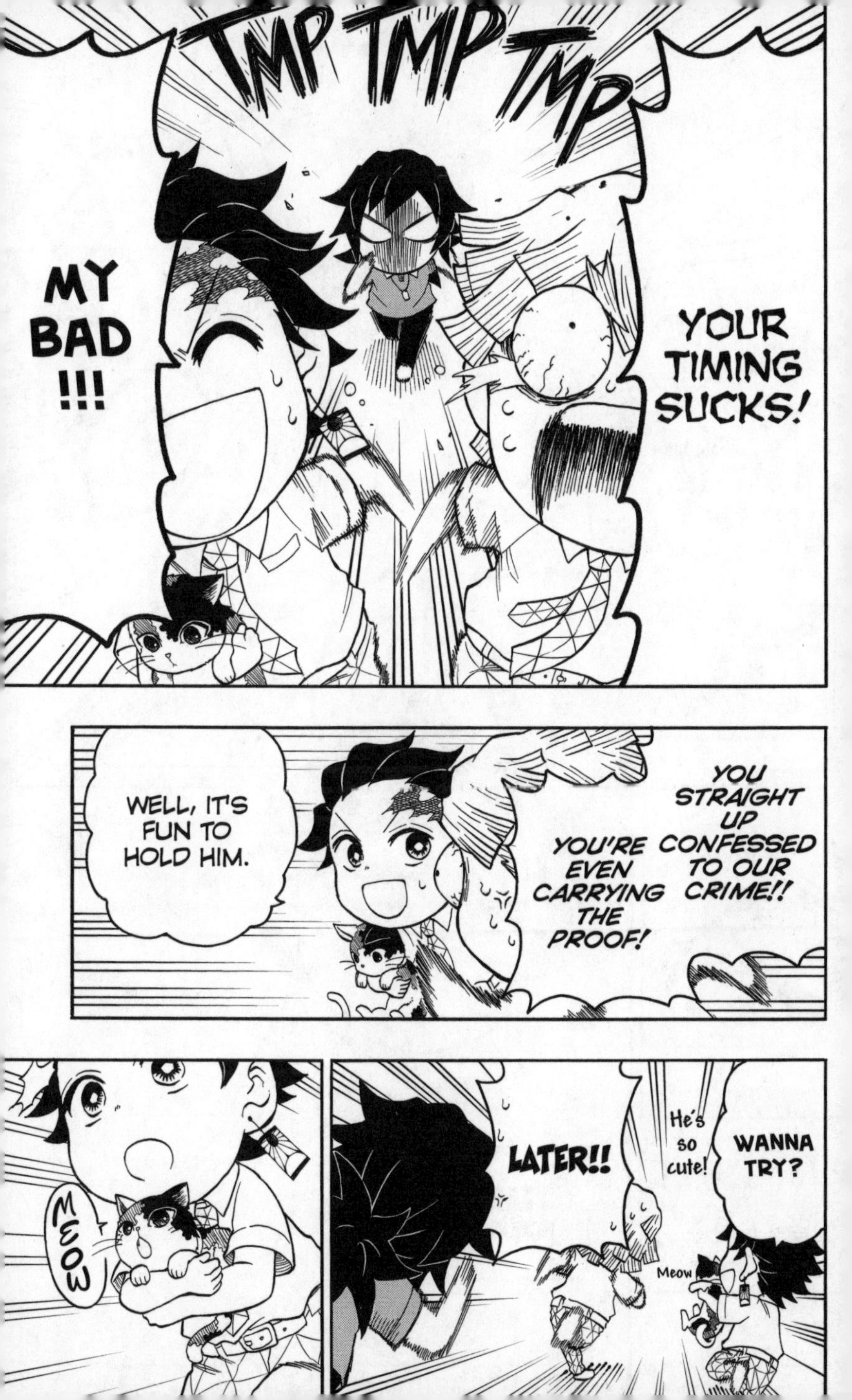
TMP TMP TMP
YOUR TIMING SUCKS!
MY BAD!!!
YOU STRAIGHT UP CONFESSED TO OUR CRIME!!
YOU'RE EVEN CARRYING THE PROOF!
WELL, IT'S FUN TO HOLD HIM.
WANNA TRY?
He's so cute!
Meow
LATER!!
MEOW

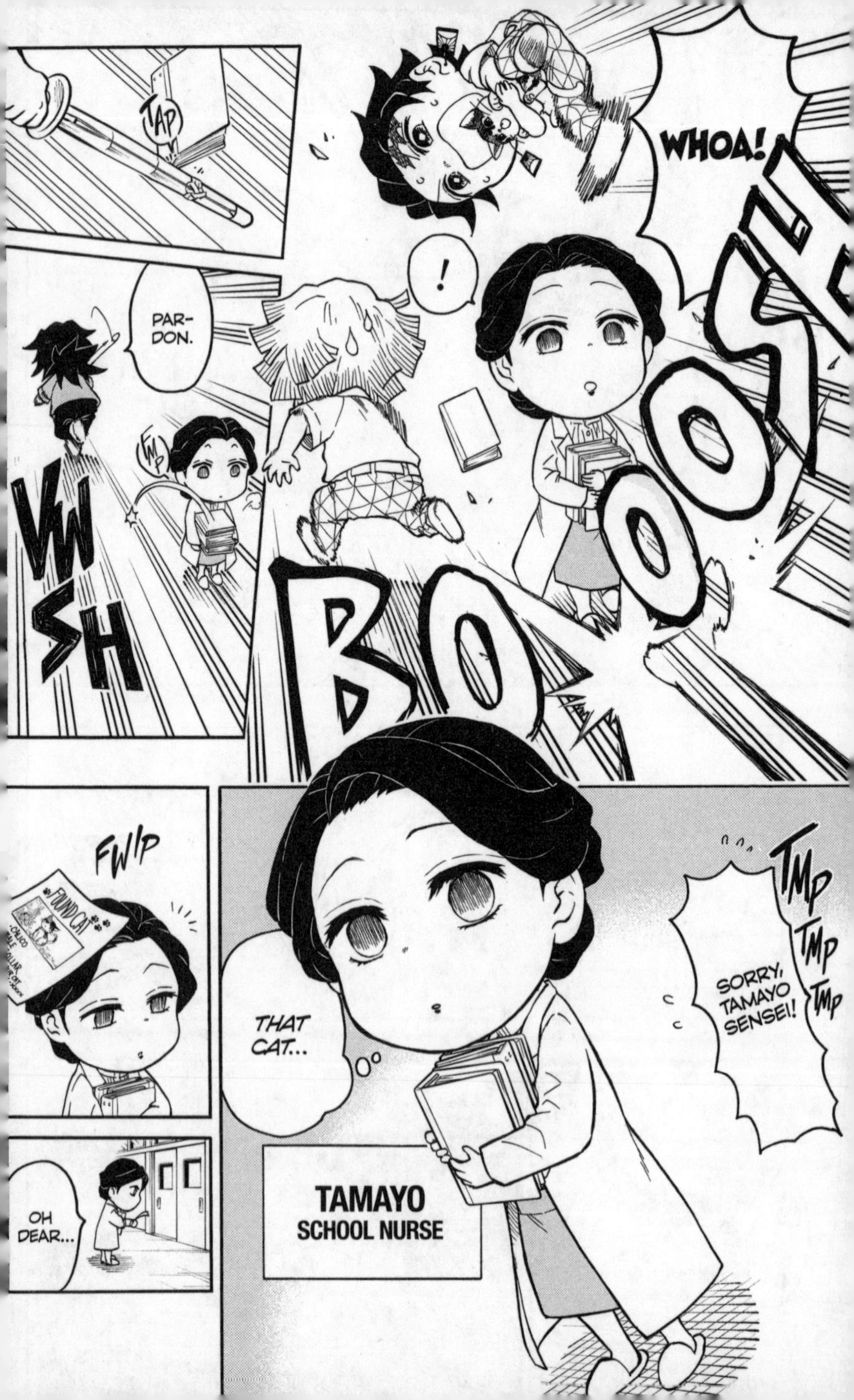
WHOA!
BOOOSH
!
TAP
PARDON.
FMP
VWSH
TMP TMP TMP
SORRY, TAMAYO SENSEI!
THAT CAT...
TAMAYO
SCHOOL NURSE
FWIP
FOUND CAT
OH DEAR...

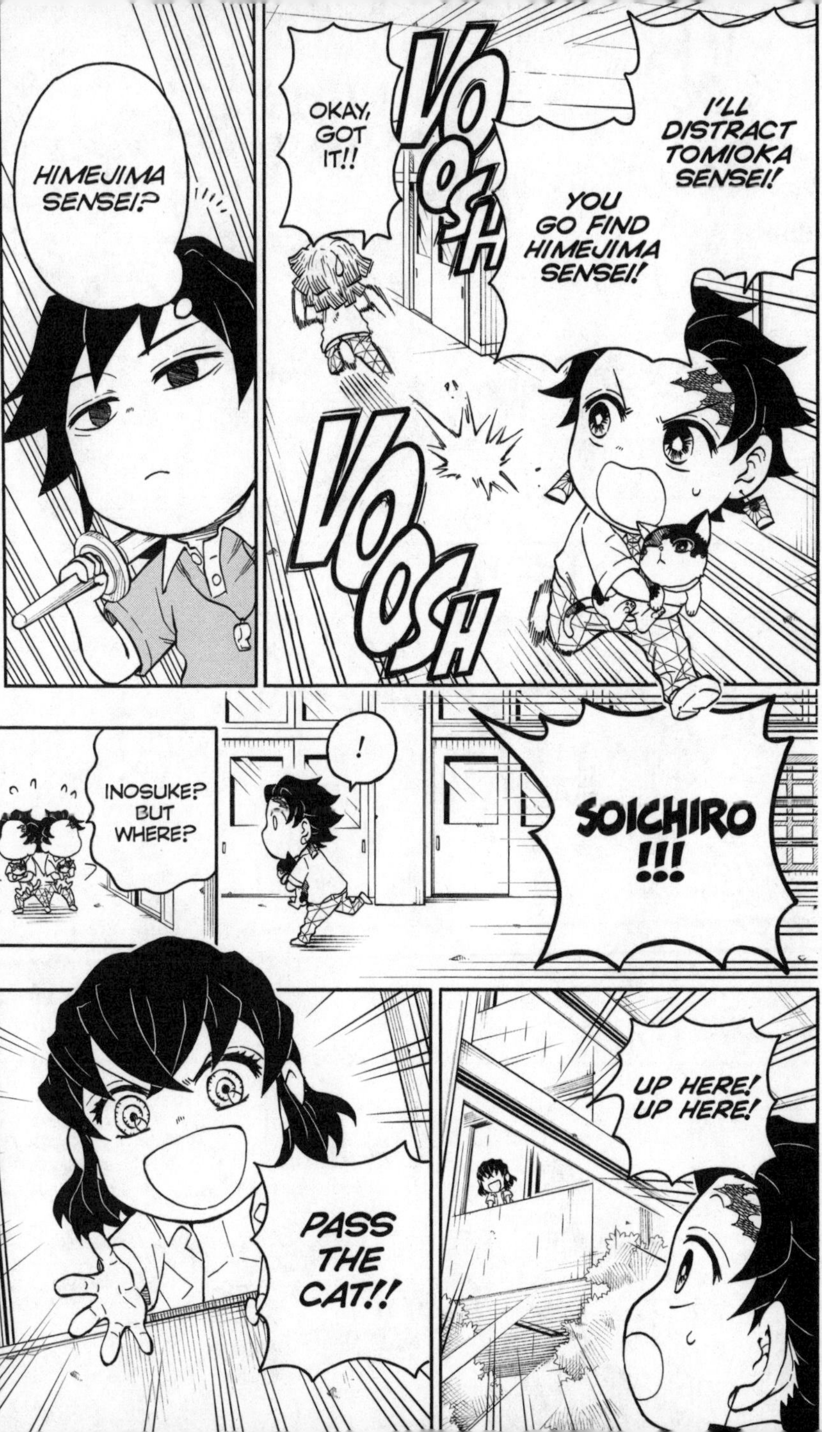
I'LL DISTRACT TOMIOKA SENSEI!
YOU GO FIND HIMEJIMA SENSEI!
OKAY, GOT IT!!
VOOSH
VOOSH
HIMEJIMA SENSEI?
SOICHIRO!!!
!
INOSUKE? BUT WHERE?
UP HERE! UP HERE!
PASS THE CAT!!

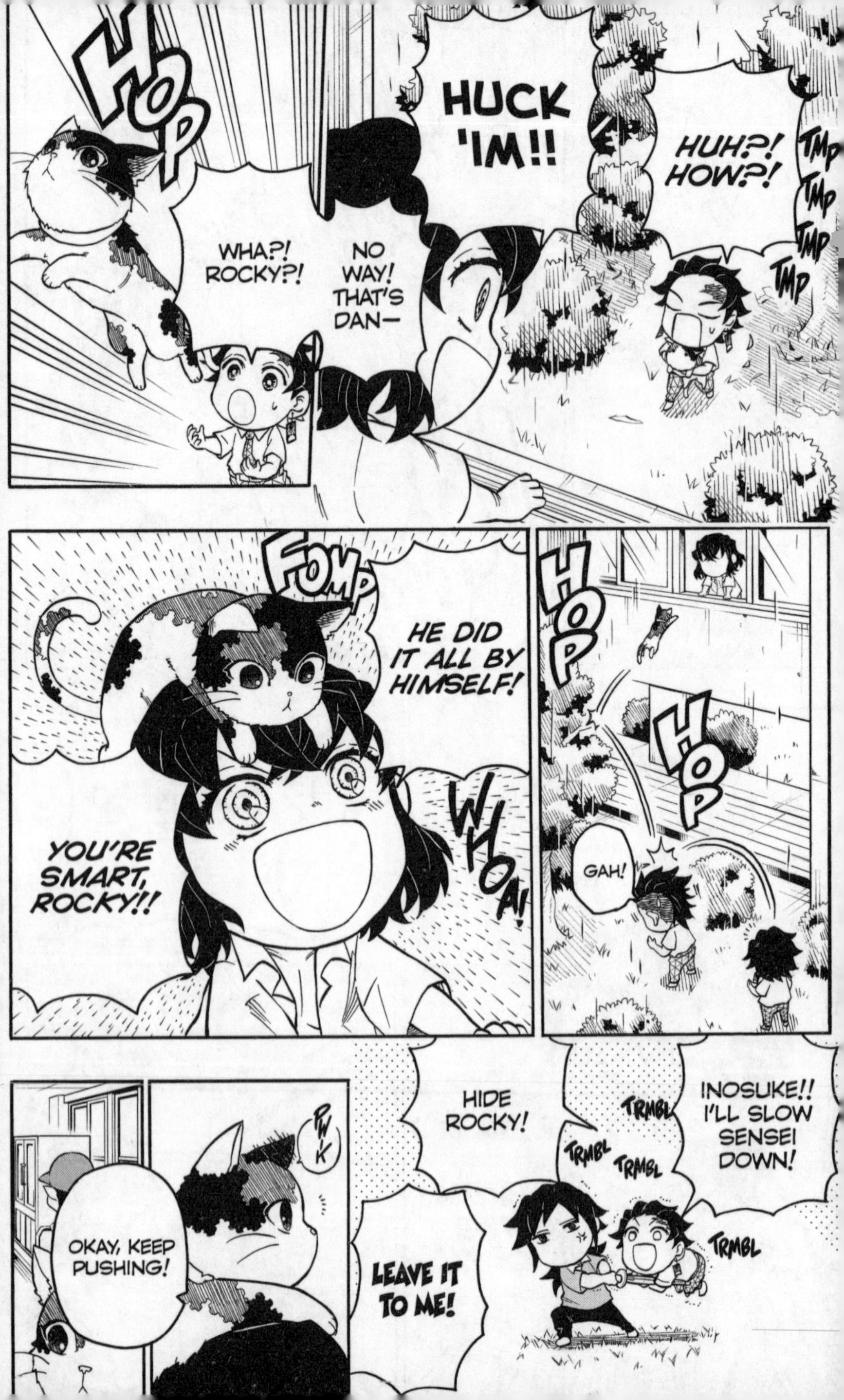
HUH?! HOW?!
TMP TMP TMP TMP
HUCK 'IM!!
NO WAY! THAT'S DAN—
WHA?! ROCKY?!
HOP
HOP
HOP
GAH!
FOMP
HE DID IT ALL BY HIMSELF!
WHOA!
YOU'RE SMART, ROCKY!!
INOSUKE!! I'LL SLOW SENSEI DOWN!
TRMBL TRMBL TRMBL TRMBL
HIDE ROCKY!
LEAVE IT TO ME!
PWIK
OKAY, KEEP PUSHING!

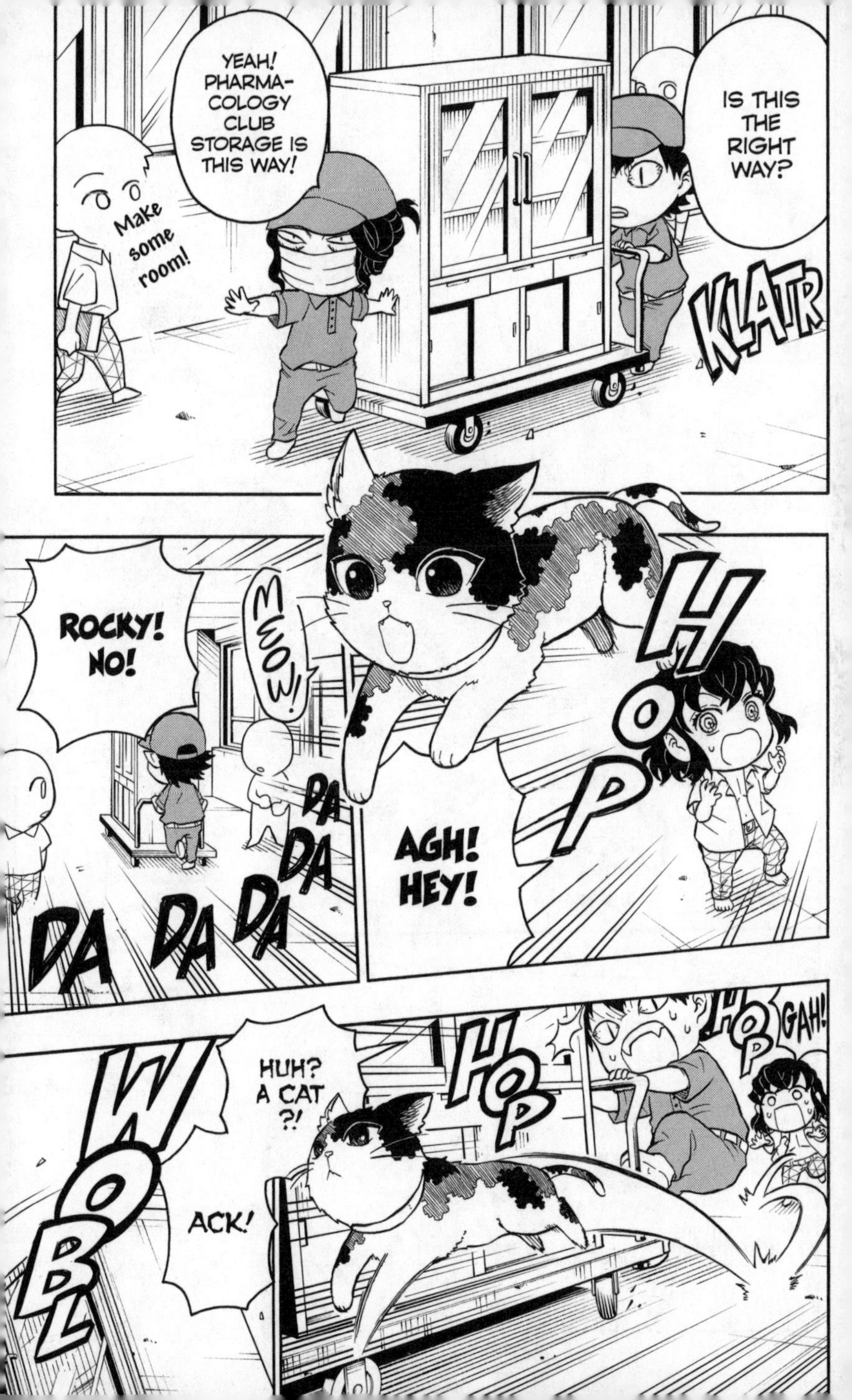
IS THIS THE RIGHT WAY?
YEAH! PHARMA-COLOGY CLUB STORAGE IS THIS WAY!
Make some room!
KLATR
MEOW!
HOP
AGH! HEY!
ROCKY! NO!
DA DA DA DA DA DA
HOP
GAH!
HOP
HUH? A CAT?!
ACK!
WOBL

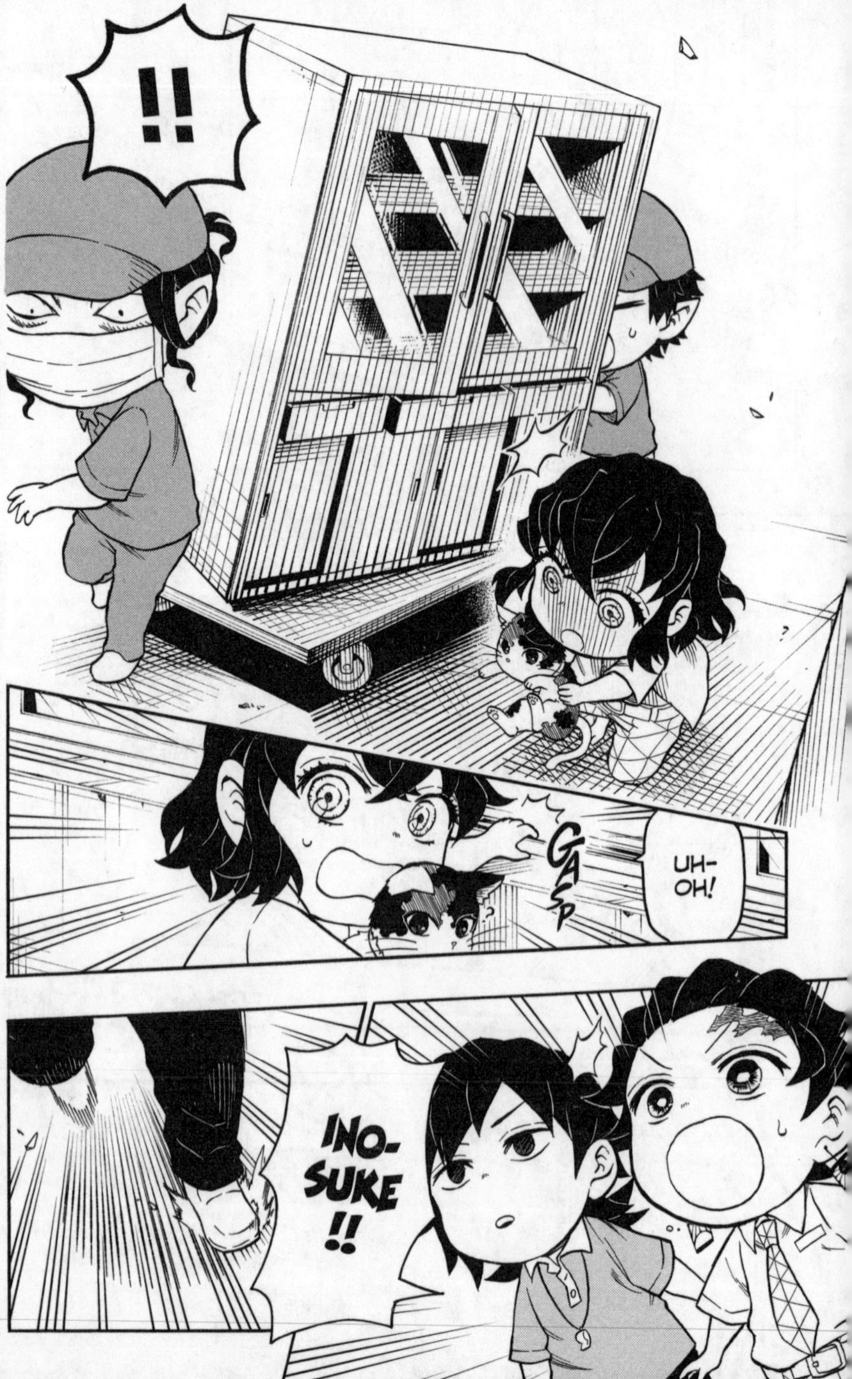
!!
UH-OH!
GASP
INO-SUKE!!

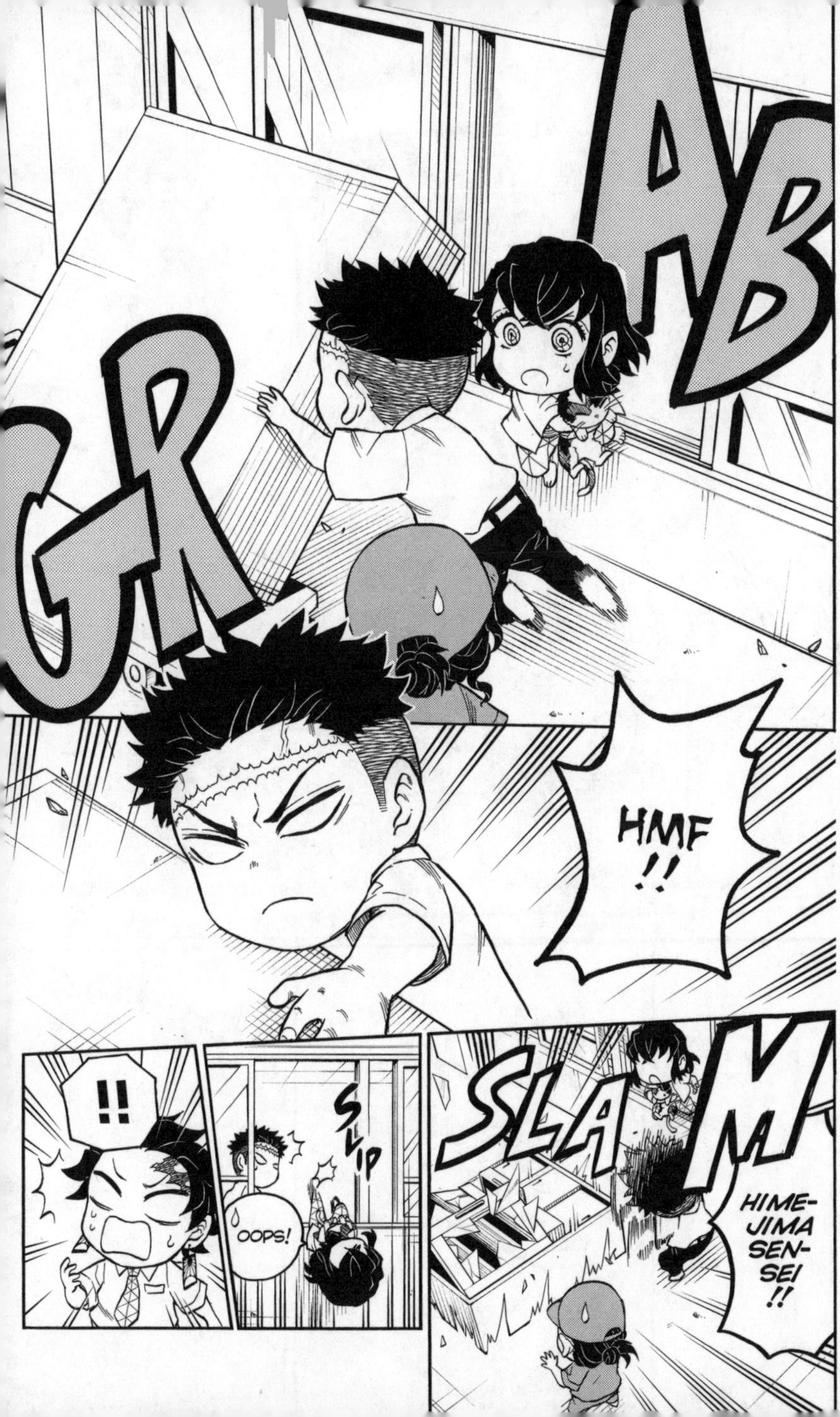

AB
GR
HMF !!
SLAM
HIME-JIMA SEN-SEI !!
SLIP
OOPS!
!!

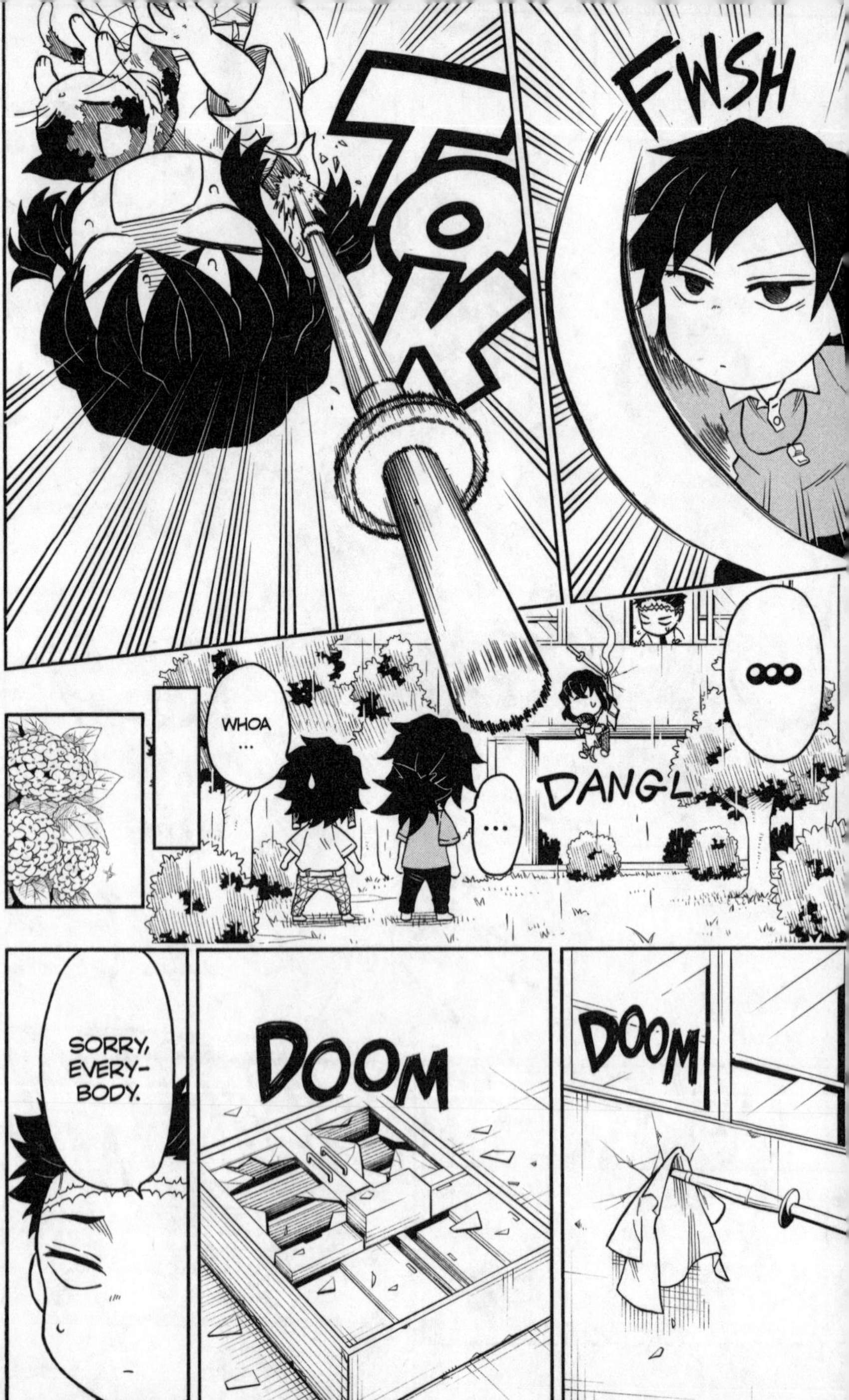
FWSH
TOK
...
DANGL
...
WHOA ...
DOOM
DOOM
SORRY, EVERY-BODY.

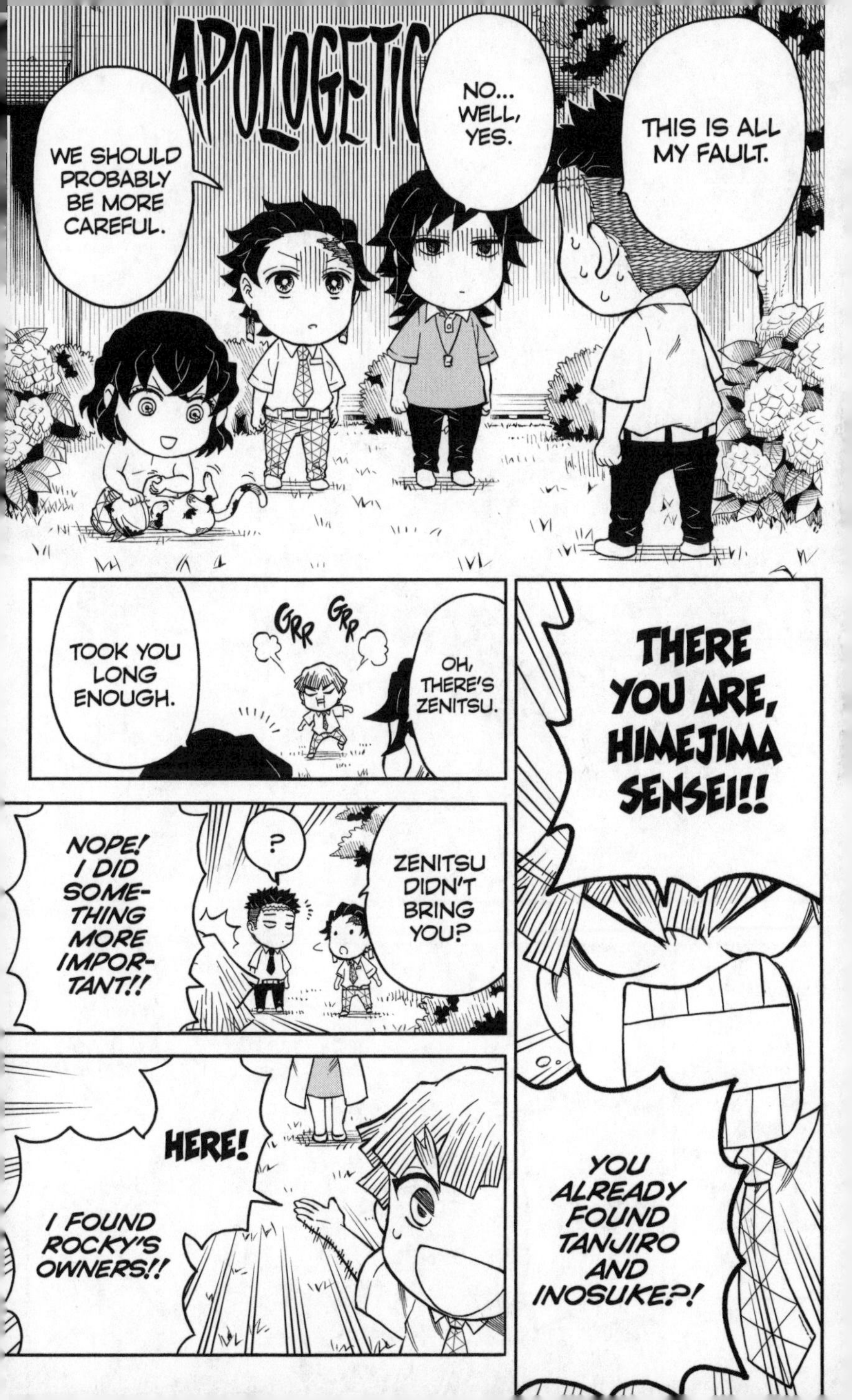

THIS IS ALL MY FAULT.
NO... WELL, YES.
APOLOGETIC
WE SHOULD PROBABLY BE MORE CAREFUL.
OH, THERE'S ZENITSU.
GRR GRR
TOOK YOU LONG ENOUGH.
THERE YOU ARE, HIMEJIMA SENSEI!!
YOU ALREADY FOUND TANJIRO AND INOSUKE?!
ZENITSU DIDN'T BRING YOU?
?
NOPE! I DID SOMETHING MORE IMPORTANT!!
HERE!
I FOUND ROCKY'S OWNERS!!

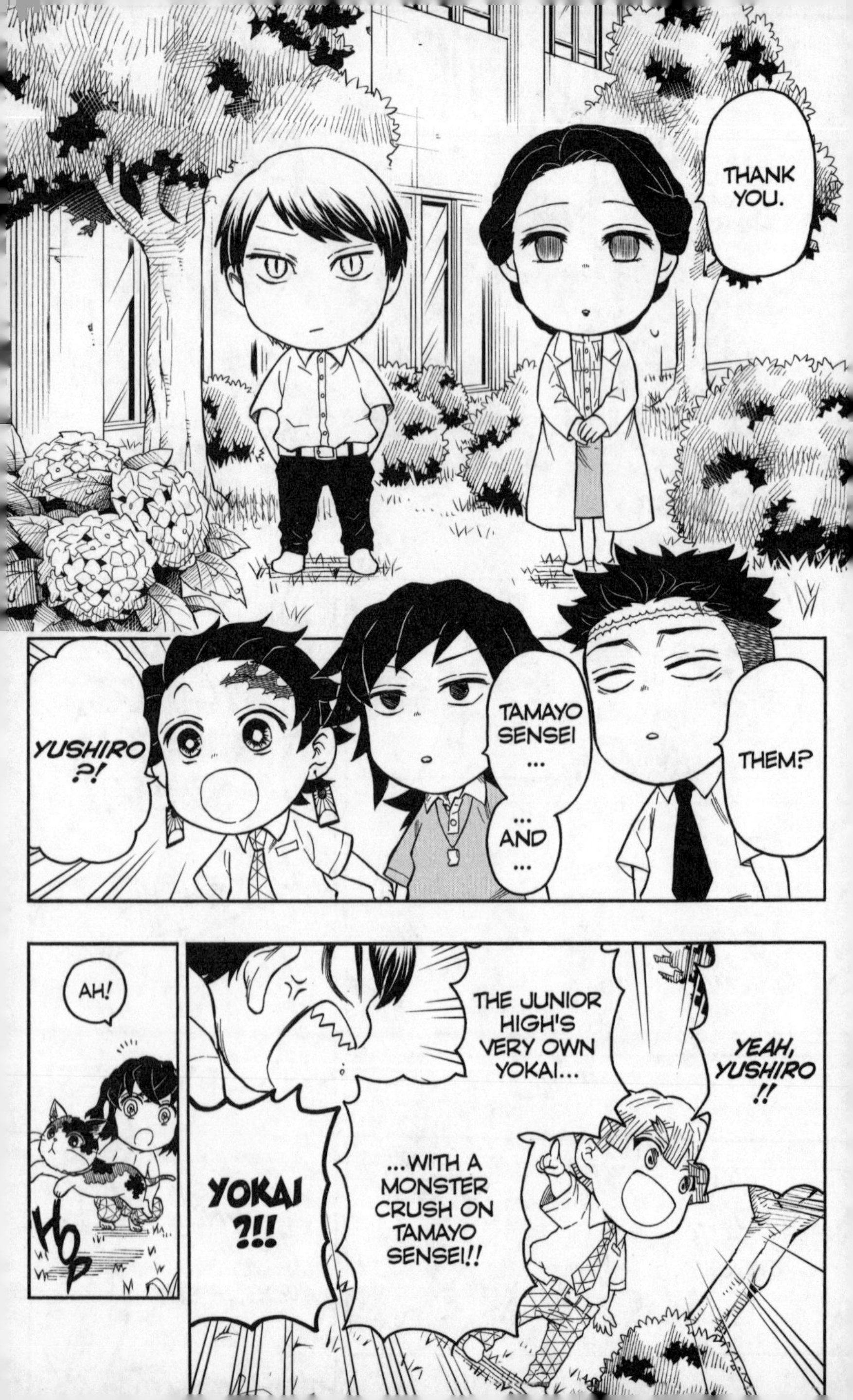
THANK YOU.
THEM?
TAMAYO SENSEI ... ... AND ...
YUSHIRO ?!
YEAH, YUSHIRO !!
THE JUNIOR HIGH'S VERY OWN YOKAI...
...WITH A MONSTER CRUSH ON TAMAYO SENSEI!!
YOKAI ?!!
AH!
HOP

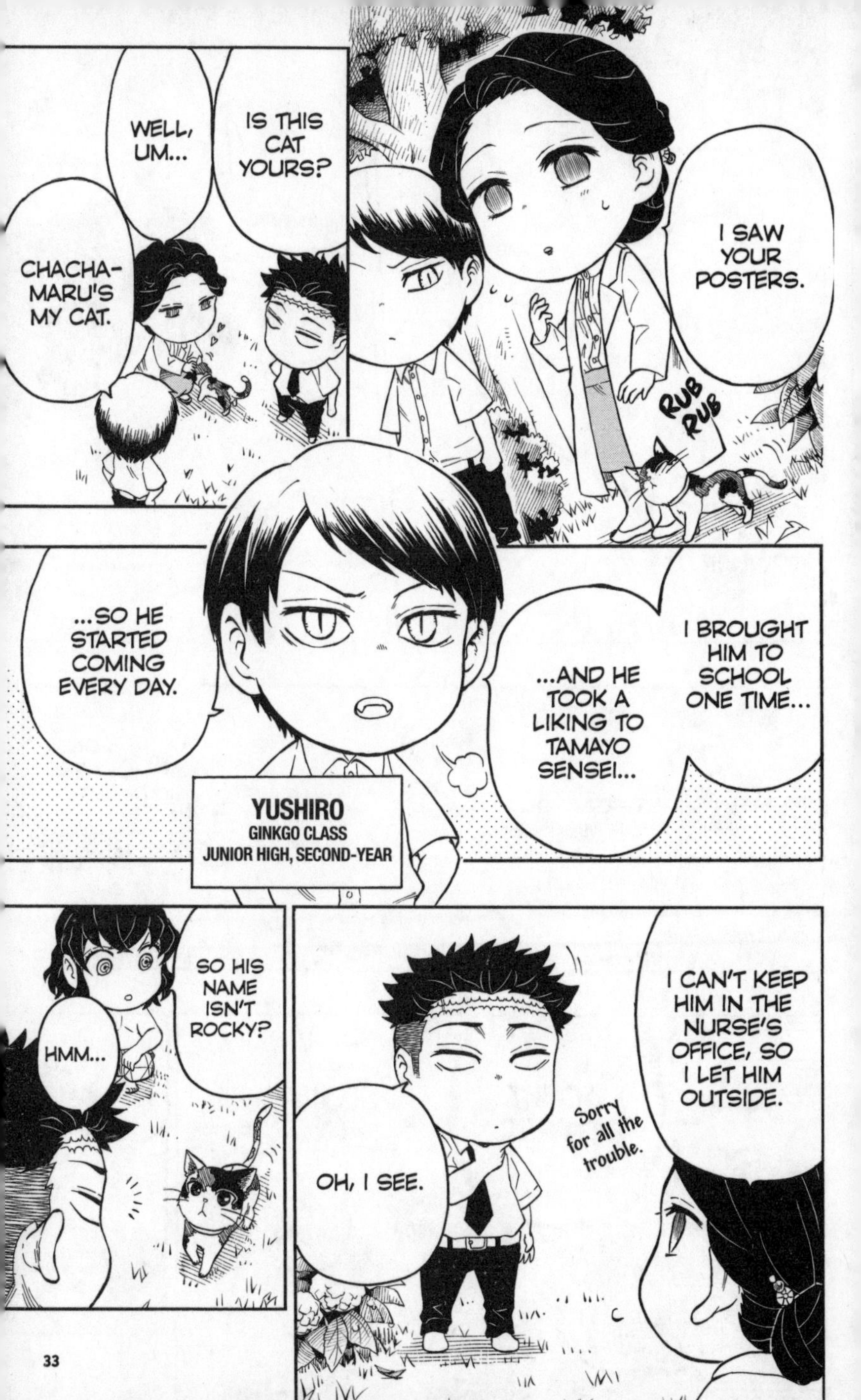
I SAW YOUR POSTERS.
RUB RUB
IS THIS CAT YOURS?
WELL, UM...
CHACHA-MARU'S MY CAT.
I BROUGHT HIM TO SCHOOL ONE TIME...
...AND HE TOOK A LIKING TO TAMAYO SENSEI...
...SO HE STARTED COMING EVERY DAY.
YUSHIRO
GINKGO CLASS
JUNIOR HIGH, SECOND-YEAR
I CAN'T KEEP HIM IN THE NURSE'S OFFICE, SO I LET HIM OUTSIDE.
Sorry for all the trouble.
OH, I SEE.
SO HIS NAME ISN'T ROCKY?
HMM...

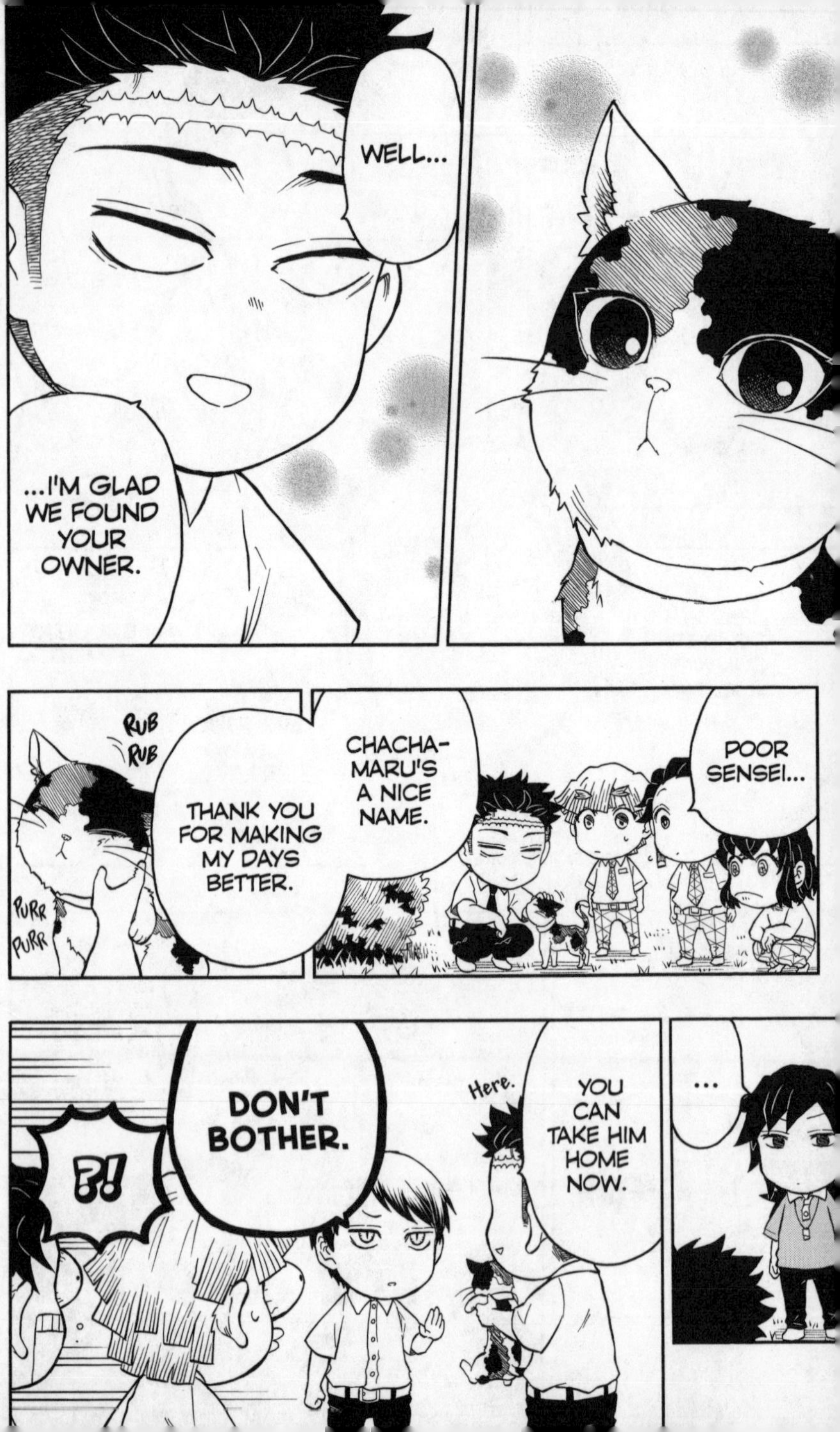
WELL...
...I'M GLAD WE FOUND YOUR OWNER.
POOR SENSEI...
CHACHA-MARU'S A NICE NAME.
RUB RUB
THANK YOU FOR MAKING MY DAYS BETTER.
PURR PURR
...
YOU CAN TAKE HIM HOME NOW.
Here.
DON'T BOTHER.
?!

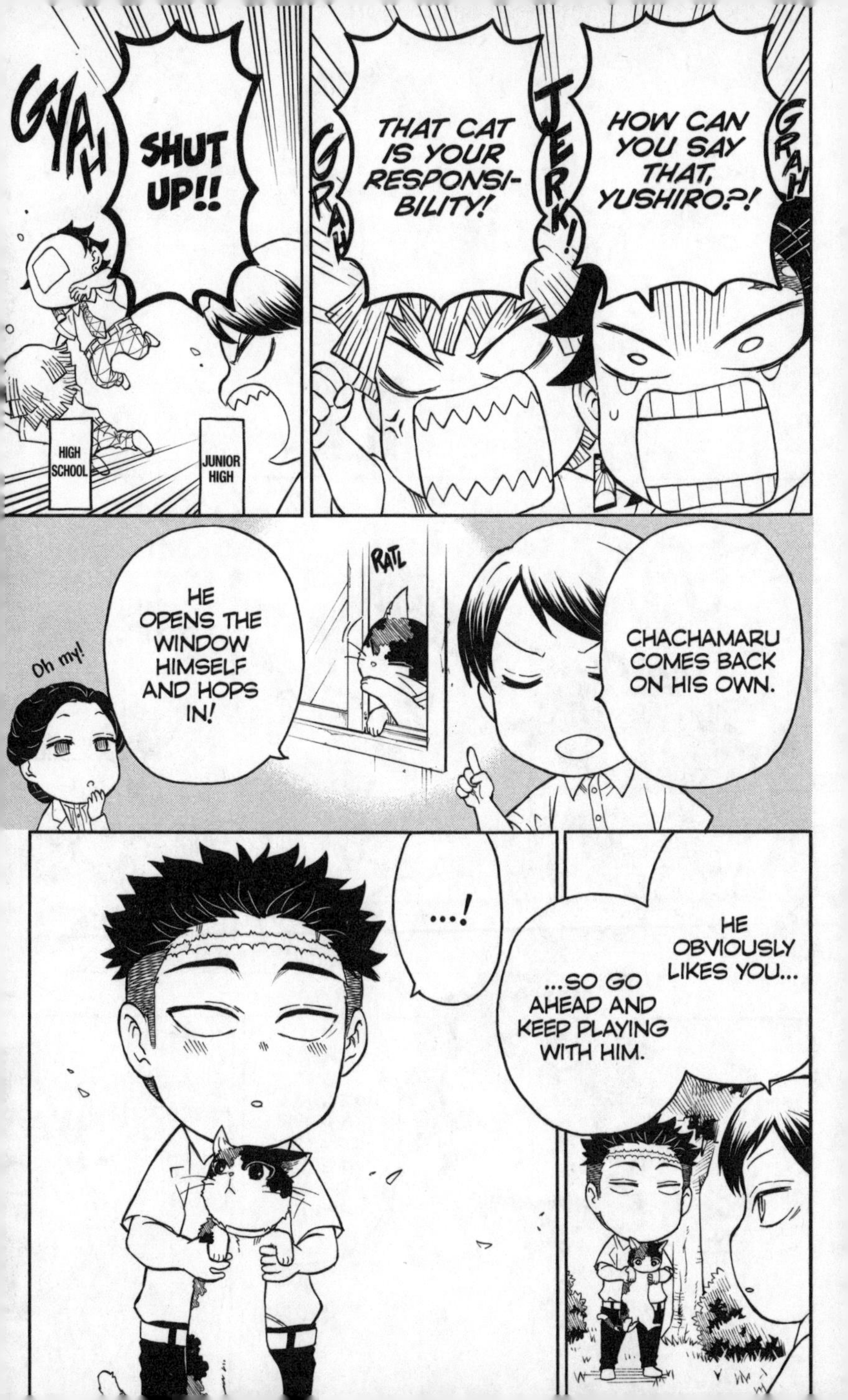
GRAH
HOW CAN YOU SAY THAT, YUSHIRO?!
JERK!
THAT CAT IS YOUR RESPONSI-BILITY!
GRAH
SHUT UP!!
GYAH
JUNIOR HIGH
HIGH SCHOOL
CHACHAMARU COMES BACK ON HIS OWN.
RATL
HE OPENS THE WINDOW HIMSELF AND HOPS IN!
Oh my!
HE OBVIOUSLY LIKES YOU...
...SO GO AHEAD AND KEEP PLAYING WITH HIM.
...!

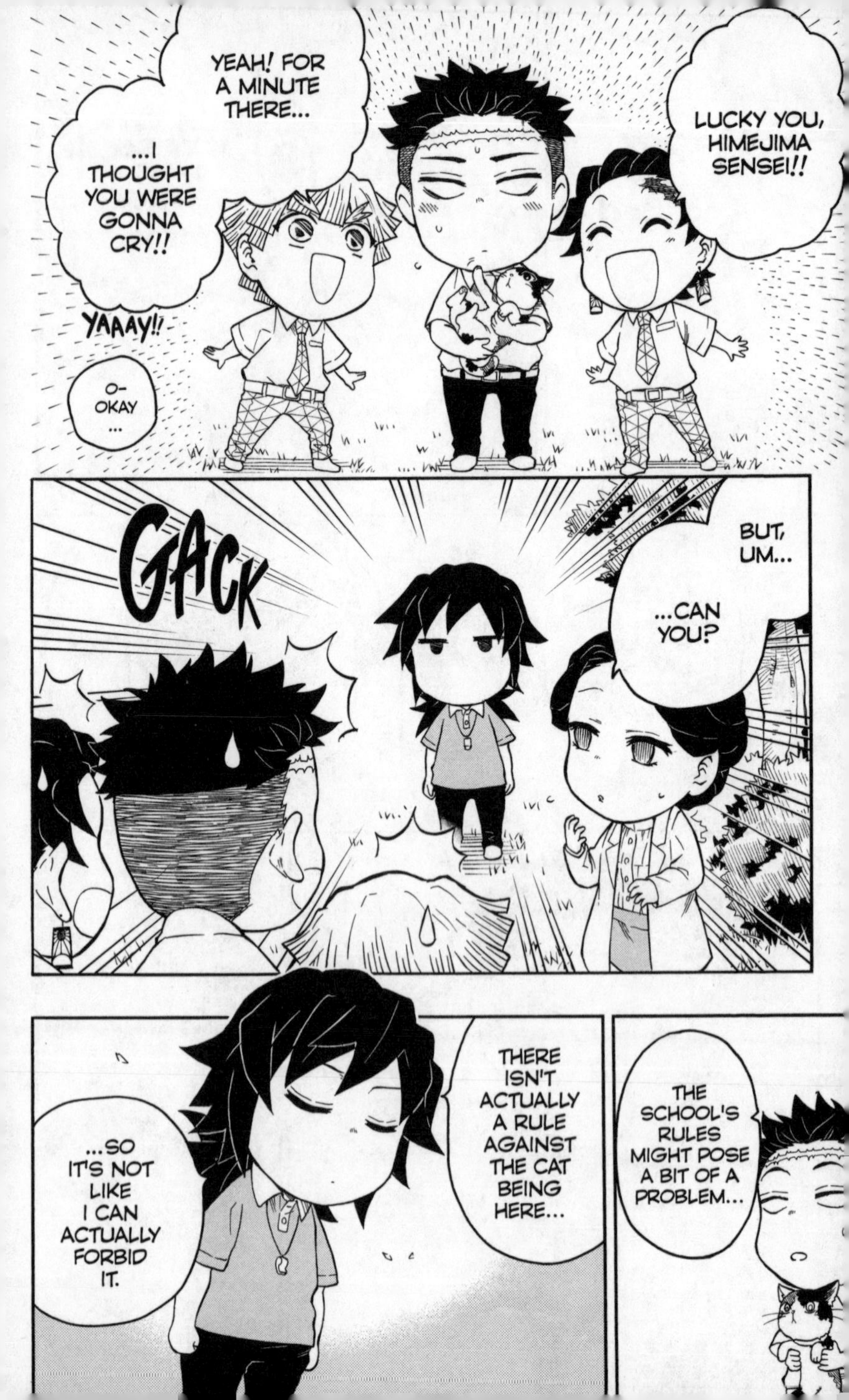

LUCKY YOU, HIMEJIMA SENSEI!!
YEAH! FOR A MINUTE THERE...
...I THOUGHT YOU WERE GONNA CRY!!
YAAAY!!
O-OKAY...
BUT, UM...
...CAN YOU?
GACK
THE SCHOOL'S RULES MIGHT POSE A BIT OF A PROBLEM...
THERE ISN'T ACTUALLY A RULE AGAINST THE CAT BEING HERE...
...SO IT'S NOT LIKE I CAN ACTUALLY FORBID IT.

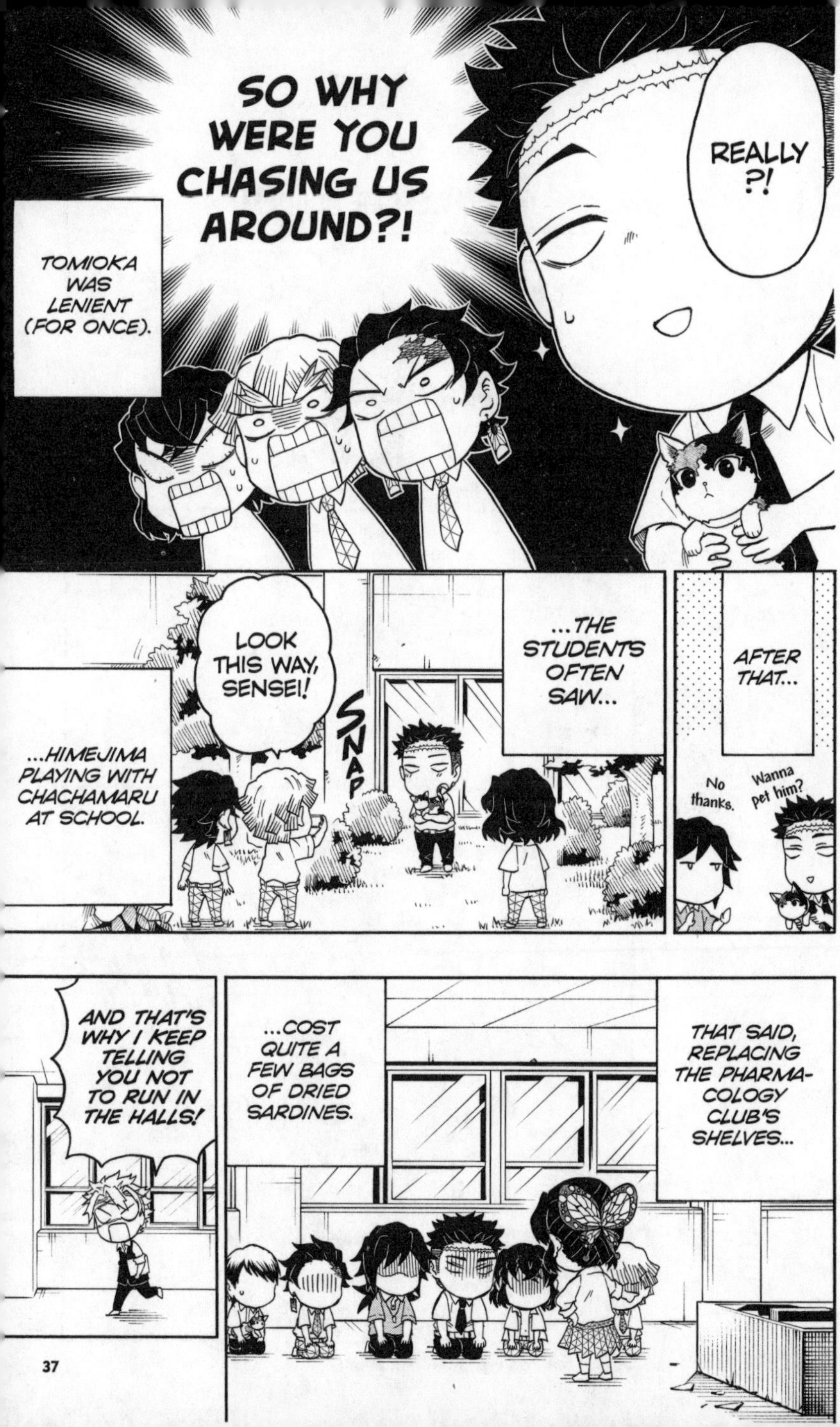
REALLY ?!
SO WHY WERE YOU CHASING US AROUND?!
TOMIOKA WAS LENIENT (FOR ONCE).
AFTER THAT...
Wanna pet him?
No thanks.
...THE STUDENTS OFTEN SAW...
LOOK THIS WAY, SENSEI!
SNAP
...HIMEJIMA PLAYING WITH CHACHAMARU AT SCHOOL.
THAT SAID, REPLACING THE PHARMA-COLOGY CLUB'S SHELVES...
...COST QUITE A FEW BAGS OF DRIED SARDINES.
AND THAT'S WHY I KEEP TELLING YOU NOT TO RUN IN THE HALLS!

AWESOME ACADEMY

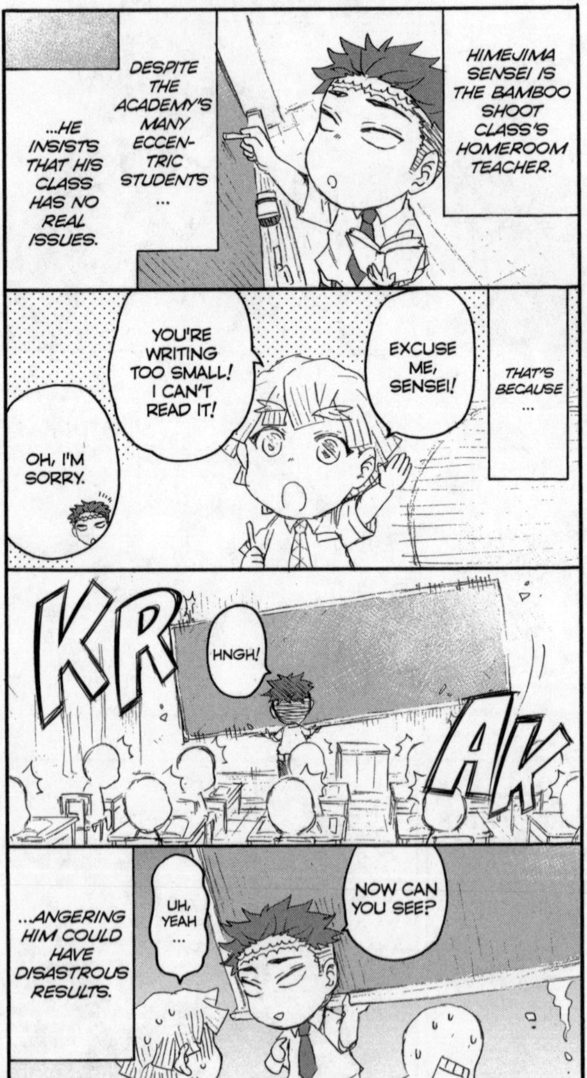
HIMEJIMA SENSEI IS THE BAMBOO SHOOT CLASS'S HOMEROOM TEACHER.
DESPITE THE ACADEMY'S MANY ECCEN-TRIC STUDENTS...
...HE INSISTS THAT HIS CLASS HAS NO REAL ISSUES.
THAT'S BECAUSE...
EXCUSE ME, SENSEI!
YOU'RE WRITING TOO SMALL! I CAN'T READ IT!
OH, I'M SORRY.
HNGH!
KRAK
NOW CAN YOU SEE?
UH, YEAH...
...ANGERING HIM COULD HAVE DISASTROUS RESULTS.

But no one has ever seen him angry.

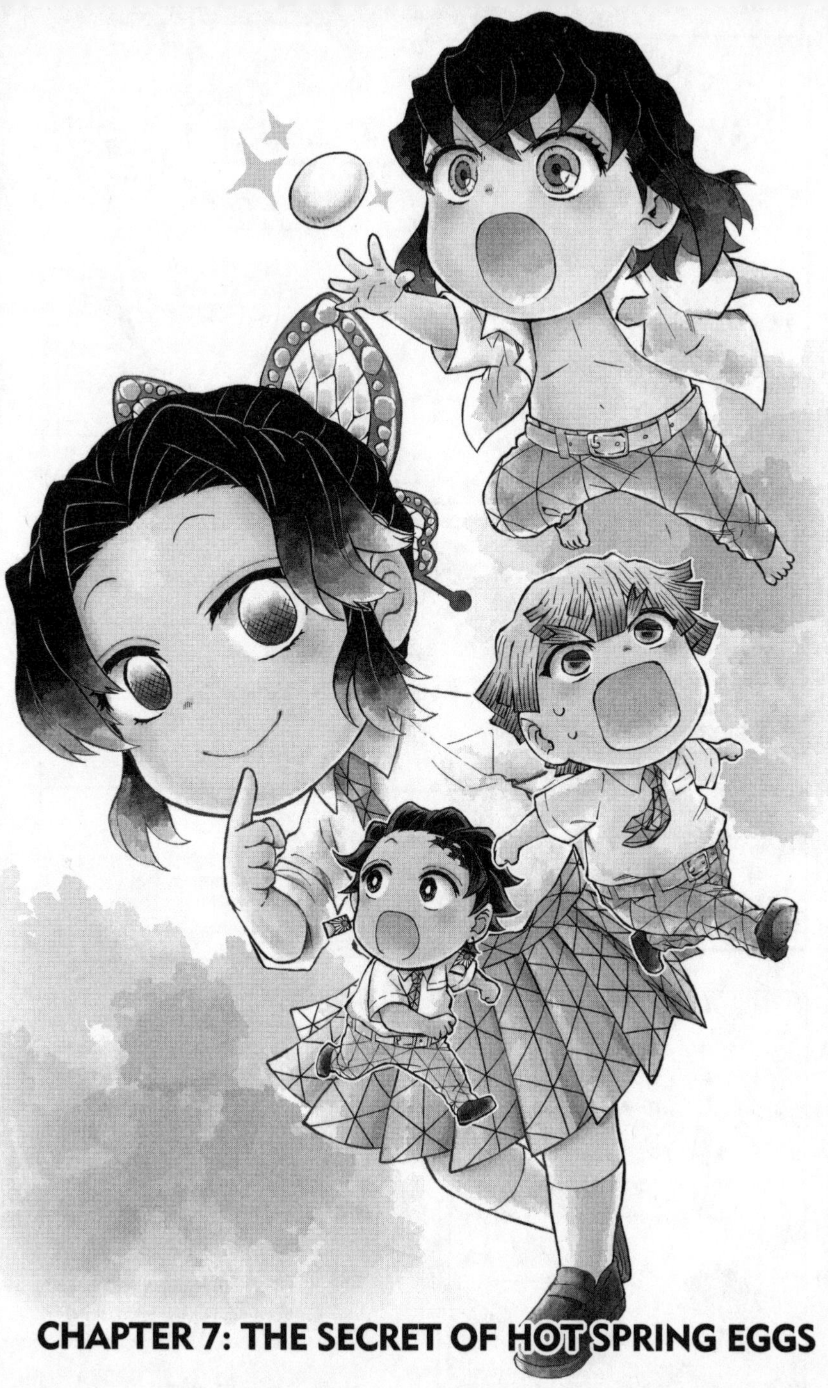

CHAPTER 7: THE SECRET OF HOT SPRING EGGS

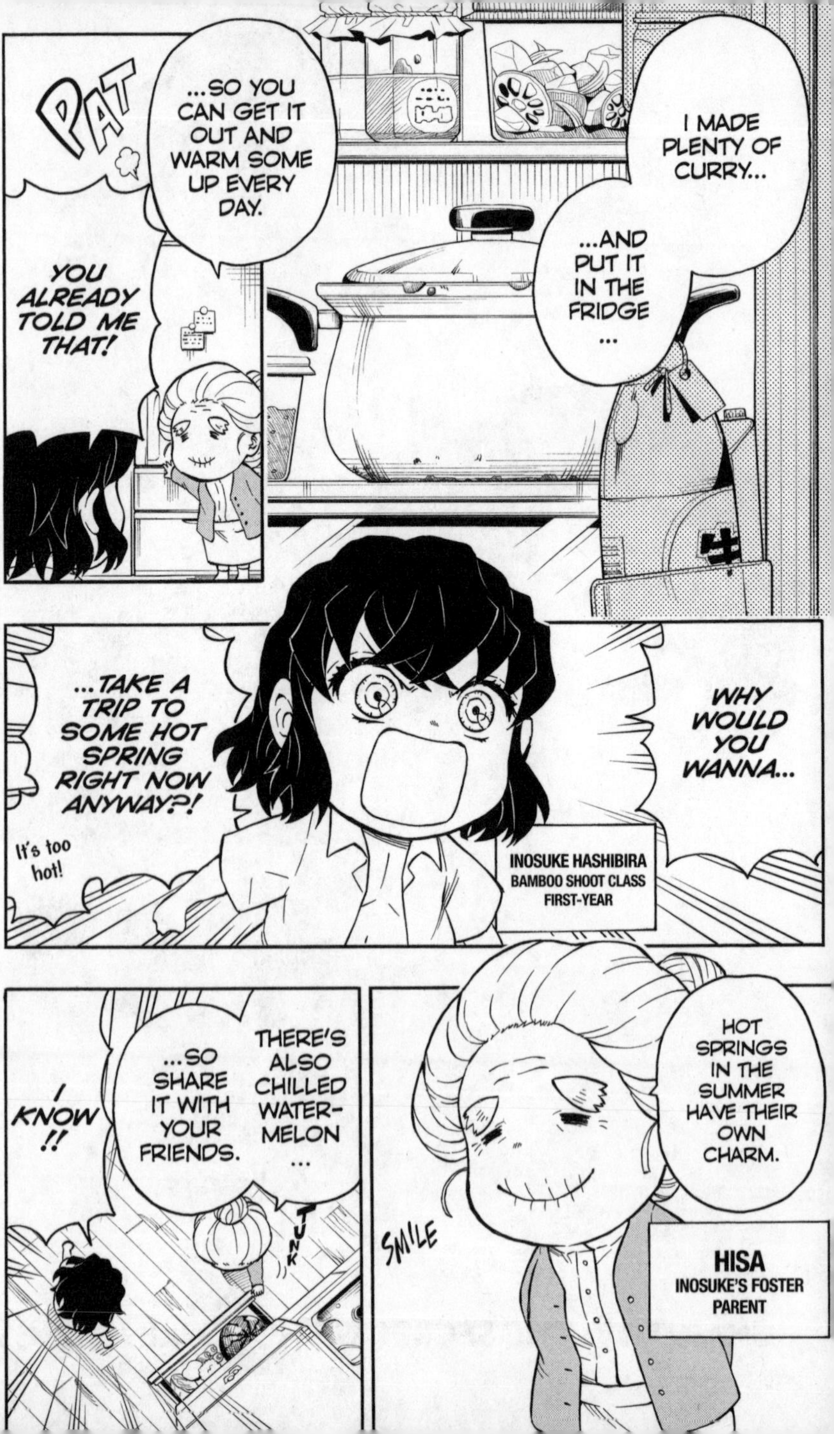
I MADE PLENTY OF CURRY...
...AND PUT IT IN THE FRIDGE ...
...SO YOU CAN GET IT OUT AND WARM SOME UP EVERY DAY.
PAT
YOU ALREADY TOLD ME THAT!
WHY WOULD YOU WANNA...
...TAKE A TRIP TO SOME HOT SPRING RIGHT NOW ANYWAY?!
It's too hot!
INOSUKE HASHIBIRA
BAMBOO SHOOT CLASS
FIRST-YEAR
HOT SPRINGS IN THE SUMMER HAVE THEIR OWN CHARM.
SMILE
HISA
INOSUKE'S FOSTER PARENT
THERE'S ALSO CHILLED WATER-MELON ...
...SO SHARE IT WITH YOUR FRIENDS.
JUNK
I KNOW!!

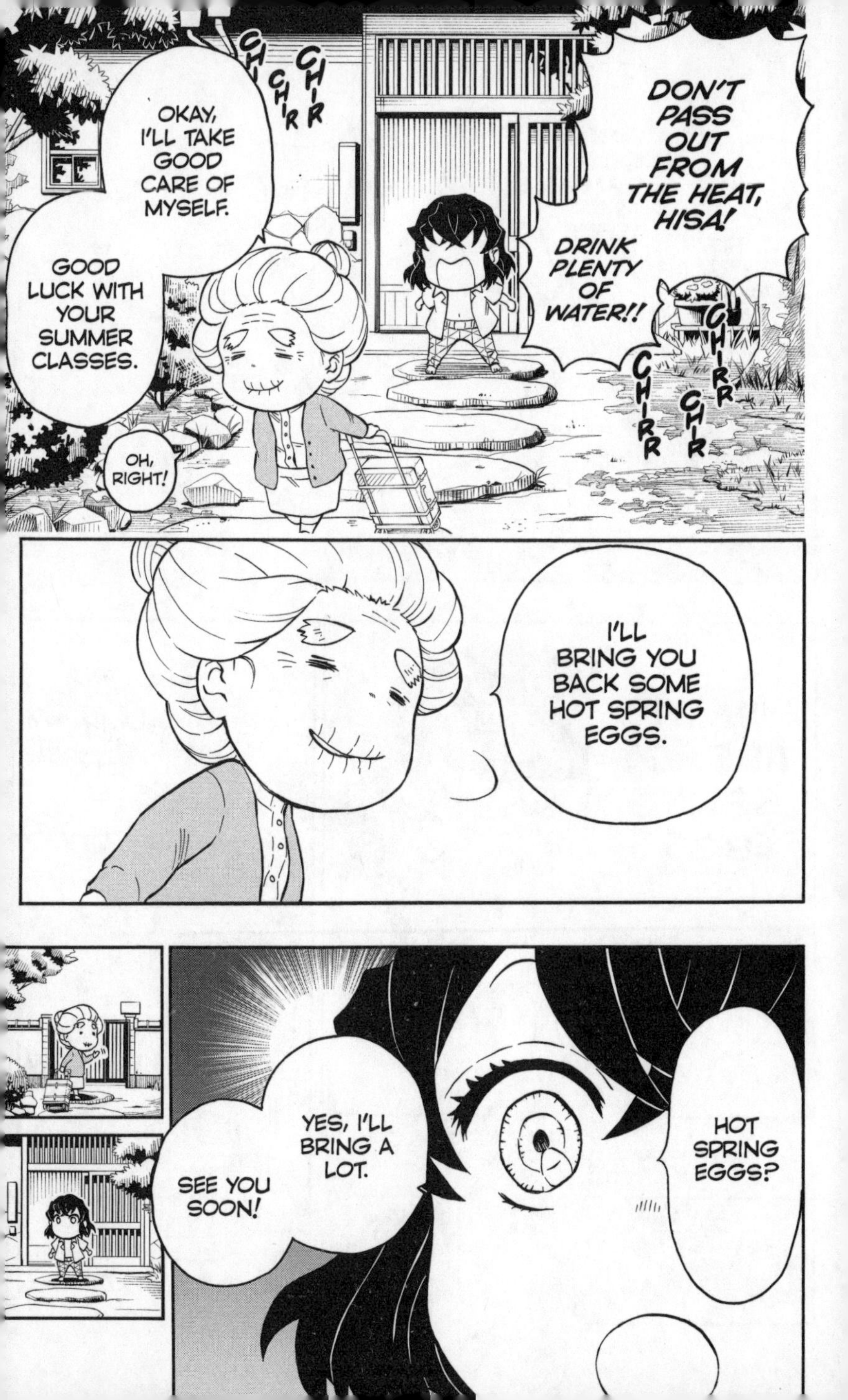
DON'T PASS OUT FROM THE HEAT, HISA!
DRINK PLENTY OF WATER!!
CHIRR CHIRR CHIRR
OKAY, I'LL TAKE GOOD CARE OF MYSELF.
CHIR CHIR
GOOD LUCK WITH YOUR SUMMER CLASSES.
OH, RIGHT!
I'LL BRING YOU BACK SOME HOT SPRING EGGS.
HOT SPRING EGGS?
YES, I'LL BRING A LOT.
SEE YOU SOON!

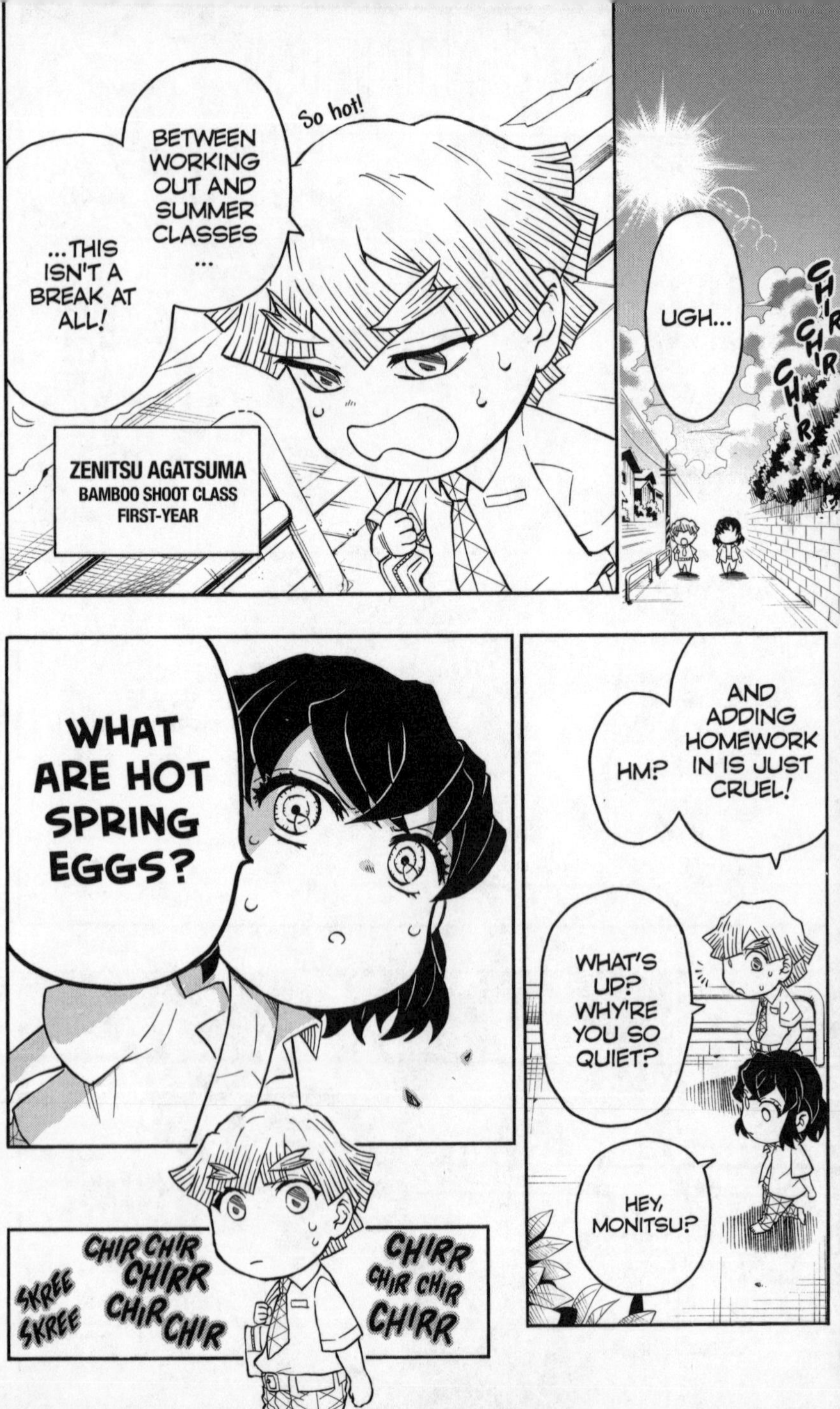
UGH...
CHIR CHIR CHIR
So hot!
BETWEEN WORKING OUT AND SUMMER CLASSES ...
...THIS ISN'T A BREAK AT ALL!
ZENITSU AGATSUMA
BAMBOO SHOOT CLASS
FIRST-YEAR
AND ADDING HOMEWORK IN IS JUST CRUEL!
HM?
WHAT'S UP? WHY'RE YOU SO QUIET?
HEY, MONITSU?
WHAT ARE HOT SPRING EGGS?
CHIRR CHIR CHIR CHIRR
CHIR CHIR CHIRR CHIR CHIR
SKREE SKREE

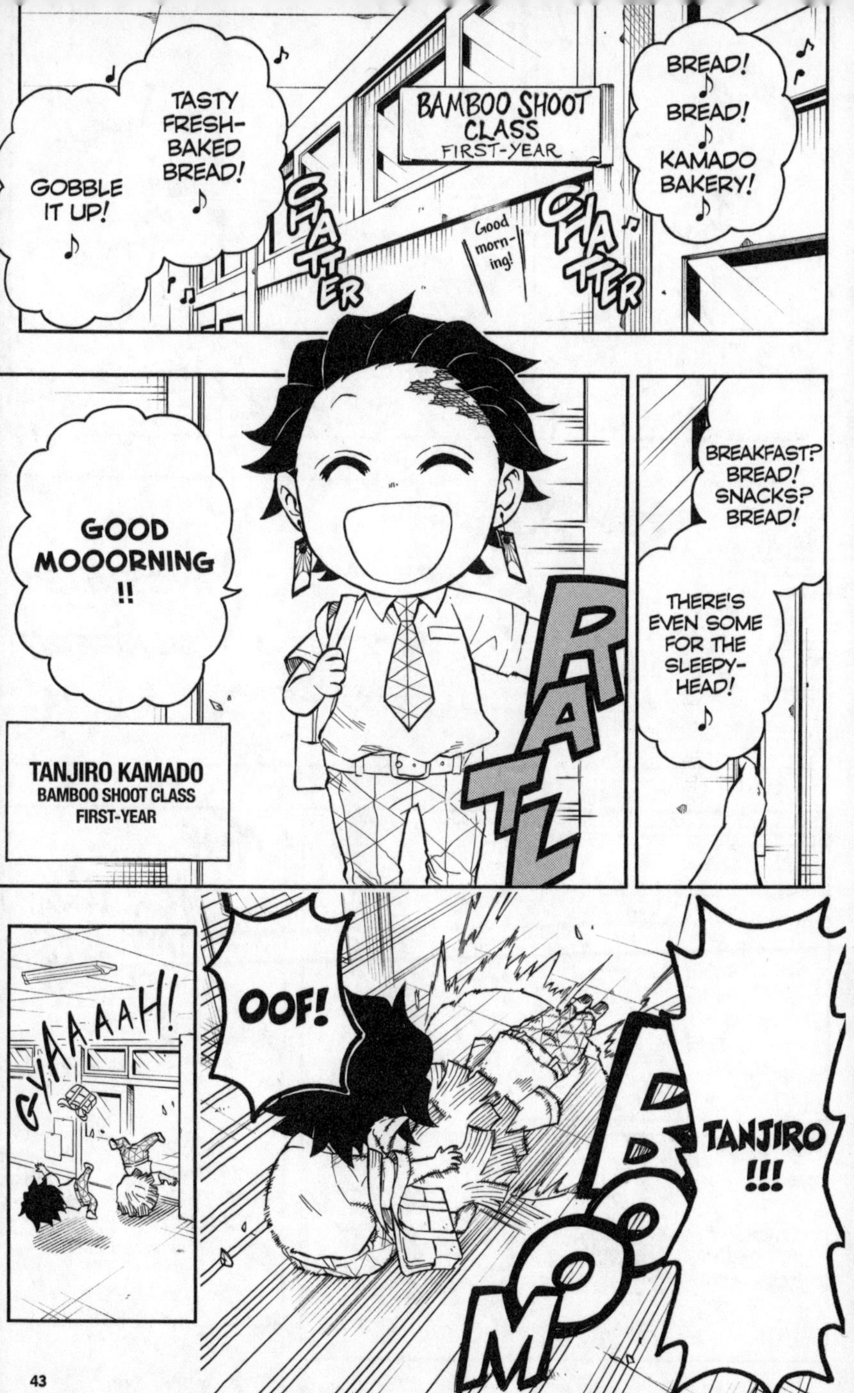
BREAD! ♪ BREAD! ♪ KAMADO BAKERY! ♪
BAMBOO SHOOT CLASS FIRST-YEAR
CHATTER
Good morning!
CHATTER
TASTY FRESH-BAKED BREAD! ♪
GOBBLE IT UP! ♪
BREAKFAST? BREAD! SNACKS? BREAD!
THERE'S EVEN SOME FOR THE SLEEPY-HEAD! ♪
RATTL
GOOD MOOORNING !!
TANJIRO KAMADO
BAMBOO SHOOT CLASS
FIRST-YEAR
TANJIRO !!!
BOOM
OOF!
GYAAAAH!

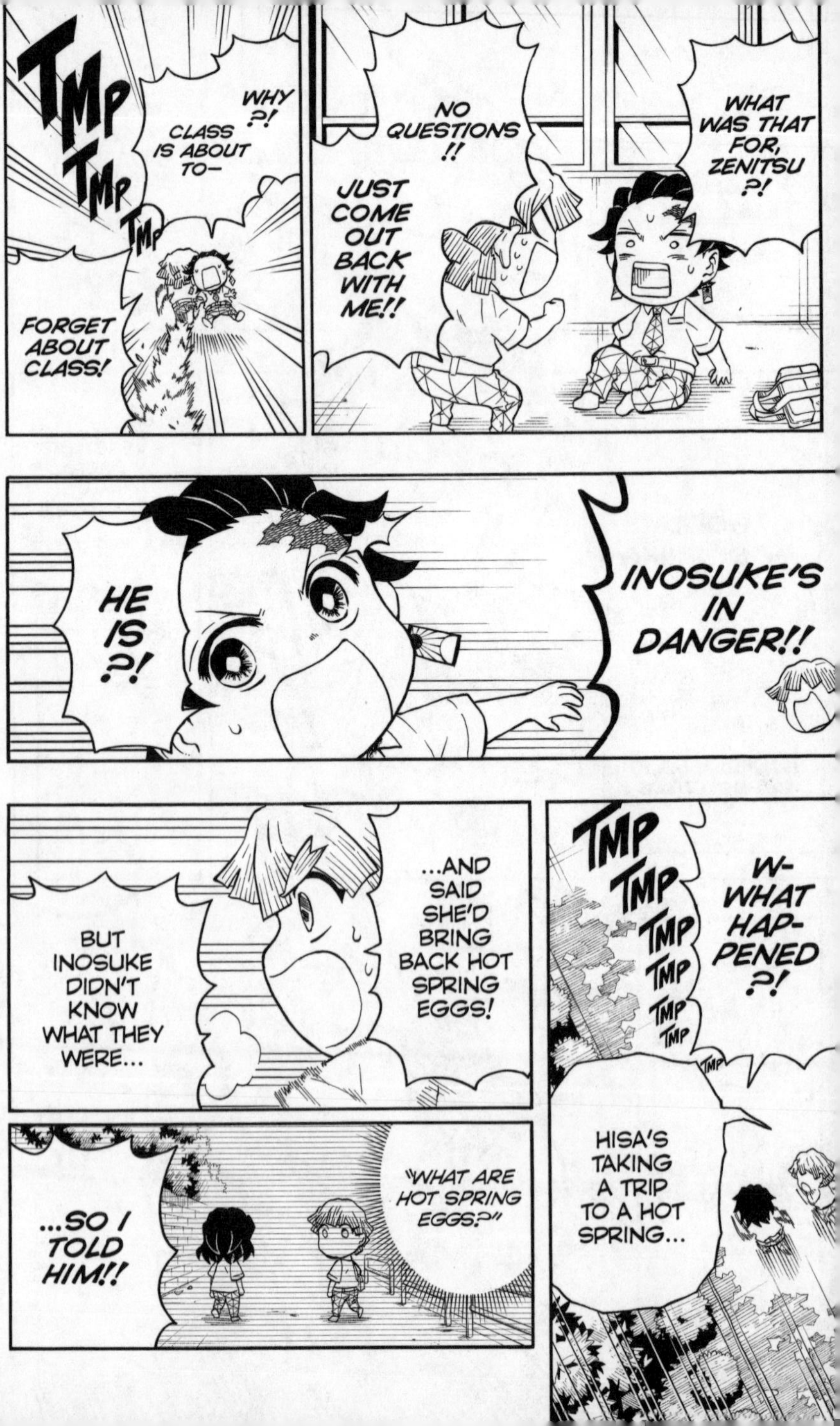
WHAT WAS THAT FOR, ZENITSU?!
NO QUESTIONS!!
JUST COME OUT BACK WITH ME!!
WHY?!
CLASS IS ABOUT TO—
TMP TMP TMP
FORGET ABOUT CLASS!
INOSUKE'S IN DANGER!!
HE IS?!
TMP TMP TMP TMP TMP TMP TMP
W-WHAT HAPPENED?!
HISA'S TAKING A TRIP TO A HOT SPRING...
...AND SAID SHE'D BRING BACK HOT SPRING EGGS!
BUT INOSUKE DIDN'T KNOW WHAT THEY WERE...
"WHAT ARE HOT SPRING EGGS?"
...SO I TOLD HIM!!

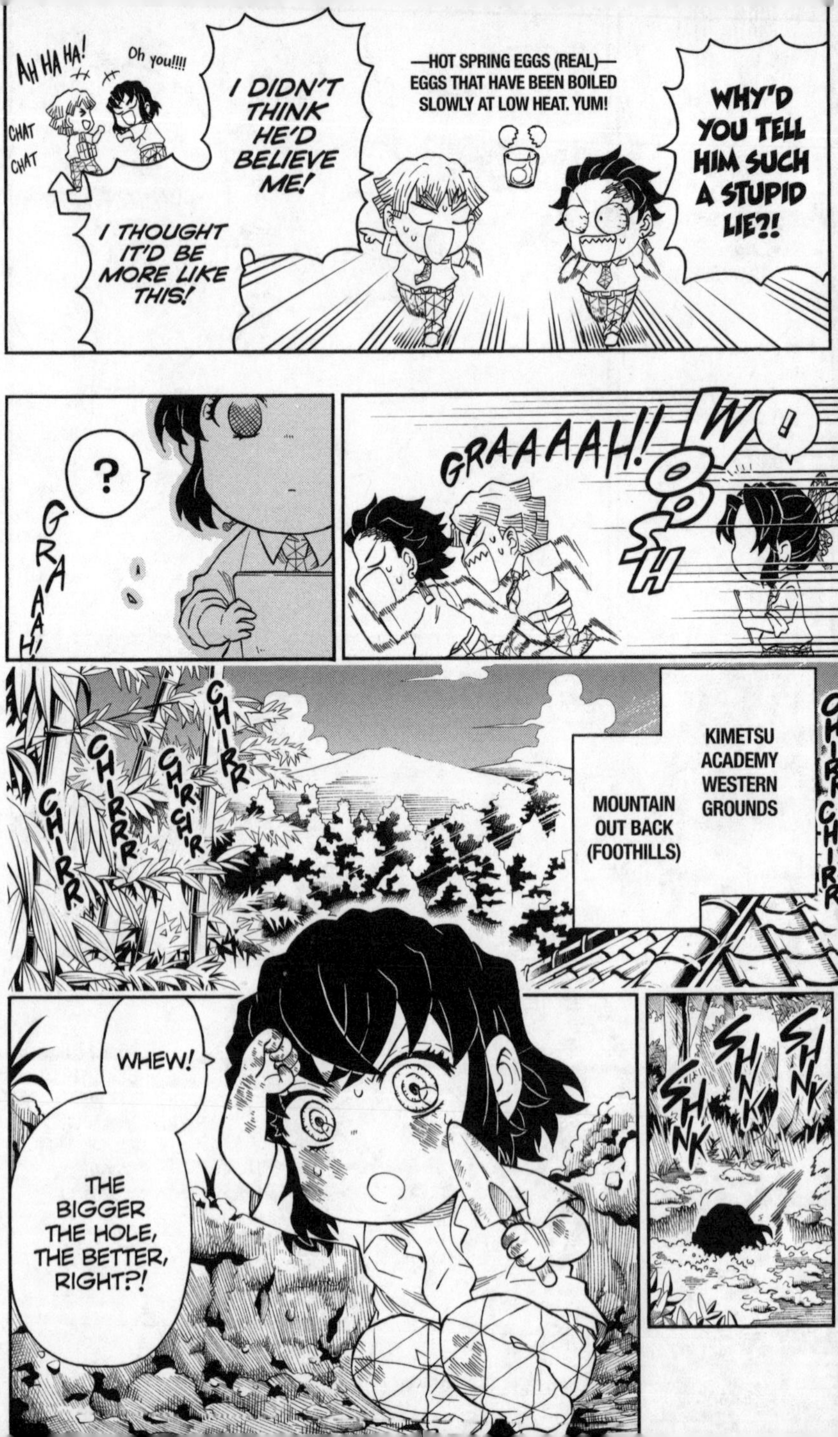
WHY'D YOU TELL HIM SUCH A STUPID LIE?!
—HOT SPRING EGGS (REAL)— EGGS THAT HAVE BEEN BOILED SLOWLY AT LOW HEAT. YUM!
I DIDN'T THINK HE'D BELIEVE ME!
I THOUGHT IT'D BE MORE LIKE THIS!
Oh you!!!!
AH HA HA!
CHAT CHAT
!
WHOOOSH
GRAAAAAH!
?
GRAAAAH!
CHIRR CHIRR
KIMETSU ACADEMY WESTERN GROUNDS
MOUNTAIN OUT BACK (FOOTHILLS)
CHIRR
CHIRR CHIR
CHIRRR
CHIRRR
SHNK
SHNK
SHNK
WHEW!
THE BIGGER THE HOLE, THE BETTER, RIGHT?!

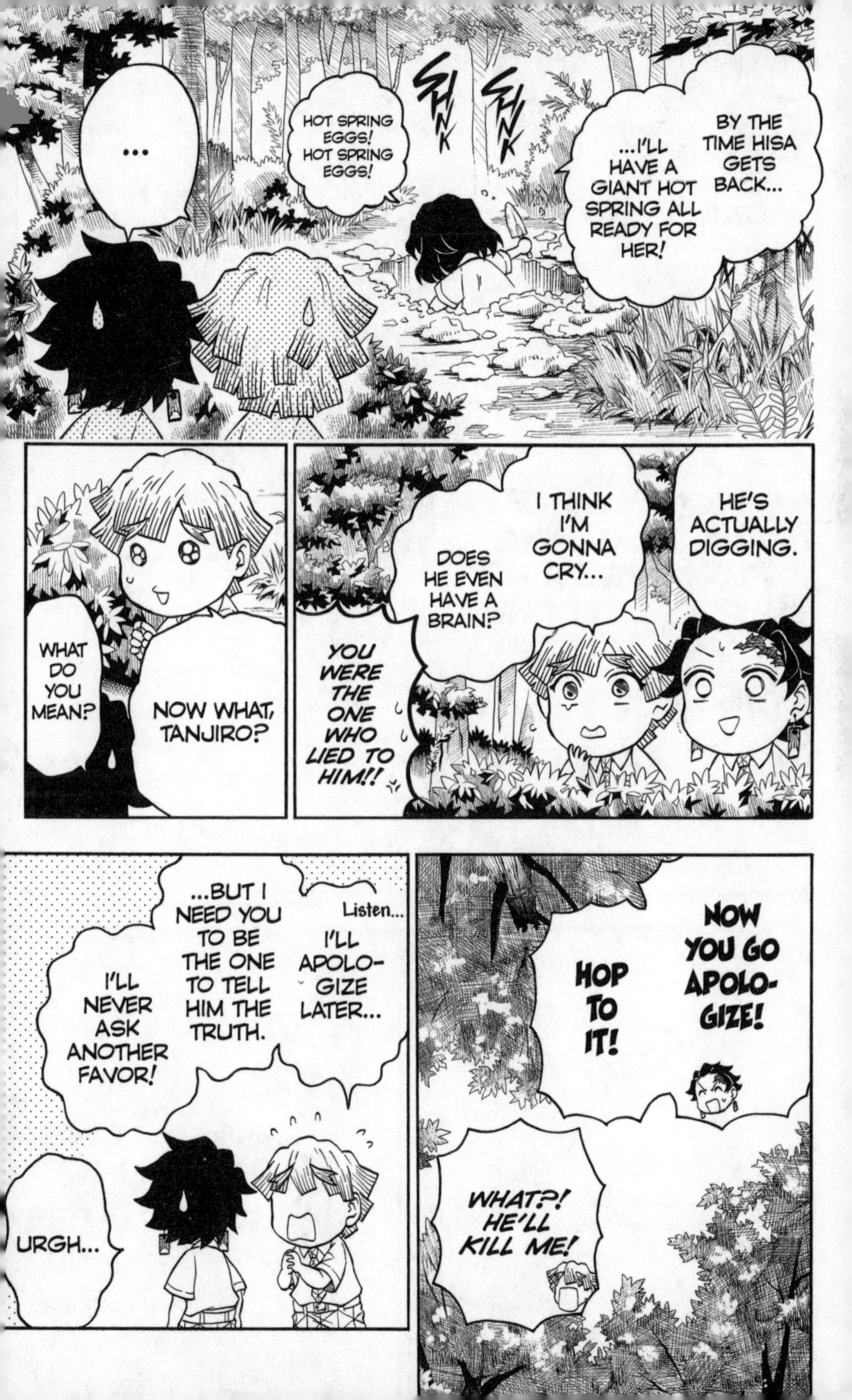

BY THE TIME HISA GETS BACK...
...I'LL HAVE A GIANT HOT SPRING ALL READY FOR HER!
SHUNK
SHUNK
HOT SPRING EGGS! HOT SPRING EGGS!
...
HE'S ACTUALLY DIGGING.
I THINK I'M GONNA CRY...
DOES HE EVEN HAVE A BRAIN?
YOU WERE THE ONE WHO LIED TO HIM!!
NOW WHAT, TANJIRO?
WHAT DO YOU MEAN?
NOW YOU GO APOLOGIZE!
HOP TO IT!
WHAT?! HE'LL KILL ME!
Listen...
I'LL APOLOGIZE LATER...
...BUT I NEED YOU TO BE THE ONE TO TELL HIM THE TRUTH.
I'LL NEVER ASK ANOTHER FAVOR!
URGH...

OH!

WELL, ACTUALLY I WANTED TO TELL YOU—

OUT FOR A WALK?

TAN-JIRO?

RJMN RJMN

YOU BETTER APOLOGIZE LATER!

UP

WE'RE GONNA HAVE A HOT SPRING SOON!!

LISTEN TO THIS, TANJIRO!!

...

...SO I NEED A GOOD SOAK!!

THE SUMMER HEAT'S GOT ME DOWN...

I can't wait!!

Oh man...

HISA'S GONNA BRING ME HOT SPRING EGGS!

Y-YEAH, ABOUT THAT...

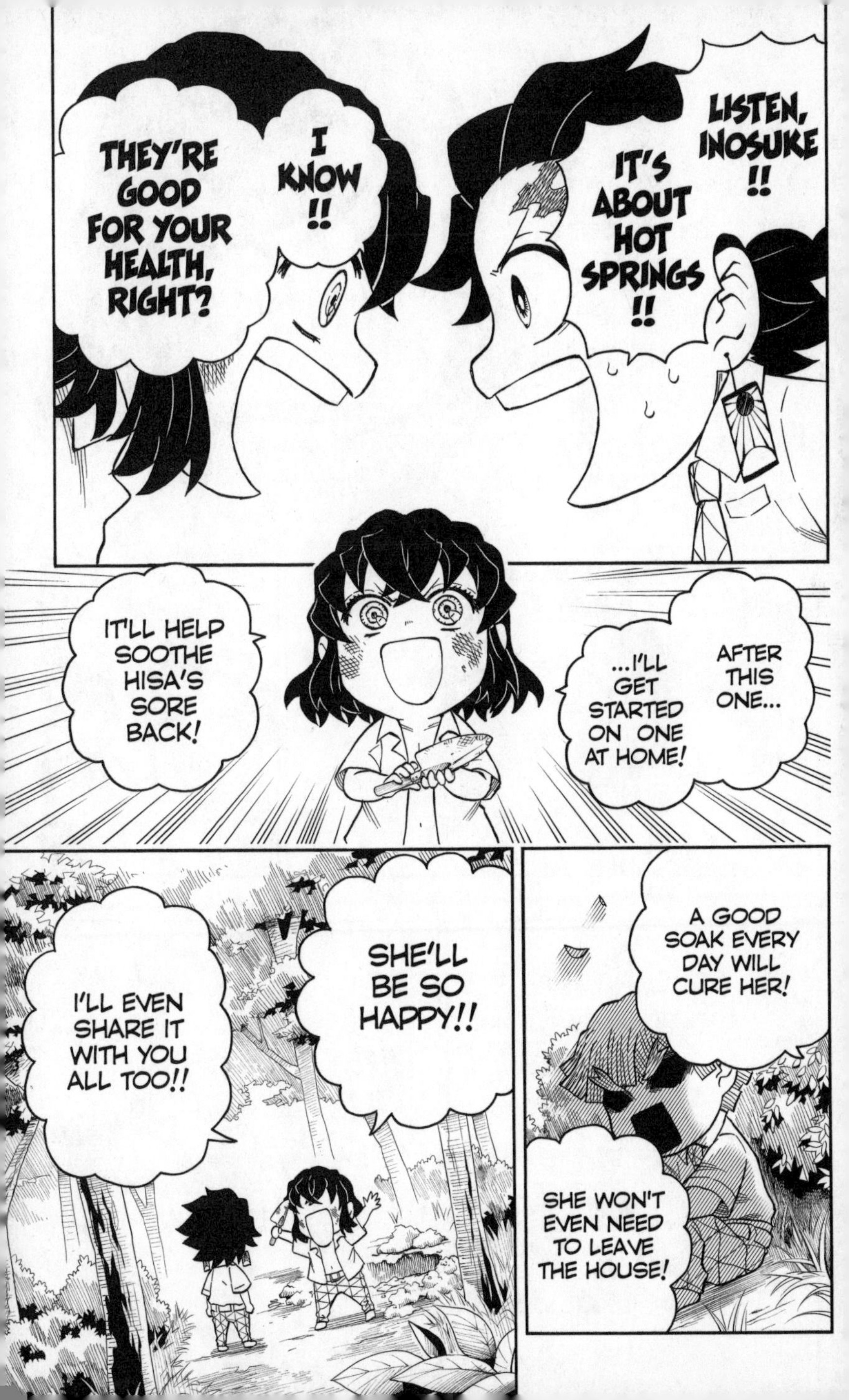
LISTEN, INOSUKE!!
IT'S ABOUT HOT SPRINGS!!
I KNOW!!
THEY'RE GOOD FOR YOUR HEALTH, RIGHT?
AFTER THIS ONE...
...I'LL GET STARTED ON ONE AT HOME!
IT'LL HELP SOOTHE HISA'S SORE BACK!
A GOOD SOAK EVERY DAY WILL CURE HER!
SHE WON'T EVEN NEED TO LEAVE THE HOUSE!
SHE'LL BE SO HAPPY!!
I'LL EVEN SHARE IT WITH YOU ALL TOO!!

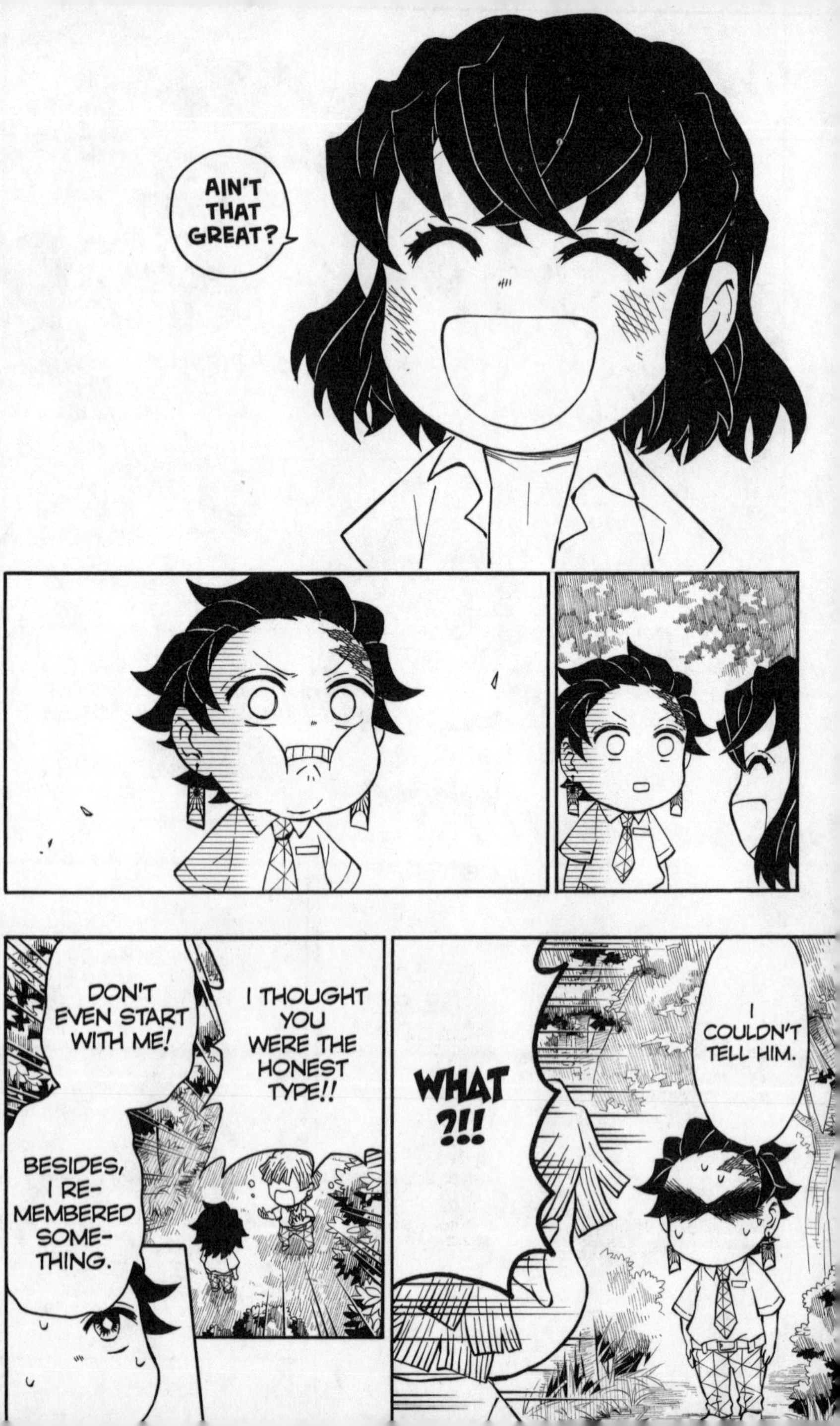
AIN'T THAT GREAT?
I COULDN'T TELL HIM.
WHAT?!!
I THOUGHT YOU WERE THE HONEST TYPE!!
DON'T EVEN START WITH ME!
BESIDES, I RE-MEMBERED SOME-THING.

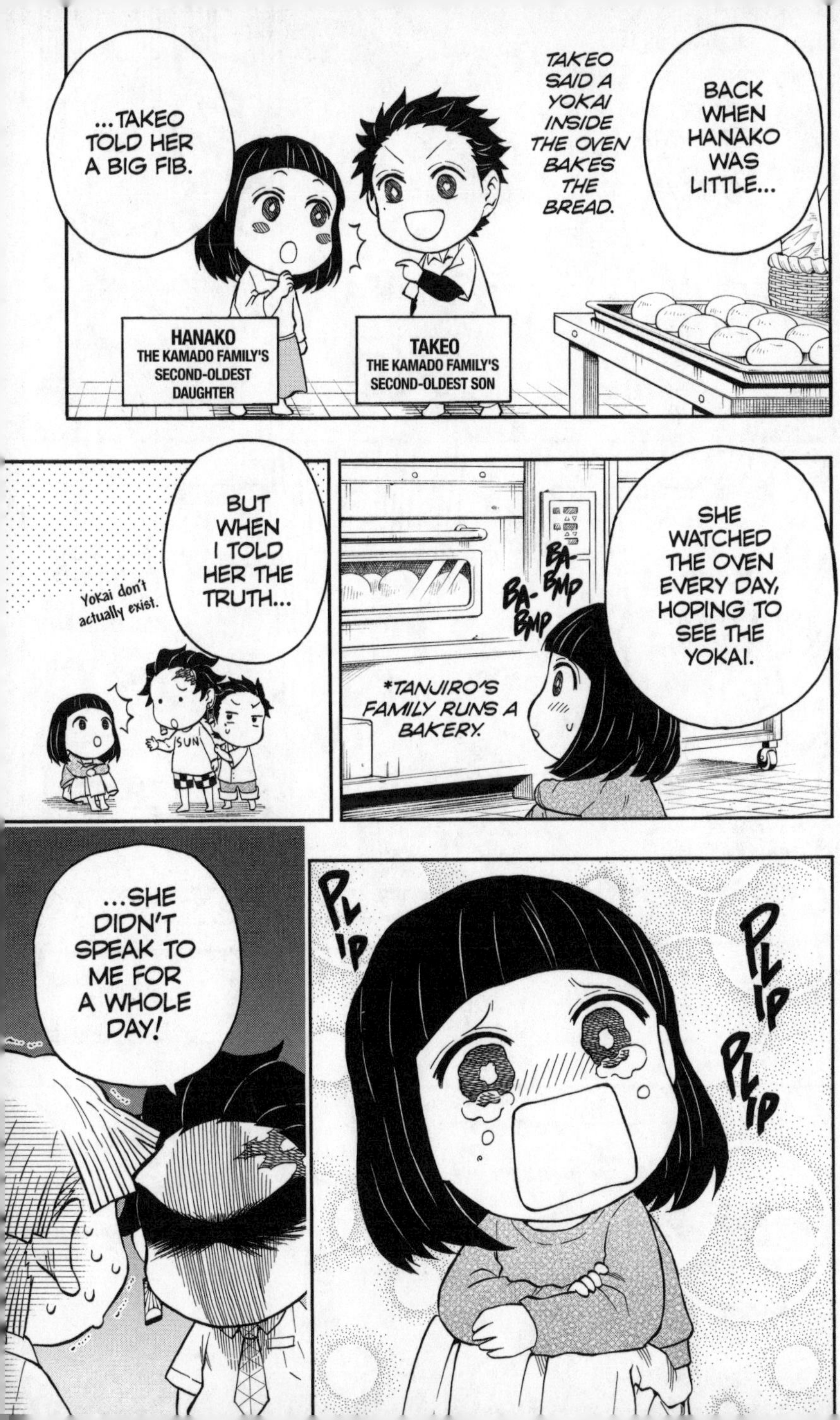
BACK WHEN HANAKO WAS LITTLE...
TAKEO SAID A YOKAI INSIDE THE OVEN BAKES THE BREAD.
...TAKEO TOLD HER A BIG FIB.
TAKEO THE KAMADO FAMILY'S SECOND-OLDEST SON
HANAKO THE KAMADO FAMILY'S SECOND-OLDEST DAUGHTER
SHE WATCHED THE OVEN EVERY DAY, HOPING TO SEE THE YOKAI.
BA-BMP
BA-BMP
*TANJIRO'S FAMILY RUNS A BAKERY.
BUT WHEN I TOLD HER THE TRUTH...
Yokai don't actually exist.
SUN
PLIP
PLIP
PLIP
...SHE DIDN'T SPEAK TO ME FOR A WHOLE DAY!

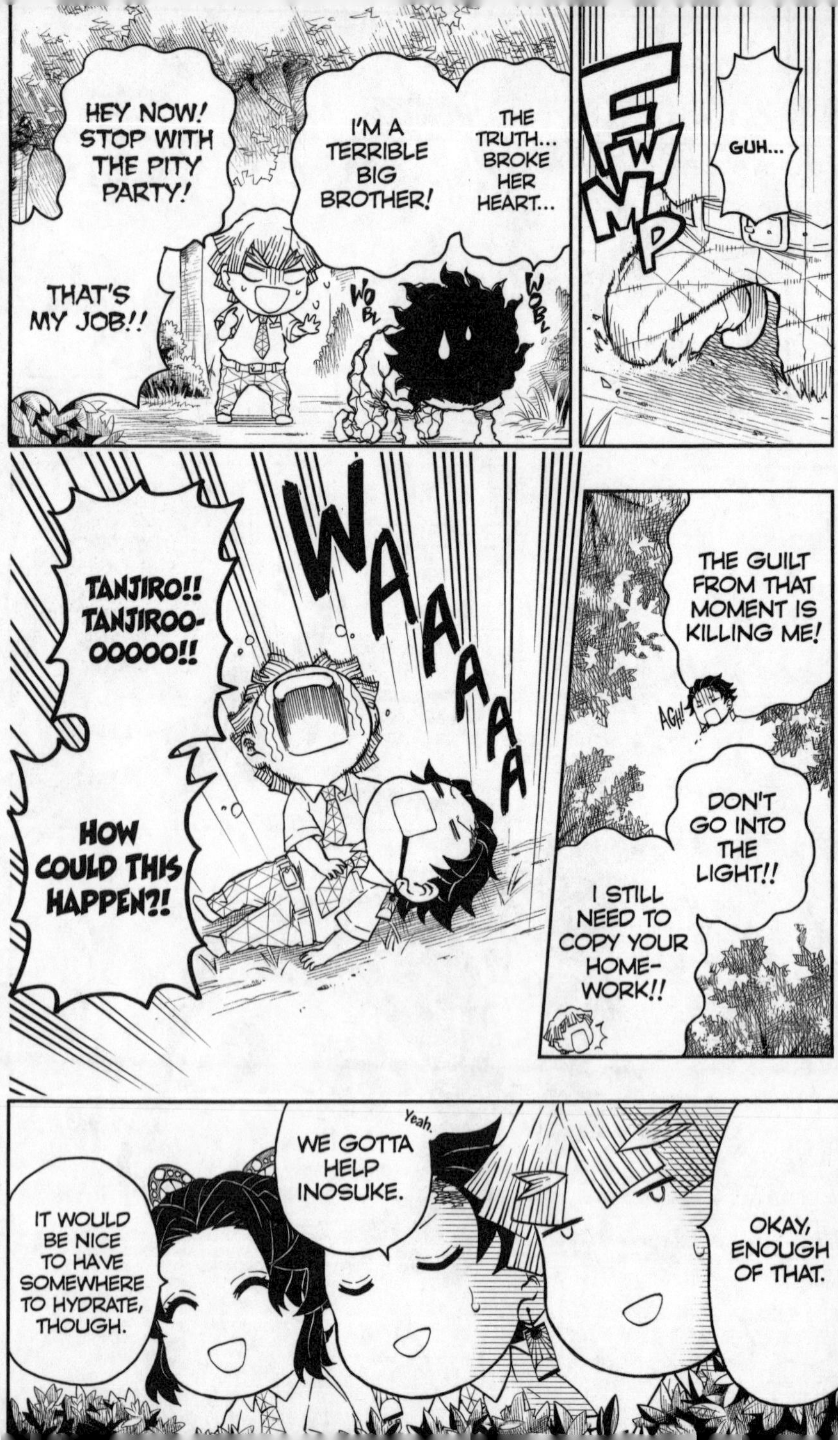
GUH...
FWMP
THE TRUTH... BROKE HER HEART...
I'M A TERRIBLE BIG BROTHER!
WOBL
WOBL
HEY NOW! STOP WITH THE PITY PARTY!
THAT'S MY JOB!!
THE GUILT FROM THAT MOMENT IS KILLING ME!
AGH!
DON'T GO INTO THE LIGHT!!
I STILL NEED TO COPY YOUR HOME-WORK!!
WAAAAAA
TANJIRO!! TANJIROO-OOOOO!!
HOW COULD THIS HAPPEN?!
OKAY, ENOUGH OF THAT.
Yeah.
WE GOTTA HELP INOSUKE.
IT WOULD BE NICE TO HAVE SOMEWHERE TO HYDRATE, THOUGH.

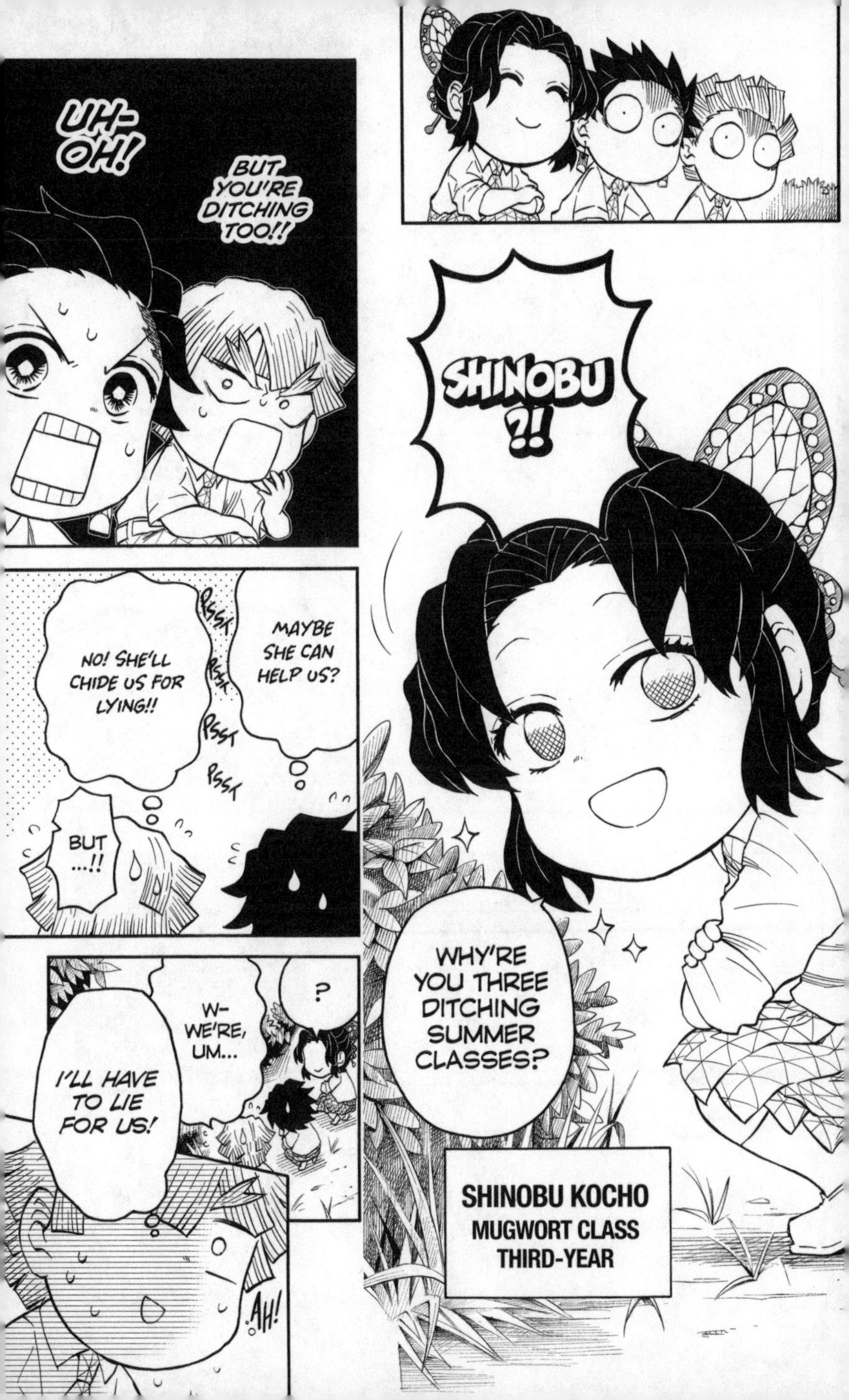
SHINOBU ?!
WHY'RE YOU THREE DITCHING SUMMER CLASSES?
SHINOBU KOCHO
MUGWORT CLASS
THIRD-YEAR
UH-OH!
BUT YOU'RE DITCHING TOO!!
MAYBE SHE CAN HELP US?
PSSK PSSK PSSK PSSK
NO! SHE'LL CHIDE US FOR LYING!!
BUT ...!!
?
W-WE'RE, UM...
I'LL HAVE TO LIE FOR US!
AH!

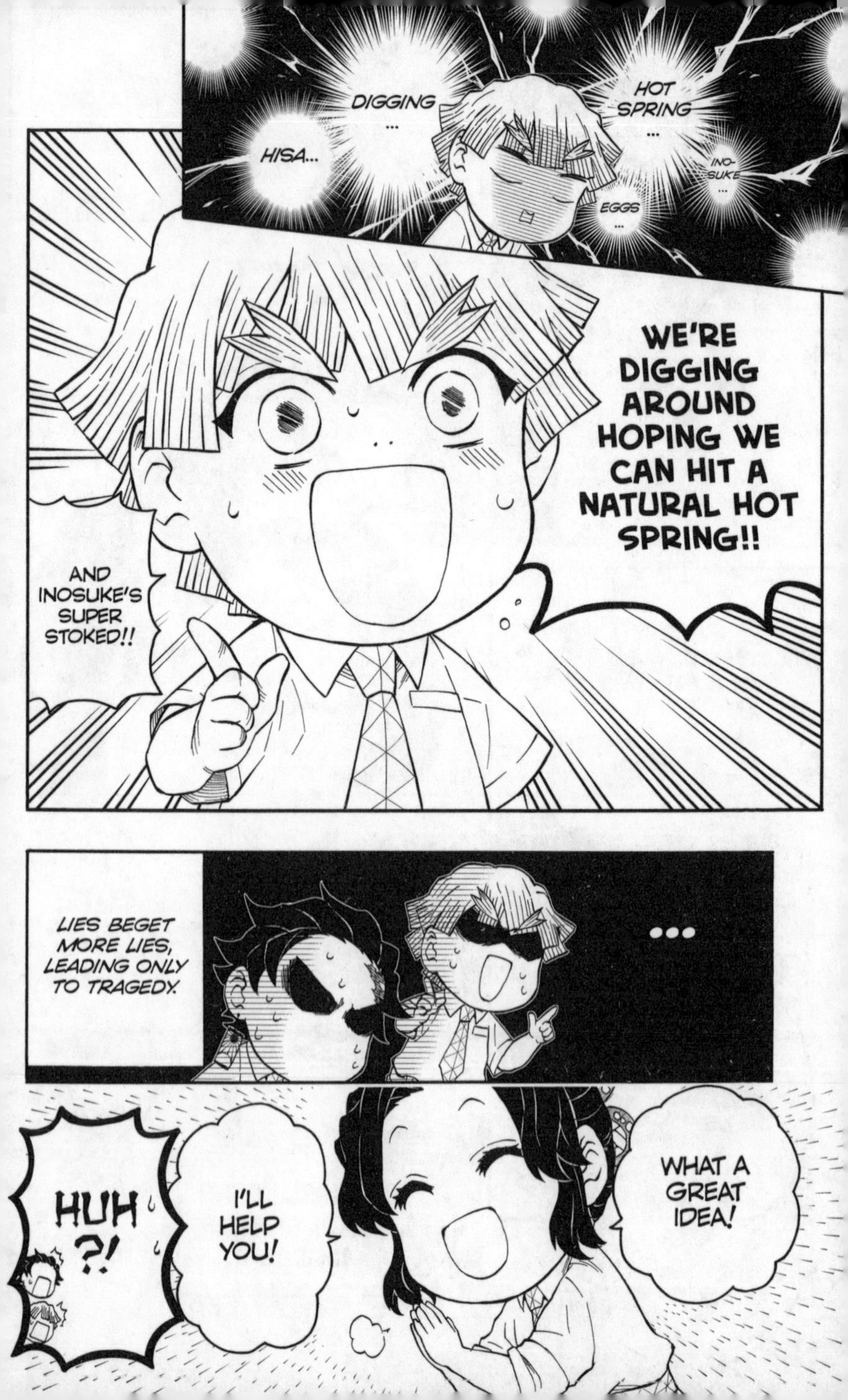
HOT SPRING ...
INO-SUKE ...
EGGS ...
DIGGING ...
HISA...
WE'RE DIGGING AROUND HOPING WE CAN HIT A NATURAL HOT SPRING!!
AND INOSUKE'S SUPER STOKED!!
...
LIES BEGET MORE LIES, LEADING ONLY TO TRAGEDY.
WHAT A GREAT IDEA!
I'LL HELP YOU!
HUH ?!

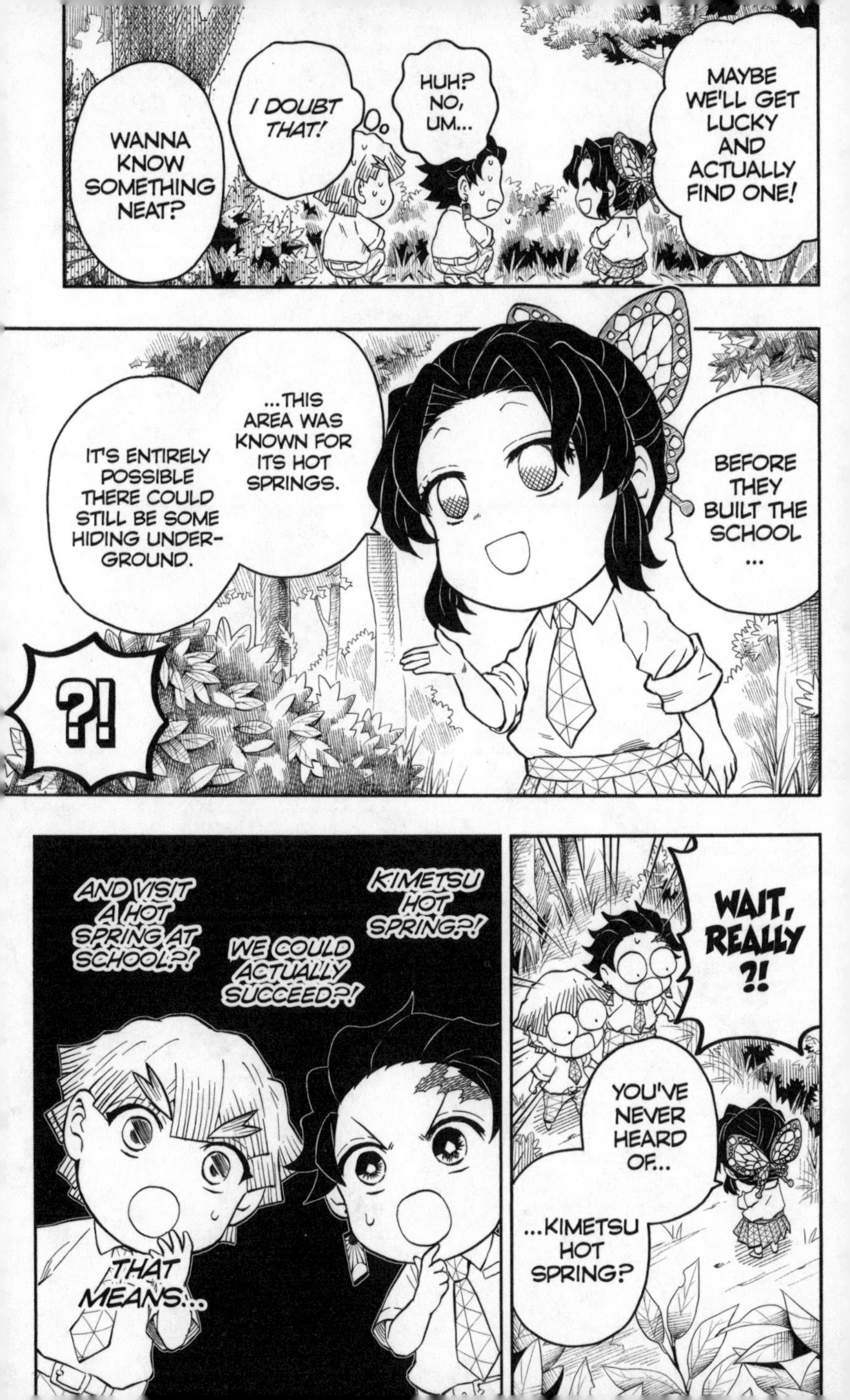
MAYBE WE'LL GET LUCKY AND ACTUALLY FIND ONE!
HUH? NO, UM...
I DOUBT THAT!
WANNA KNOW SOMETHING NEAT?
BEFORE THEY BUILT THE SCHOOL ...
...THIS AREA WAS KNOWN FOR ITS HOT SPRINGS.
IT'S ENTIRELY POSSIBLE THERE COULD STILL BE SOME HIDING UNDER-GROUND.
?!
WAIT, REALLY ?!
YOU'VE NEVER HEARD OF...
...KIMETSU HOT SPRING?
KIMETSU HOT SPRING?!
THAT MEANS...
WE COULD ACTUALLY SUCCEED?!
AND VISIT A HOT SPRING AT SCHOOL?!

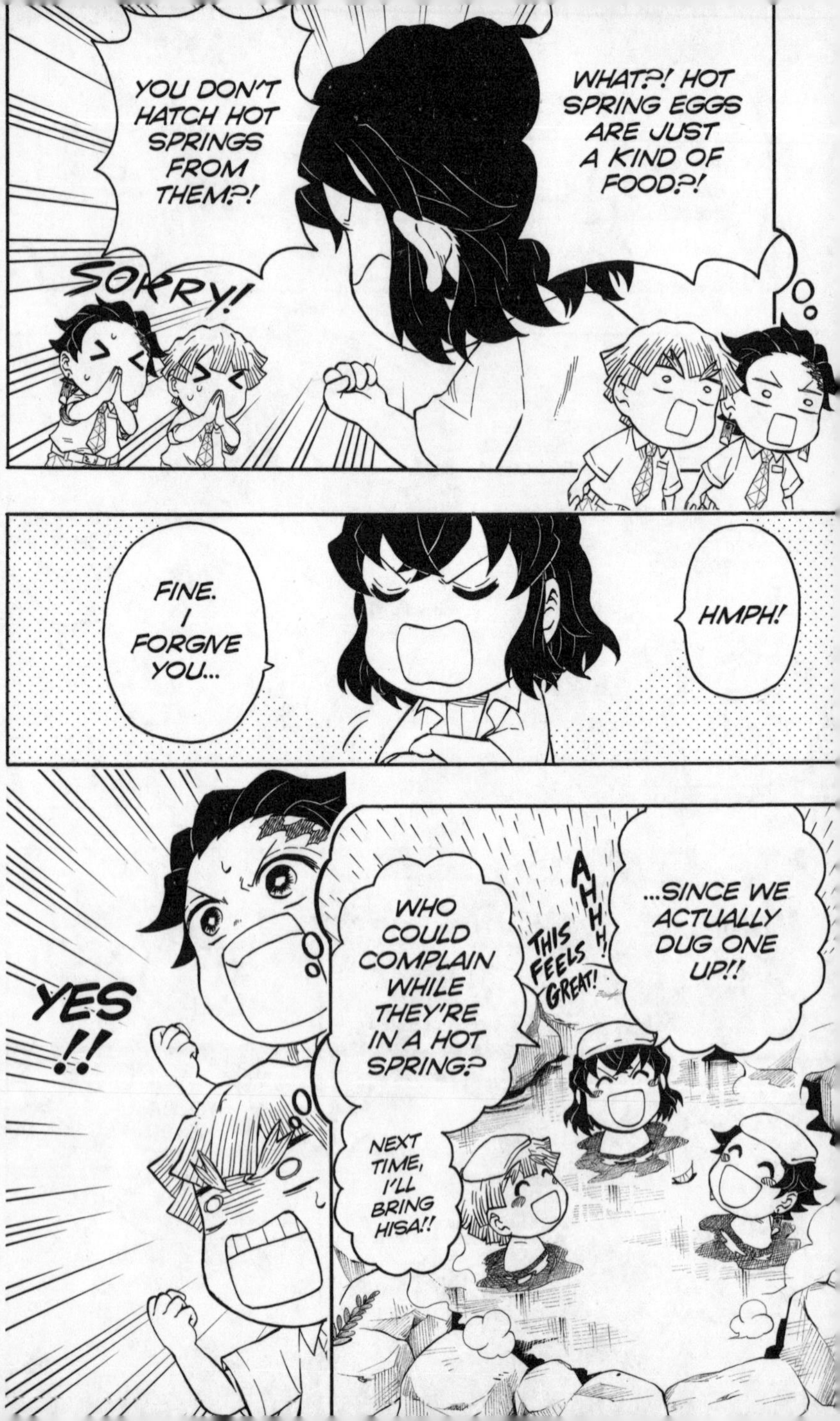
WHAT?! HOT SPRING EGGS ARE JUST A KIND OF FOOD?!
YOU DON'T HATCH HOT SPRINGS FROM THEM?!
SORRY!
HMPH!
FINE. I FORGIVE YOU...
...SINCE WE ACTUALLY DUG ONE UP!!
AHHH! THIS FEELS GREAT!
WHO COULD COMPLAIN WHILE THEY'RE IN A HOT SPRING?
NEXT TIME, I'LL BRING HISA!!
YES!!

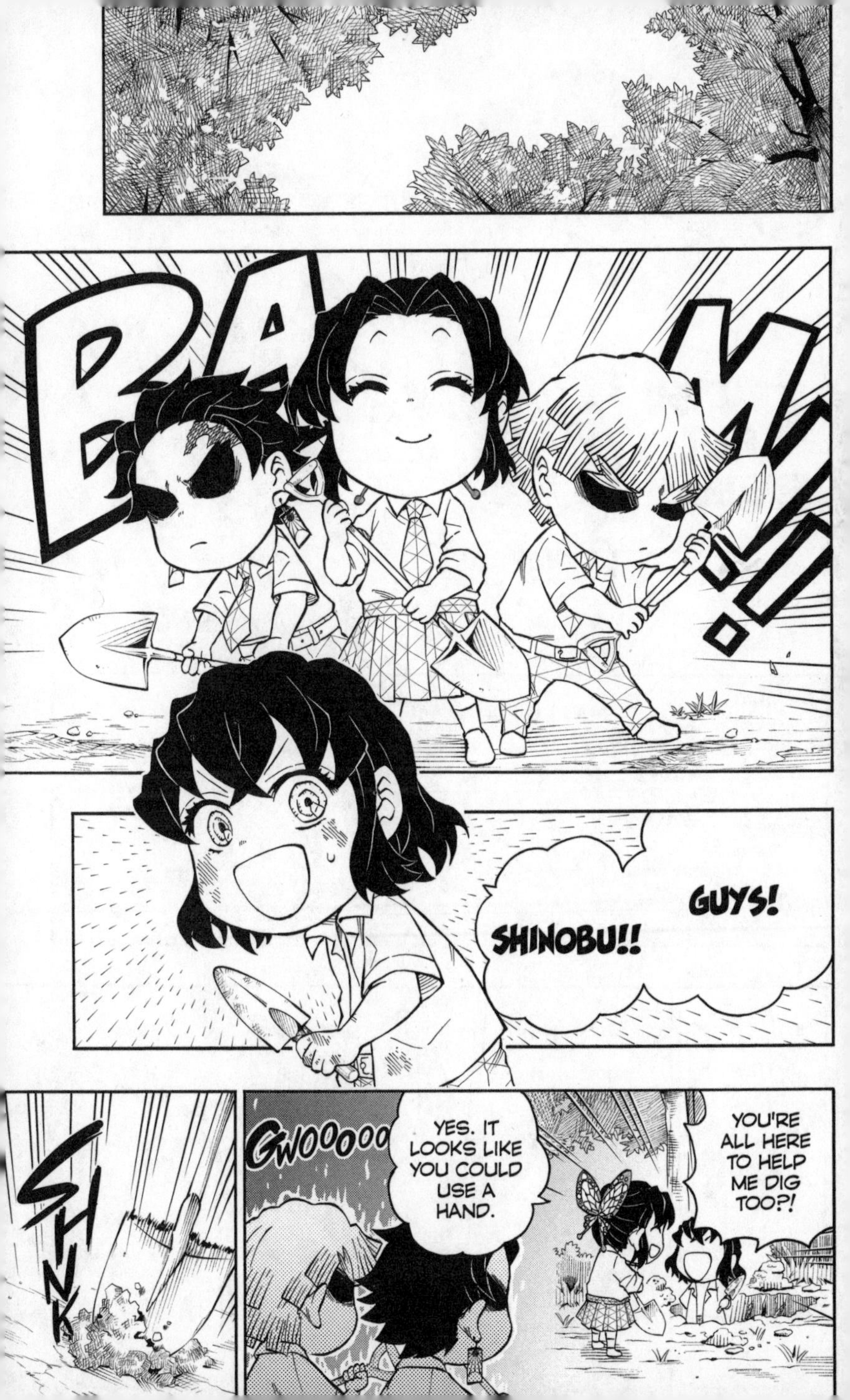
BAM!!
GUYS!
SHINOBU!!
YOU'RE ALL HERE TO HELP ME DIG TOO?!
YES. IT LOOKS LIKE YOU COULD USE A HAND.
GWOOOOO
SHNK

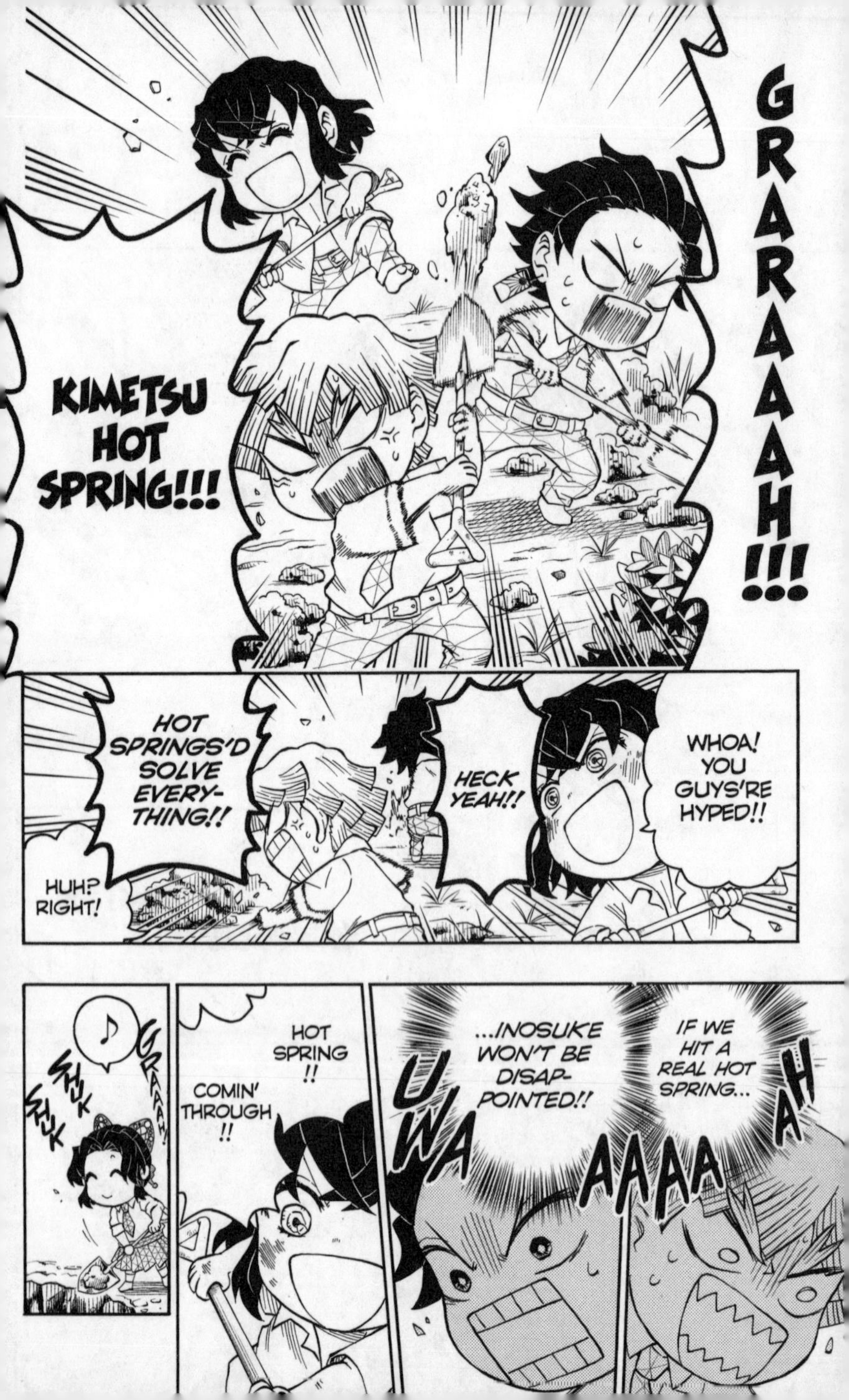
GRAAAAH!!!
KIMETSU HOT SPRING!!!
WHOA! YOU GUYS'RE HYPED!!
HECK YEAH!!
HOT SPRINGS'D SOLVE EVERY-THING!!
HUH? RIGHT!
IF WE HIT A REAL HOT SPRING...
...INOSUKE WON'T BE DISAP-POINTED!!
UWAAAAAAH
HOT SPRING!!
COMIN' THROUGH!!
♪
GRAAAH!
SHUK SHUK

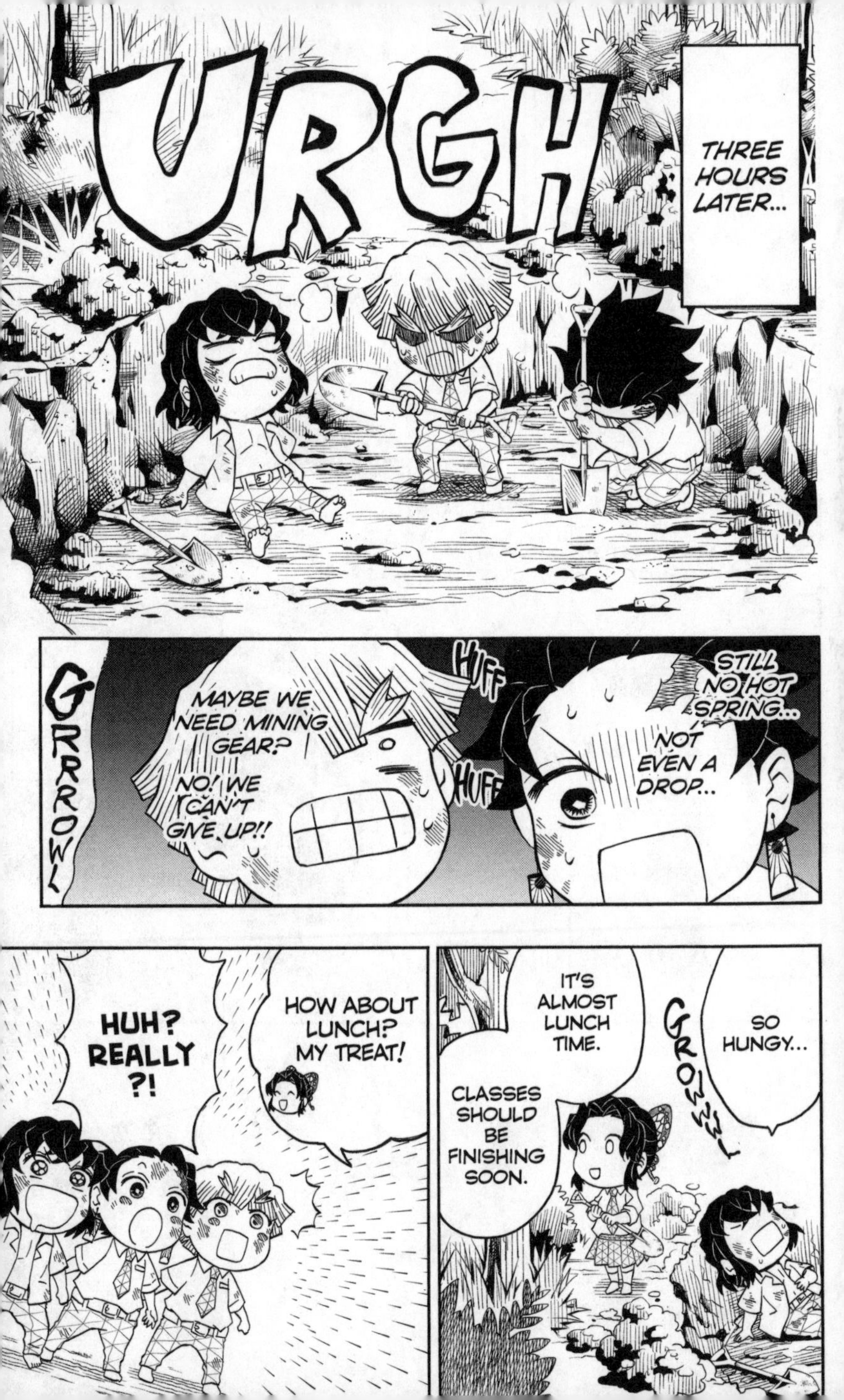
THREE HOURS LATER...
URGH
STILL NO HOT SPRING...
NOT EVEN A DROP...
HUFF
HUFF
MAYBE WE NEED MINING GEAR?
NO! WE CAN'T GIVE UP!!
GRRROWL
SO HUNGY...
GROWWWL
IT'S ALMOST LUNCH TIME.
CLASSES SHOULD BE FINISHING SOON.
HOW ABOUT LUNCH? MY TREAT!
HUH? REALLY?!

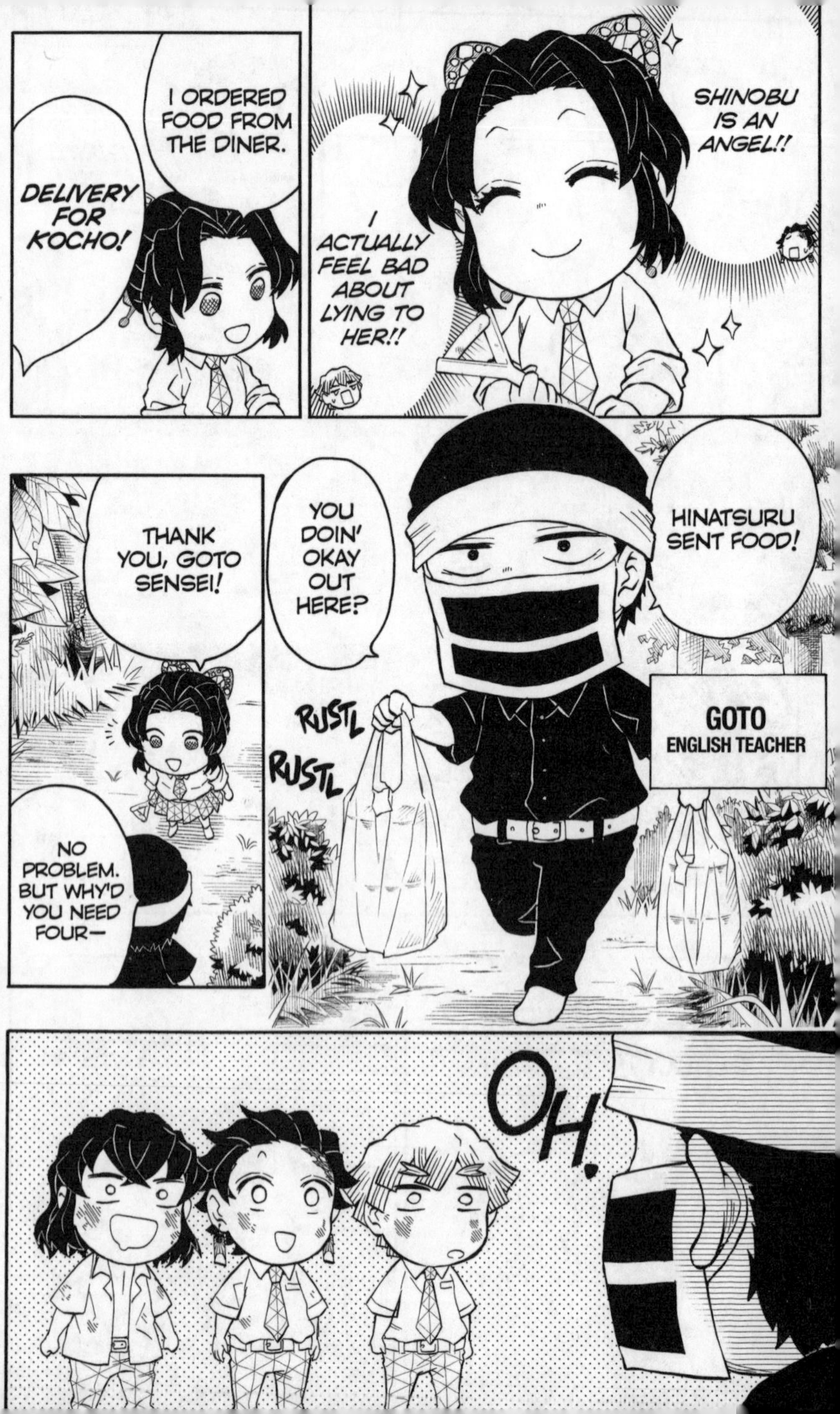

SHINOBU IS AN ANGEL!!
I ACTUALLY FEEL BAD ABOUT LYING TO HER!!
I ORDERED FOOD FROM THE DINER.
DELIVERY FOR KOCHO!
HINATSURU SENT FOOD!
GOTO
ENGLISH TEACHER
YOU DOIN' OKAY OUT HERE?
RUSTL
RUSTL
THANK YOU, GOTO SENSEI!
NO PROBLEM. BUT WHY'D YOU NEED FOUR—
OH.

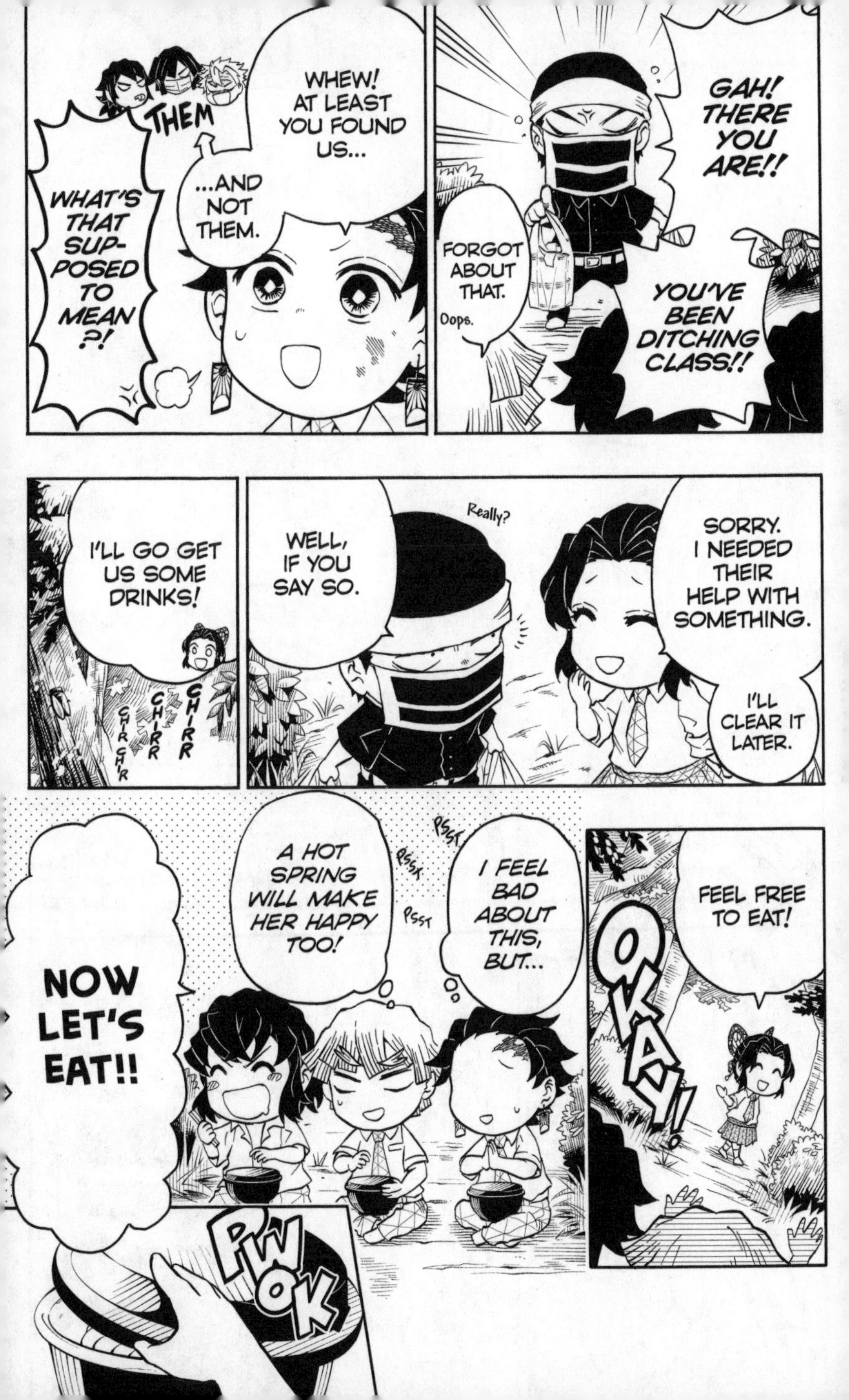

GAH! THERE YOU ARE!!
YOU'VE BEEN DITCHING CLASS!!
FORGOT ABOUT THAT.
Oops.
WHEW! AT LEAST YOU FOUND US...
...AND NOT THEM.
THEM
WHAT'S THAT SUP-POSED TO MEAN?!
SORRY. I NEEDED THEIR HELP WITH SOMETHING.
I'LL CLEAR IT LATER.
Really?
WELL, IF YOU SAY SO.
I'LL GO GET US SOME DRINKS!
CHIRR CHIRR CHIR CHIR
FEEL FREE TO EAT!
OKAY!
I FEEL BAD ABOUT THIS, BUT...
PSST PSSST PSST
A HOT SPRING WILL MAKE HER HAPPY TOO!
NOW LET'S EAT!!
PWOK

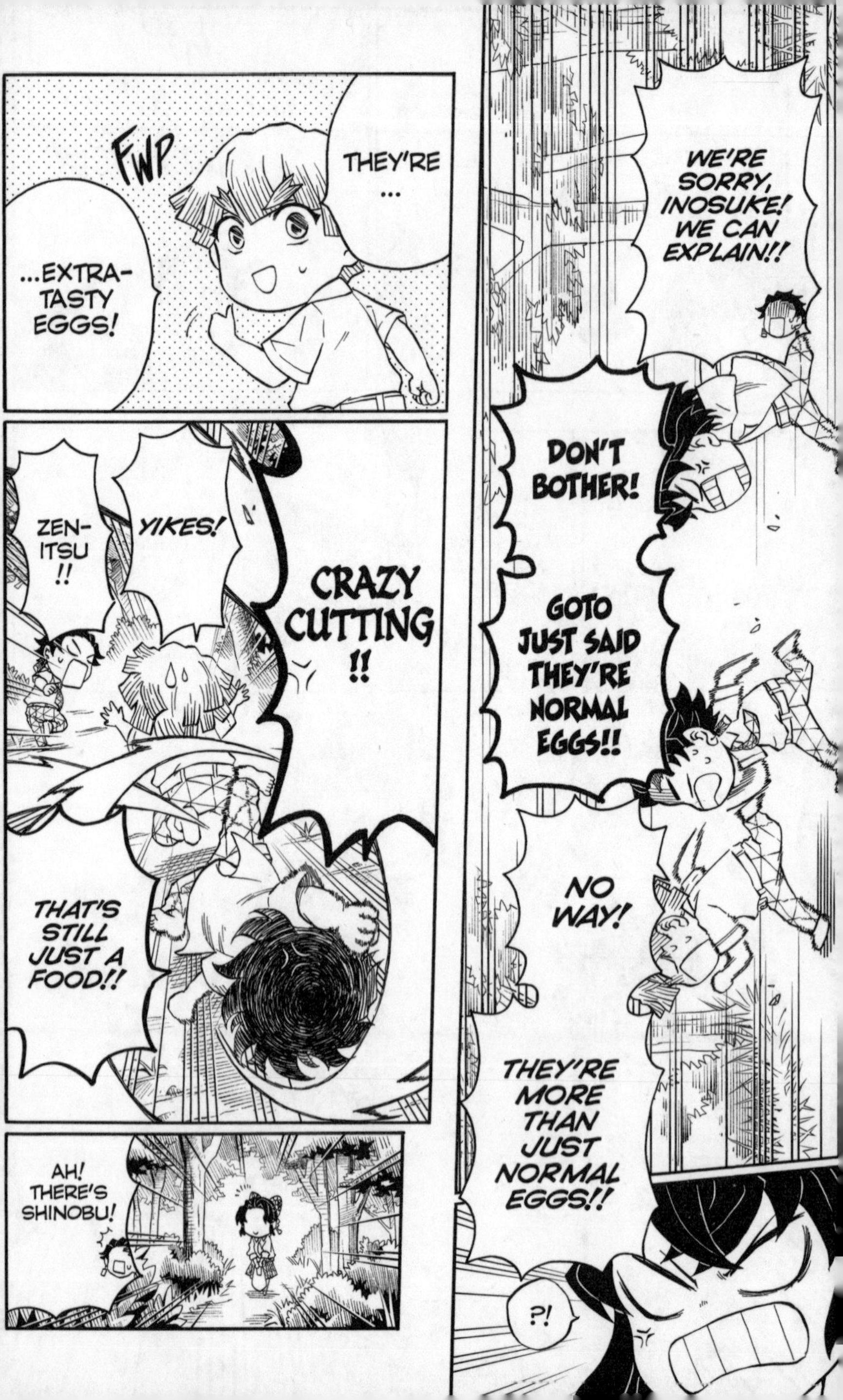

WE'RE SORRY, INOSUKE! WE CAN EXPLAIN!!
DON'T BOTHER!
GOTO JUST SAID THEY'RE NORMAL EGGS!!
NO WAY!
THEY'RE MORE THAN JUST NORMAL EGGS!!
?!
THEY'RE ...
FWP
...EXTRA-TASTY EGGS!
YIKES!
ZEN-ITSU!!
CRAZY CUTTING!!
THAT'S STILL JUST A FOOD!!
AH! THERE'S SHINOBU!

BLAH
BLAH
BLAH

WE'LL TELL YOU EVERYTHING!

WSH

ARE YOU FIGHTING?

WSH

SENPAI! HELP US!

OH, IS THAT WHAT HAPPENED?

DON'T BE MAD, OKAY?

Er...

SORRY, INOSUKE.

WHAT A SILLY LIE THAT WAS, ZENITSU!

POUT

AND THAT'S WHY YOU WERE RUNNING?

YEAH... SORRY.

WE'RE REALLY, REALLY...

...SORRY...!!

INOSUKE...

COLD

NO TEA

THEY'RE A NATURAL OCCUR-ANCE...

...THAT ONLY APPEAR IN CERTAIN PLACES.

THAT'S WHY THEY'RE SO VALUABLE.

...HOT SPRINGS OCCUR...

...WHEN GEOTHERMAL ACTIVITY HEATS GROUNDWATER.

HOT SPRING

GROUNDWATER

HERE YOU GO!!

MAGMA

67

A FEW DAYS LATER...

HUH?

YOU'LL NEVER FIND A HOT SPRING HERE!

KIMETSU HOT SPRING? SERIOUSLY?

...THE BOYS DISCOVERED THEIR HOLE...

...HAD BEEN TRANSFORMED INTO AN ARTIFICIAL POND WHERE THE PHARMACOLOGY CLUB COULD GROW HERBS.

...UNTIL AFTER THE POND WAS FINISHED.

SHE USED US...

...FOR FREE LABOR?

THEY DIDN'T FIGURE IT OUT...

DON'T LEAVE IT TO HER

SHINOBU KOCHO LEADS BOTH THE PHARMACOLOGY AND FENCING CLUBS.

SHE'S SKILLED WITH THE PEN AND THE SWORD.

YES? WHAT'S UP?

SHINOBU SENPAI!

SHINOBU SENPAI!

YOUNGER STUDENTS LOOK UP TO HER.

IT'S SO CUTE!

AND BLACK...

...LIKE BLACK INK...

Hmm...

It's a girl!

WOULD YOU NAME IT FOR US?

OH! I'M HONORED!

AND WE'RE IN CHARGE!

CHEER!

A CHICK WAS BORN!

BUT SHE SUCKS AT NAMING THINGS.

CHIC-TOPUS!

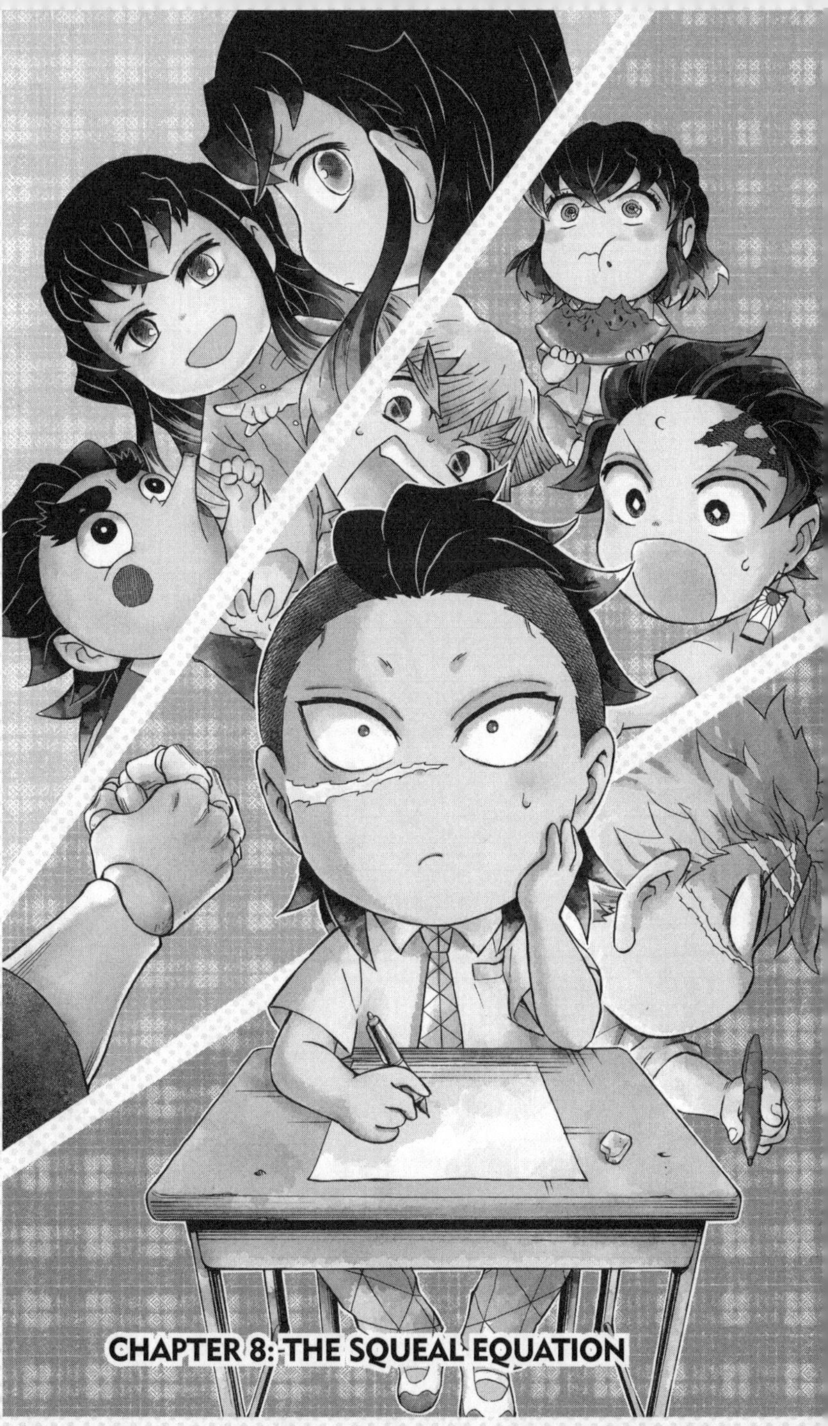
CHAPTER 8: THE SQUEAL EQUATION

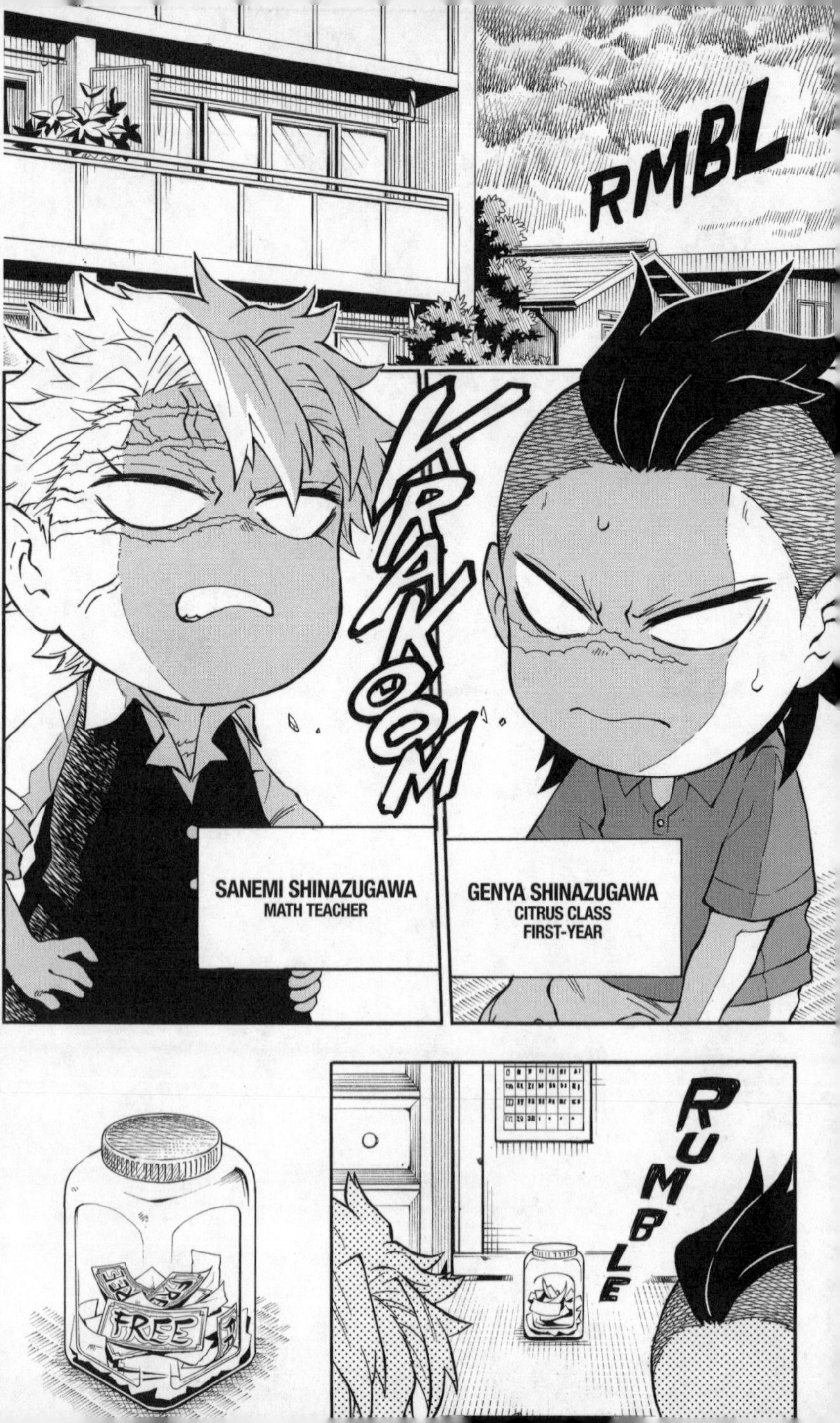
RMBL
KRAKOOM
GENYA SHINAZUGAWA
CITRUS CLASS
FIRST-YEAR
SANEMI SHINAZUGAWA
MATH TEACHER
RUMBLE
FREE

WE HAD A FIGHT ABOUT MY GRADES!!

I CAN'T ASK HIM!

BAM

MY FINAL EXAM SCORES SUCKED!

WHAT HAPPENED?

YOU CAN FIGHT HIM? RESPECT!

GOT THAT, GENYA?

IF YOU SCORE THIS BADLY AGAIN...

FLASH-BACK

NEVER SCORE THIS LOW AGAIN!

RMMMM

THE GAME'S OPERATOR WON'T LIKE THAT!

WITHOUT SPENDING ANYTHING?!

MARKS-MANSHIP CLUB ACE →

I WANT TO WIN ALL THE PRIZES AT THE MARKSMANSHIP GAME.

...BUT WHAT WAS YOUR RANK ON FINALS?

I DON'T MIND...

Well...

RIGHT?

ANYWAY, WE'LL HELP YOU.

13/90

THIRTEENTH.

HOW THE HECK ARE WE SUP-POSED TO HELP YOU?!

SMARTY-PANTS!

NO WAY!

ARE YOU FOR REAL?!

GYAH! YOU DON'T UNDER-STAND!

SALT

47TH

72ND

28TH

NOM NOM

SALT YAKISOBA

SAUCE YAKISOBA

RX4MEN

RAMEN

REFILL PLEASE.

YES, INOSUKE?

KANAO

SHINOBU

SO...NOT KANAO OR SHINOBU?

PICK A GUY! NO GIRLS!

NERVOUS AROUND GIRLS

HMM

HE'S AWAY AT SOCCER CAMP.

SPARKL

HOW ABOUT MURATA?

6

TOKITO

DING DONG

I KNOW!

IT DOESN'T HAVE TO BE AN *OLDER* STUDENT!

HI! I'M HERE TO HANG OUT!!

KO- TETSU?!

HUH?! YOU'RE HERE, TANJIRO?!

KOTETSU
ELEMENTARY SCHOOL, FOURTH-YEAR

SERI- OUSLY ?!

I FORGOT WE'D MADE PLANS FOR TODAY.

Thanks.

It's a snack

MUICHIRO, THIS IS FROM KANAMORI.

CAN WE BORROW THE YOU-KNOW- WHAT?

WE'LL ENLIST HIS HELP AS WELL.

NO.

IF YOU HAVE PLANS, WE CAN—

?

I'D BE DEAD!!!

IT'S GOOD FOR MOTIVATION.

✻ WATERMELON

...THAT'LL BE YOUR HEAD.

THAT WOULD KILL ME!!

AND WHAT'D YOU DO TO ITS HANDS?!

THAT'S NOT JUST A DOLL, THEN!

YOU PROGRAM IT?!

TAK TAK TAK TAK

I'LL PROGRAM IT TO STOP FOR CORRECT ANSWERS.

HOW IS THAT GONNA MOTIVATE ME?!

I have plenty.

WE'LL JUST HAVE IT SPLIT ANOTHER WATERMELON INSTEAD.

FROM TETSUIDO

OH, OKAY.

TOKITO, I THINK THIS IS A LITTLE TOO DANGEROUS.

...AFTER THE DOLL SPLITS THE WATER-MELON...

...I'LL HAVE NO CHOICE BUT TO THROW AWAY THE LEFTOVERS.

OKAY, IN THAT CASE...

CHOMP MUNCH CHOMP

AT THAT POINT YOU'RE JUST WASTING WATER-MELON!!

← LOVES WATERMELON

IF THAT'S ALL IT TAKES, WHY'RE WE EVEN USING THAT THING?!

GRAAAAAH

I CAN'T LET THAT HAPPEN!!

THAT'D BE TERRIBLE!!

UM...

SHOULDN'T YOU THREE...

...BE STUDYING TOO?

HUH?

DOESN'T THAT WORRY YOU?

YOUR GRADES ARE WORSE THAN HIS, RIGHT?

YOU GET BAD GRADES WHEN YOU'RE LAZY.

HARSH

TICK TICK TICK

YOU HAVE 20 SECONDS!!

$$y = -3(x-1)^2 + 5$$
$$-3 \leqq x \leqq -1$$

FIND THE MAXIMUM AND MINIMUM VALUES FOR THIS EQUATION!!

FIRST QUESTION!!

W-WELL, UM...

...

UM...X=-3 FOR A MINIMUM OF -43 AND X=-1 FOR A MAX OF -7!!!

COR-RECT!

SHING

BESIDES, YORIICHI IS BUSY WITH GENYA.

CHOP

GAH!

DURING SUMMER BREAK IT IS WISE TO STUDY HARD BUT WHO WOULD BOTHER?

—A SUMMER HAIKU BY THREE NINCOMPOOPS

TING
TING

GENYA'S DEDI-CATED!

I'M NOT GETTING PUNCHED BY THAT THING!

GAH!

I DIALED IT DOWN TO GOOSE-EGG MODE.

NO WORRIES! I'VE GOT ANOTHER ONE!!

NO WAY!

GETTING PUNCHED BY HIM WOULD HURT A LOT LESS!

NAH, YUICHIRO WILL TEACH US!!

JUST USE YORIICHI TYPE ZERO!!

IN THE END...

HUH?

YOU'RE FINE WITH THAT, RIGHT?!

Don't you understand this?

...TANJIRO AND FRIENDS STUDIED...

WATERMELOOOON! AAAAGH!

CHOP

...AT THE TOKITOS' HOUSE WHILE THEIR PARENTS WERE AWAY.

We're traveling!

I KNOW THAT'S THE RIGHT ATTITUDE, BUT...

Y-YEAH...

LET'S ALL DO OUR BEST!!

DON'T WORRY! YOU'LL GET YOUR VOUCHERS BACK!!

?

YOU THINK SO?

HE'S LIKE AN INFORMATION SPONGE.

...I CAN'T BELIEVE THAT TOKITO...

...ALREADY KNOWS ALL THIS.

IF I WAS GIFTED LIKE TOKITO...

GRRR

You try it!

Come on already!

STAY BACK!

YIIIKES!

Goose-egg mode

CHATTER

CHATTER

C'mon! Just try it!

...THEN MY BROTHER WOULDN'T GET MAD AT ME...

...FOR BEING A LOSER.

HE MUST BE ASHAMED OF ME.

CONTEMPLATIVE

GENYA...

HIS FAVO-RITE?!

YOU'RE HIS FAVORITE!

HE GETS ANGRY BECAUSE HE CARES ABOUT YOU.

...YOU'RE NOT A LOSER.

...BUT HE'S SUPER HARD ON YOU.

I'VE NEVER SEEN HIM SCOLD ANYONE ELSE FOR THEIR GRADES...

...ISN'T IT?

THAT'S A KIND OF FAVORITISM...

...HAVE A PROBLEM WITH WHAT HE DOES...

BUT IF YOU DO...

IF YOU DO WELL, I BET HE'LL EVEN REWARD YOU!!!

YOU REALLY THINK THAT, HUH?

I'LL BACK YOU UP.

...THEN YOU SHOULD TELL HIM.

AH HA HA HA!

NOT A CHANCE.

STOP GAWKING AT MY TEST!

IT'S NOT JUST A MYTH?!

I DIDN'T KNOW THAT WAS POSSIBLE!

Holy moly!

A HUNDRED POINTS!!

A FEW DAYS LATER...

...OUTSIDE THE SHINAZU-GAWA RESI-DENCE...

SHUT UP!

Move it, Genya!

HURRY!! WE'RE HEADIN' TO THE FESTIVAL!!

URK!

NOW GO INSIDE...

...AND GET YOUR VOUCHERS BACK!

AH!

BDMP BDMP

ARE YOU HERE...?

BIG BRO?

I'M HOME...

KREEK

WILL HE...

...REALLY GIVE THEM BACK?

CHATTER

CHATTER

CANDIED APPLES!

SHAVED ICE!!

YAKI-SOBA!

GENYA! I WANT TAKOYAKI!

GAH! WHAT THE?!

STOP DROOLING OVER MY VOUCHERS!!

LET'S GO TO THE FESTIVAL!

WHY'RE YOU UP HERE, SANEMI?

SIGH...

AH HA HA! AH HA HA!

Let's go!

OKAY, OKAY...

THE GUY RUNNING THE MARKSMANSHIP GAME IS THE ONE WHO REALLY WON HERE.

PLAYING AGAIN? THAT'S 300 YEN!

WA HA HA HA

YOU'RE GONNA TAKE ALL THE PRIZES AT THIS RATE!

TOKITOS

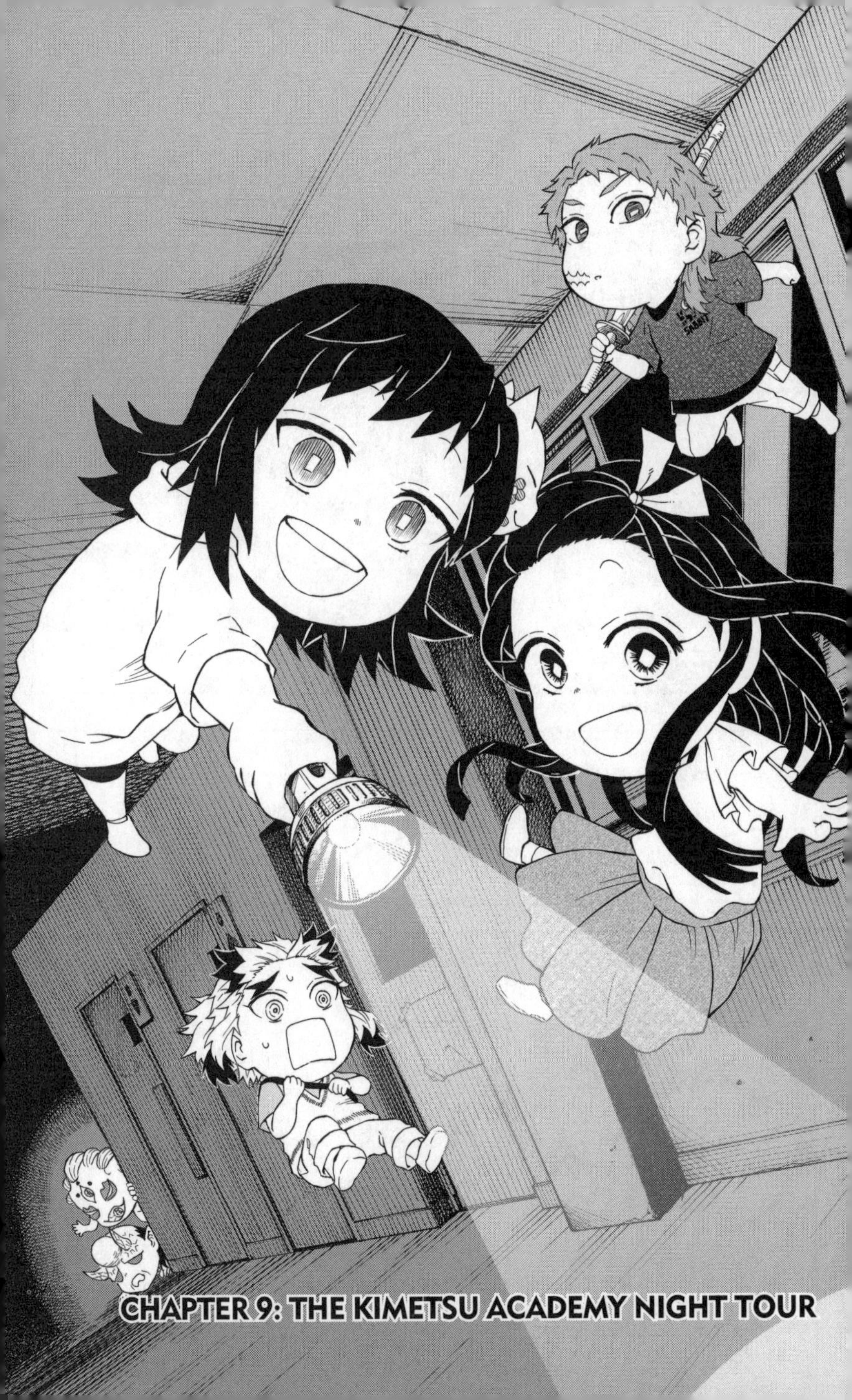

CHAPTER 9: THE KIMETSU ACADEMY NIGHT TOUR

IDEAS FOR THE SCHOOL'S SEVEN MYSTERIES?

YEAH! THE SCHOOL PAPER...

...PUT OUT A CALL FOR IDEAS!

"ONCE WE HAVE SEVEN, WE'LL ANNOUNCE THE CHOSEN MYSTERIES."

Cool!

SPOOKY STORIES, HUH?

"...SO WE'RE LOOKING FOR YOUR SPOOKY STORIES."

"LIKE OTHER SCHOOLS, KIMETSU ACADEMY SHOULD HAVE SEVEN MYSTERIOUS HAUNTINGS ..."

IT SAYS, UM...

I BET WE COULD COME UP WITH SOME THINGS!

I'VE NEVER HEARD ANYTHING SPOOKY ABOUT THIS SCHOOL.

THE LEMON-HEADED LUNATIC STALKER!!

HUFF... HUFF... WHERE'S NEZUKO?

SNORT

THE TERRIFYING BOAR-MAN UNDER THE FLOOR!!

THE JUNIOR HIGH'S GOING TO GET IN ON THIS TOO, RIGHT?

I CAN'T WAIT TO SEE WHAT PEOPLE COME UP WITH!

GRAAAH

WHAT'D YOU CALL ME?!

THAT'S WHY WE'LL KEEP IT A SECRET!

THERE'S NO WAY THE TEACHERS OR OUR PARENTS WOULD LET US!

WAIT, WE CAN'T!

ADVENTURE...

YAY

HMM

BRING A FLASHLIGHT AND JUNK FOOD!

TELL YOUR PARENTS YOU'RE SLEEPING OVER AT MY HOUSE!

...

SABITO
TARO CLASS JUNIOR HIGH, SECOND-YEAR

COULD BE!

THAT'S WHY WE'LL NEED A BODY-GUARD!

WILL IT BE DANGEROUS?

YAY! NOW WE'LL BE SAFE!!

YAHOO!!

WOO WOO HOO

WELL, I GUESS I COULD...

BODY-GUARD

NEZUKO AGREED TO GO.

HM?

...EXCUSE ME?

UM...

YOU CAN INVITE A FRIEND IF YOU WANT!

DON'T BE A SPOIL-SPORT!

BUT ISN'T THIS A BIT KIDDY FOR JUNIOR HIGH?

...AND THIS CLASS WRITTEN ON IT.

I FOUND THIS, AND IT HAD YOUR NAME...

SENJURO RENGOKU
AUTUMN LEAVES CLASS
JUNIOR HIGH, FIRST-YEAR

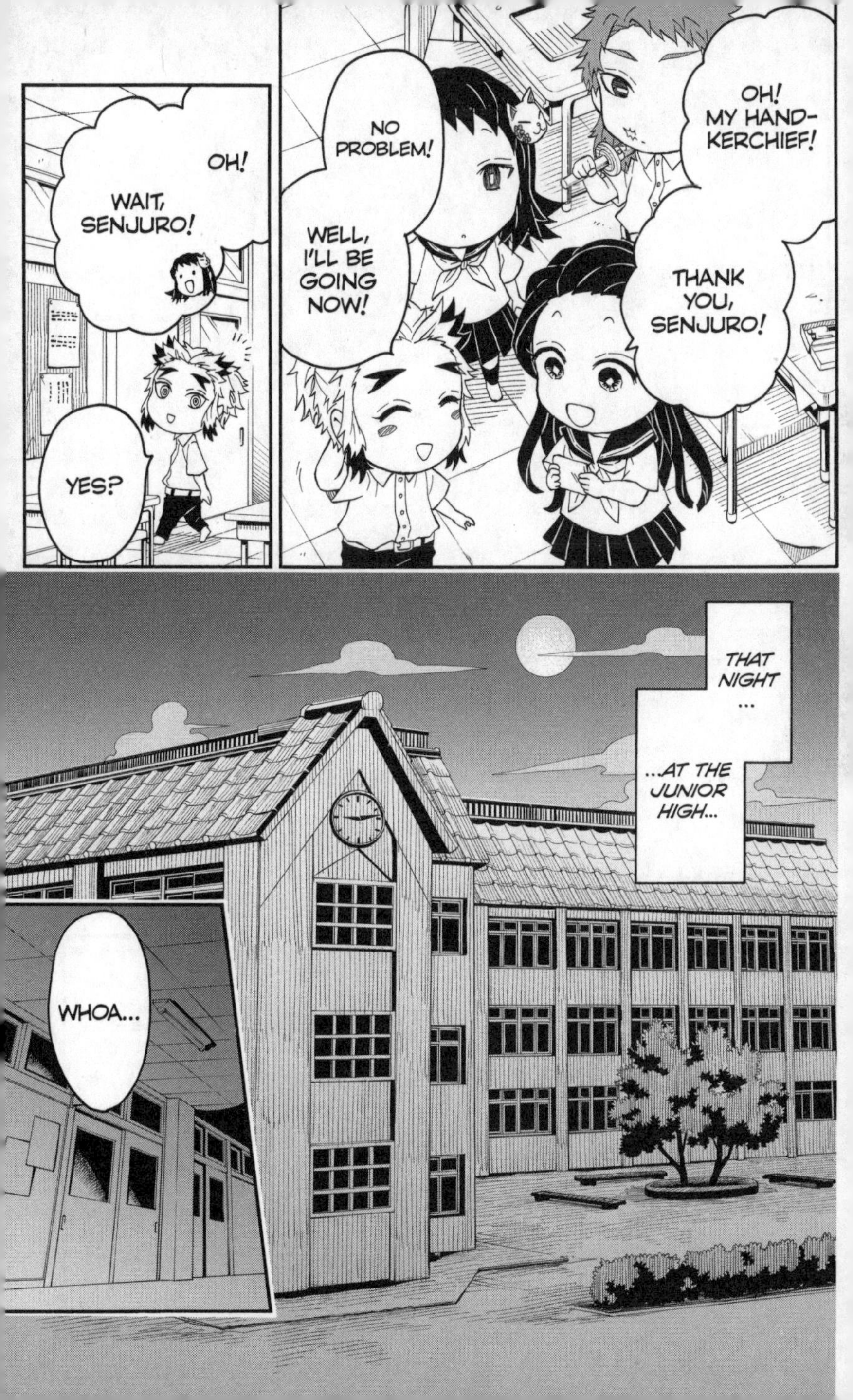
OH! MY HAND-KERCHIEF!
NO PROBLEM!
THANK YOU, SENJURO!
WELL, I'LL BE GOING NOW!
OH!
WAIT, SENJURO!
YES?
THAT NIGHT ...
...AT THE JUNIOR HIGH...
WHOA...

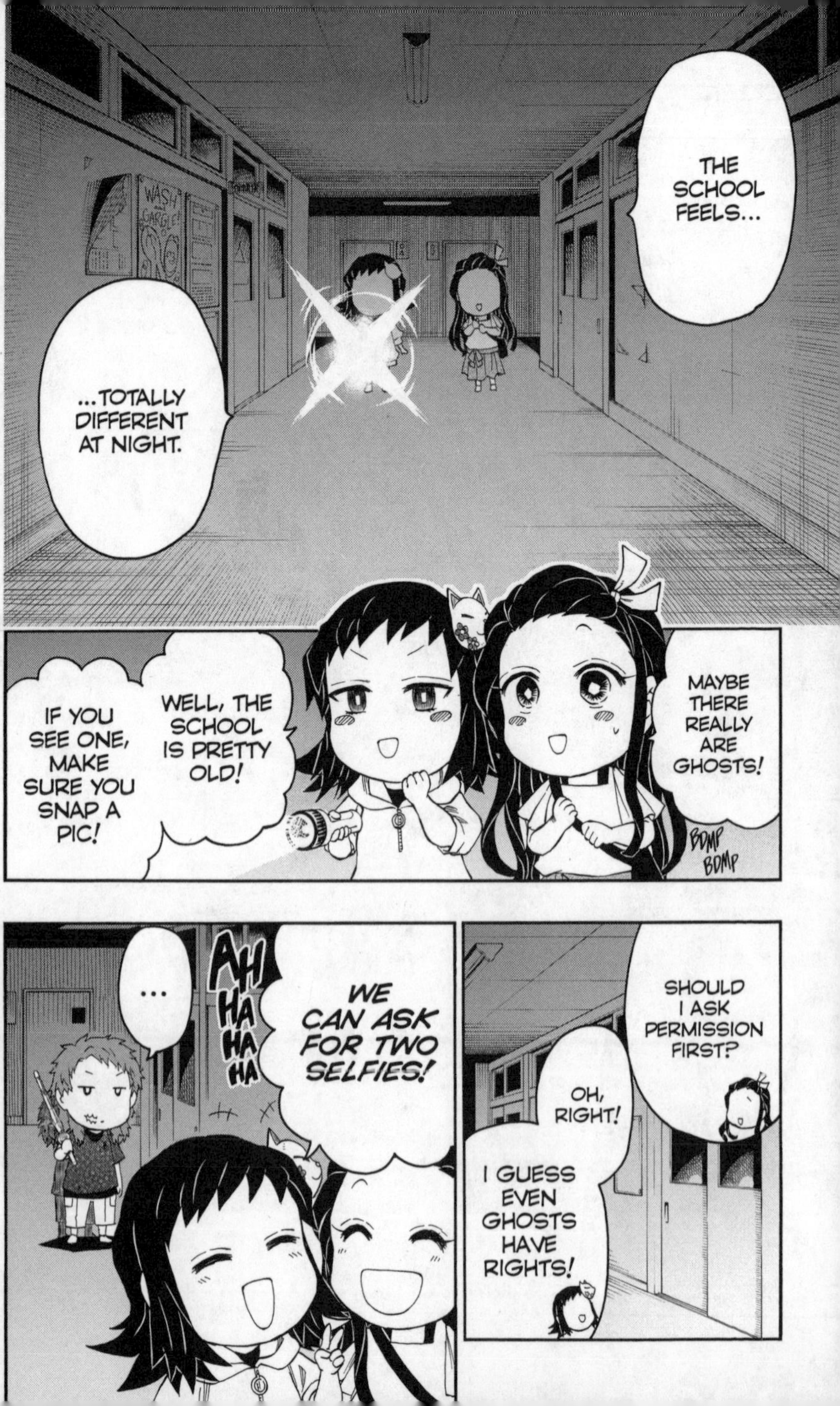
THE SCHOOL FEELS...
WASH GARGLE!
...TOTALLY DIFFERENT AT NIGHT.
MAYBE THERE REALLY ARE GHOSTS!
BDMP BDMP
WELL, THE SCHOOL IS PRETTY OLD!
IF YOU SEE ONE, MAKE SURE YOU SNAP A PIC!
SHOULD I ASK PERMISSION FIRST?
OH, RIGHT!
I GUESS EVEN GHOSTS HAVE RIGHTS!
WE CAN ASK FOR TWO SELFIES!
AH HA HA HA
...

SO WHY'D THEY NEED ME?

THEY AREN'T SCARED AT ALL.

WOo

YAY

I wanna go home...

MAKOMO INVITED HIM.

HUFF HUFF

TRMBL TRMBL

AND WHY'D HE COME?

Yikes! Why're you being so mean?

THEN STOP CLINGING TO ME!

I CAN'T! THIS IS A TEST OF COURAGE FOR ME!

IF YOU'RE SCARED, GO HOME.

IT'LL HELP ME BE BRAVER!!

STOP BULLYING HIM, SABITO!

WALK ON YOUR OWN!!

GWUP

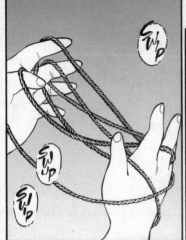

SWIP

SWIP

SWIP

!

SHH!

MAYBE THE SCIENCE ROOM?

SO! WHERE SHOULD WE LOOK?

SWIP

SWIP

LOOK!

WHAT'S WRONG, SABITO?

SOME-ONE'S IN THE CLASS-ROOM!

WHAT ?!

TH-THEN IS THAT...

...A G-G-GHOST?

NO ONE ELSE SHOULD BE HERE THIS LATE!

AH!

WHERE?

YEEEEEEK!

PIPE DOWN.

SO WHO'S THAT KID?

UM, HE'S...

M-MY LEGS GAVE OUT...

ARE YOU ALL RIGHT, SENJURO?

THAT WAS SCARY.

PHEW!

...MY CLASSMATE *RUI AYAKI!*

RUI AYAKI
AUTUMN LEAVES CLASS
JUNIOR HIGH, FIRST-YEAR

WHAT'RE *YOU* DOING HERE?

I JUST DO THIS SOMETIMES.

WHAT ARE YOU DOING HERE AT NIGHT?

I ENJOY PRACTICING CAT'S CRADLE...

BUT UNLIKE YOU, I DON'T MAKE A BUNCH OF NOISE.

...IN A NICE, QUIET, PEACEFUL ENVIRONMENT!

VEEN

DO WHAT?

HANG OUT AT SCHOOL AT NIGHT.

SORRY. THEY'RE ALL IDIOTS.

...

CAN YOU MAKE TOKYO TOWER?!

YOU DON'T NEED TO BE SO GRUMPY.

OOH, *ATTITUDE* MUCH?

...TRY THE HIGH SCHOOL.

IF YOU WANT SPOOKS...

NO IDEA.

TMP TMP

CAN YOU S-SENSE SPIRITS?

SERI-OUSLY?

THERE'S A WEIRD FEELING IN THE AIR.

HUH? WHY?

NO.

COME WITH US, RUI!

SHALL WE CHECK IT OUT?

DON'T NEED 'EM.

WE'LL GIVE YOU SNACKS!

AW, C'MON!

THE HIGH SCHOOL

HE'S KIMETSU TOWN'S CAT'S CRADLE CHAMP!

RUI'S KINDA WEIRD, HUH?

...

NICE!

FUMP

WHY ASK ME?

PICKING UP ANY VIBES, SABITO?

HERE WE ARE, BUT...

What should we do?

CHAK

Hmm...

I NEVER CONSIDERED THAT!

...BUT THE HIGH SCHOOL'S GONNA BE LOCKED UP TIGHT.

I WAS ABLE TO LEAVE ONE OF THE JUNIOR HIGH'S WINDOWS UNLOCKED...

DID SOMEONE JUST OPEN IT?

RATTLE

LUCKY US!

HEY! THIS WINDOW'S UNLOCKED!

WHAT'S WRONG, NEZUKO?

HM? WHAT WAS THAT?

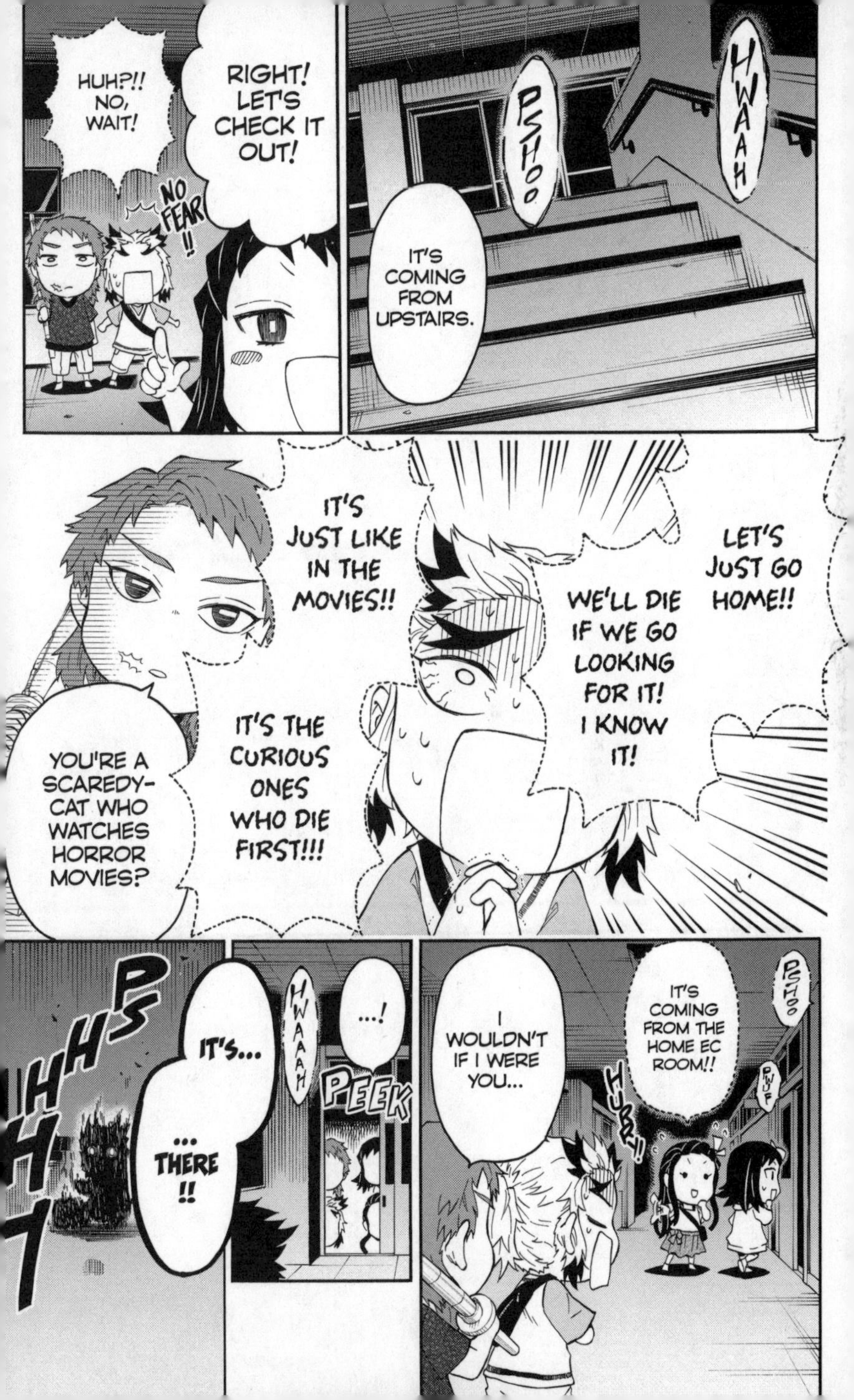
HWAAH
PSHOO
IT'S COMING FROM UPSTAIRS.
RIGHT! LET'S CHECK IT OUT!
NO FEAR!!
HUH?!! NO, WAIT!
LET'S JUST GO HOME!!
WE'LL DIE IF WE GO LOOKING FOR IT! I KNOW IT!
IT'S JUST LIKE IN THE MOVIES!!
IT'S THE CURIOUS ONES WHO DIE FIRST!!!
YOU'RE A SCAREDY-CAT WHO WATCHES HORROR MOVIES?
PSHOO
IT'S COMING FROM THE HOME EC ROOM!!
PWUF
HURK!!
I WOULDN'T IF I WERE YOU...
...!
HWAAAH
PEEK
IT'S...
... THERE !!
PSHHHH

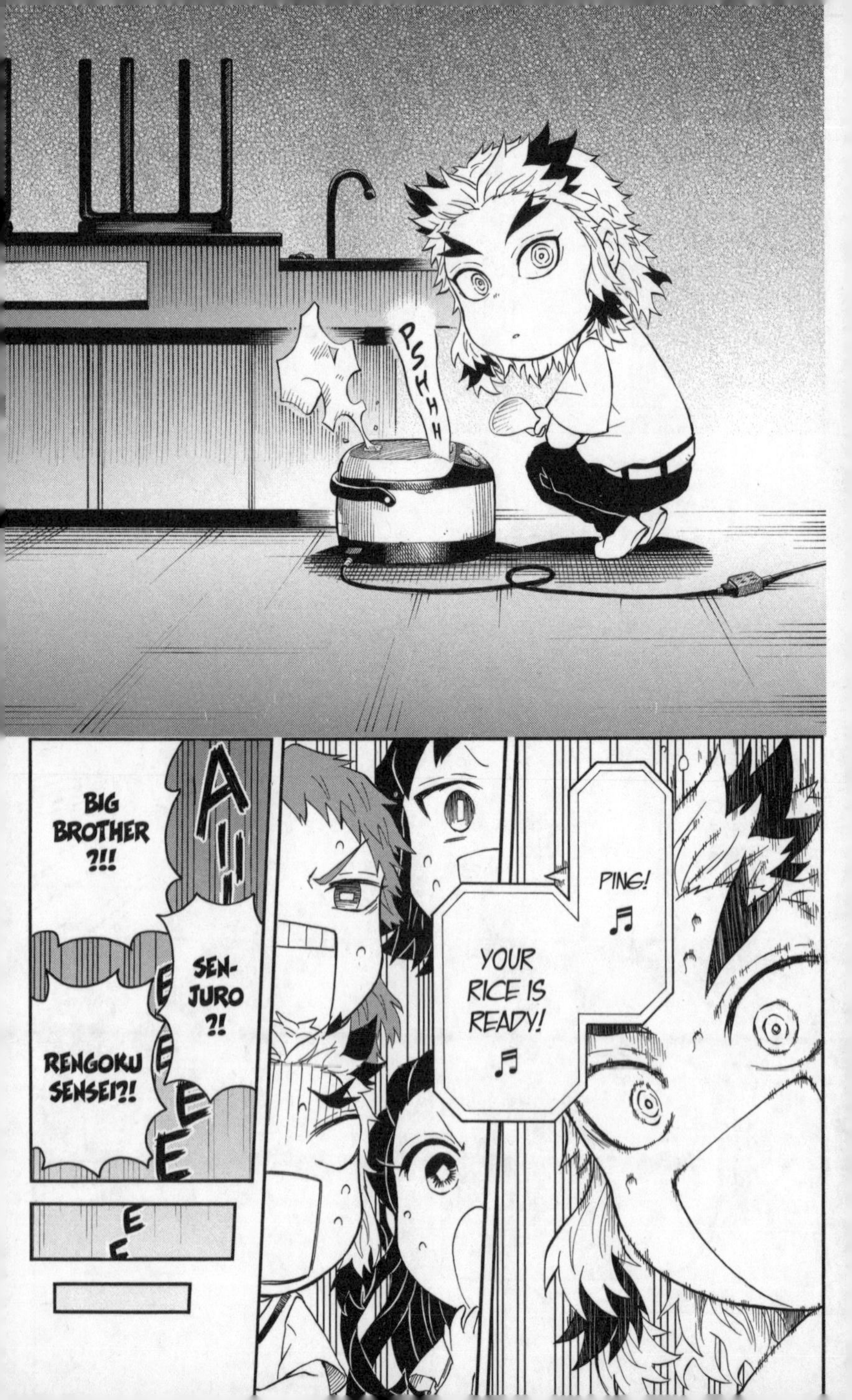
PSHHH
PING! ♬
YOUR RICE IS READY! ♬
AIIEEEEEEE
BIG BROTHER ?!!
SEN-JURO ?!
RENGOKU SENSEI?!

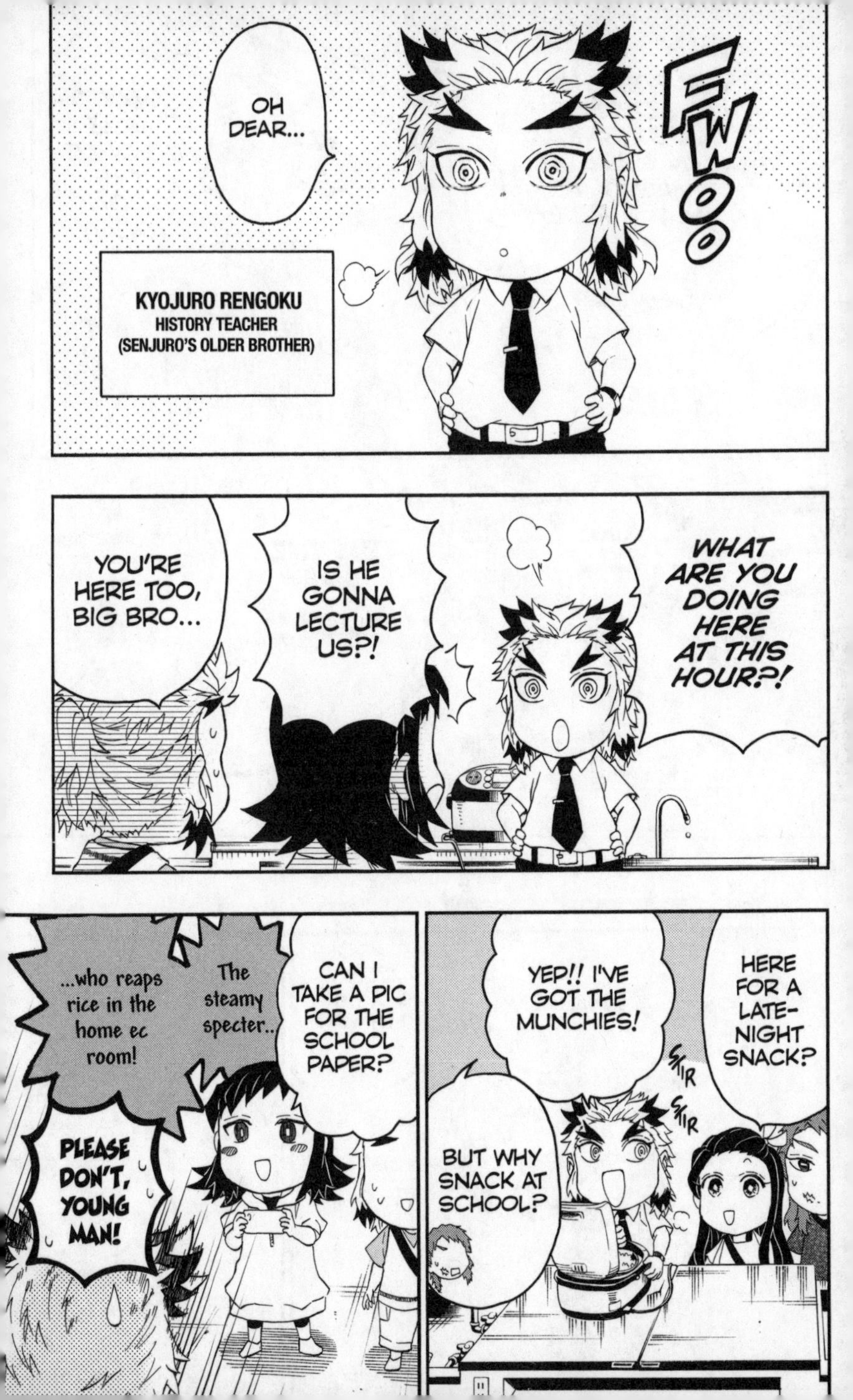
OH DEAR...
FWOOO
KYOJURO RENGOKU
HISTORY TEACHER
(SENJURO'S OLDER BROTHER)
WHAT ARE YOU DOING HERE AT THIS HOUR?!
IS HE GONNA LECTURE US?!
YOU'RE HERE TOO, BIG BRO...
HERE FOR A LATE-NIGHT SNACK?
YEP!! I'VE GOT THE MUNCHIES!
SKIR
SKIR
BUT WHY SNACK AT SCHOOL?
CAN I TAKE A PIC FOR THE SCHOOL PAPER?
The steamy specter...
...who reaps rice in the home ec room!
PLEASE DON'T, YOUNG MAN!

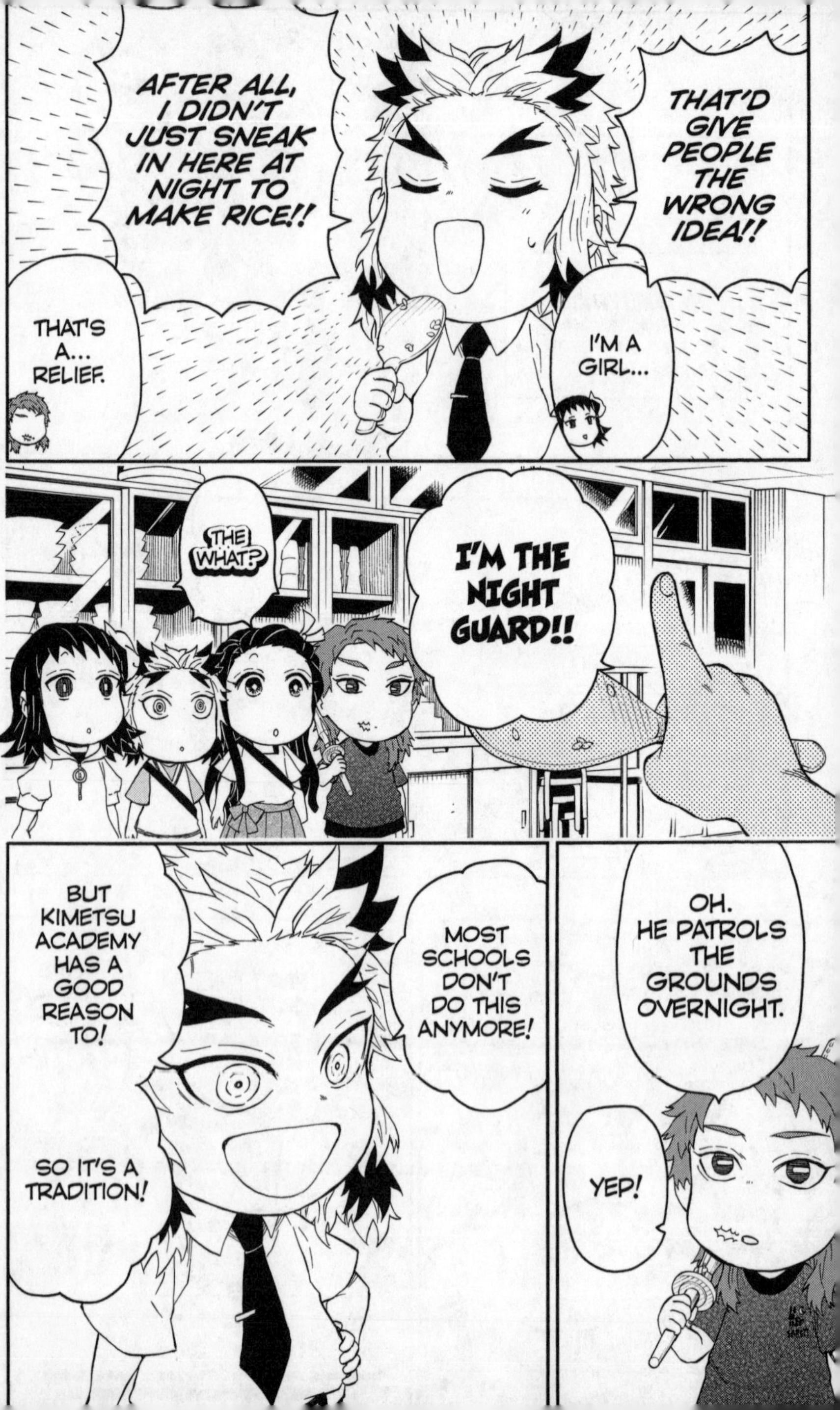
AFTER ALL, I DIDN'T JUST SNEAK IN HERE AT NIGHT TO MAKE RICE!!
THAT'D GIVE PEOPLE THE WRONG IDEA!!
THAT'S A... RELIEF.
I'M A GIRL...
THE WHAT?
I'M THE NIGHT GUARD!!
BUT KIMETSU ACADEMY HAS A GOOD REASON TO!
MOST SCHOOLS DON'T DO THIS ANYMORE!
SO IT'S A TRADITION!
OH. HE PATROLS THE GROUNDS OVERNIGHT.
YEP!

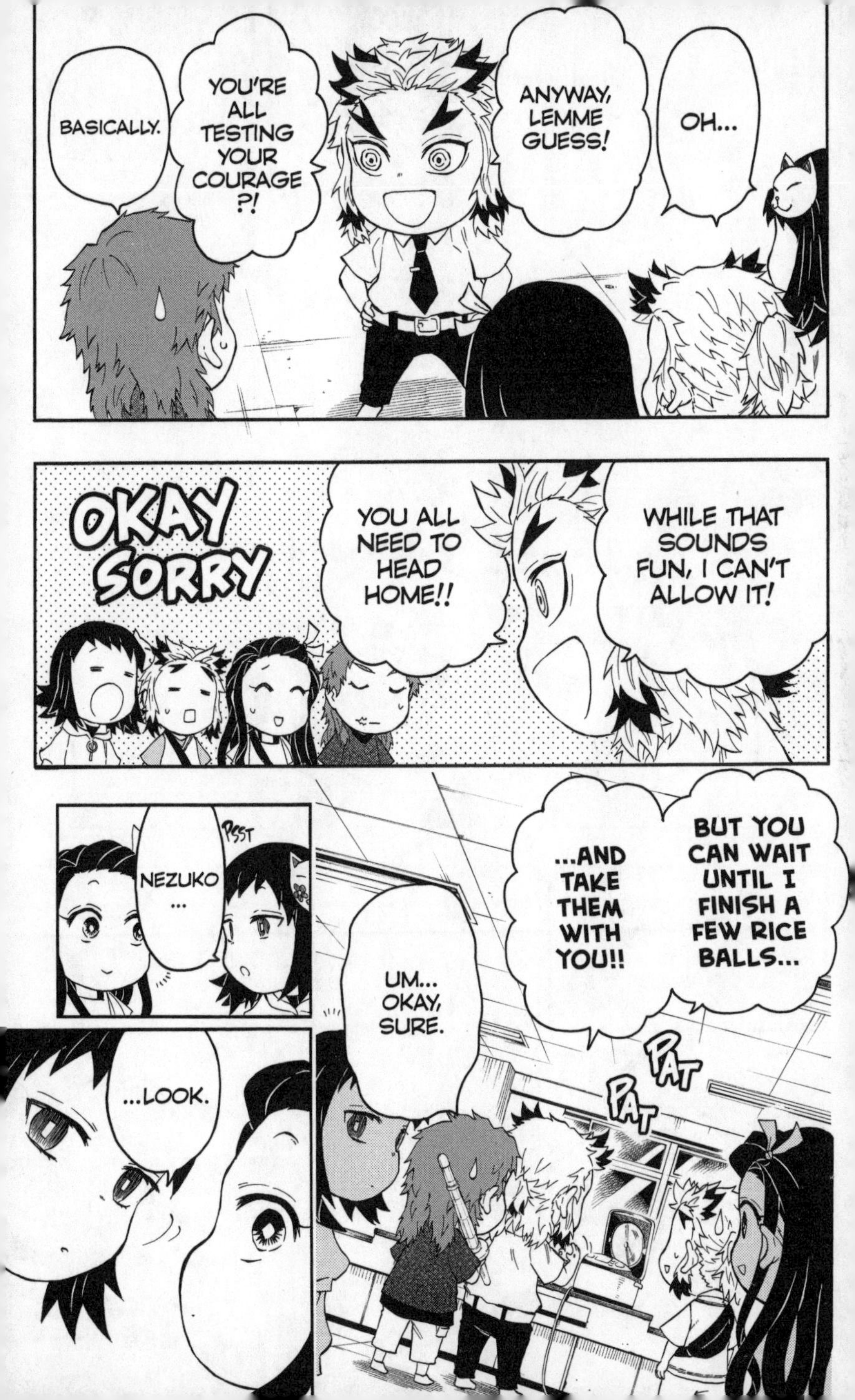
OH...
ANYWAY, LEMME GUESS!
YOU'RE ALL TESTING YOUR COURAGE?!
BASICALLY.
WHILE THAT SOUNDS FUN, I CAN'T ALLOW IT!
YOU ALL NEED TO HEAD HOME!!
OKAY SORRY
BUT YOU CAN WAIT UNTIL I FINISH A FEW RICE BALLS...
...AND TAKE THEM WITH YOU!!
PAT
PAT
UM... OKAY, SURE.
PSST
NEZUKO...
...LOOK.

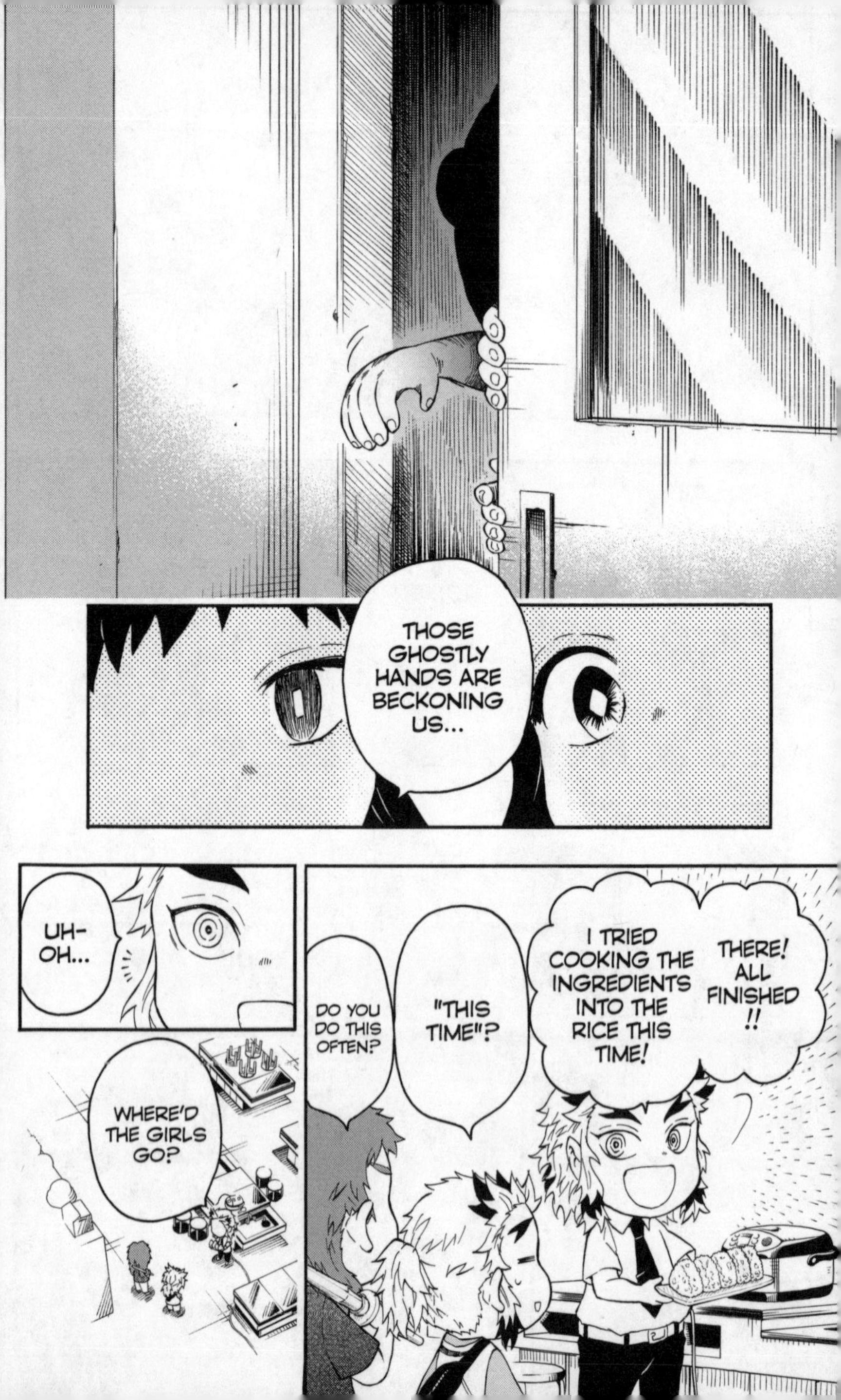
THOSE GHOSTLY HANDS ARE BECKONING US...
THERE! ALL FINISHED!!
I TRIED COOKING THE INGREDIENTS INTO THE RICE THIS TIME!
"THIS TIME"?
DO YOU DO THIS OFTEN?
UH-OH...
WHERE'D THE GIRLS GO?

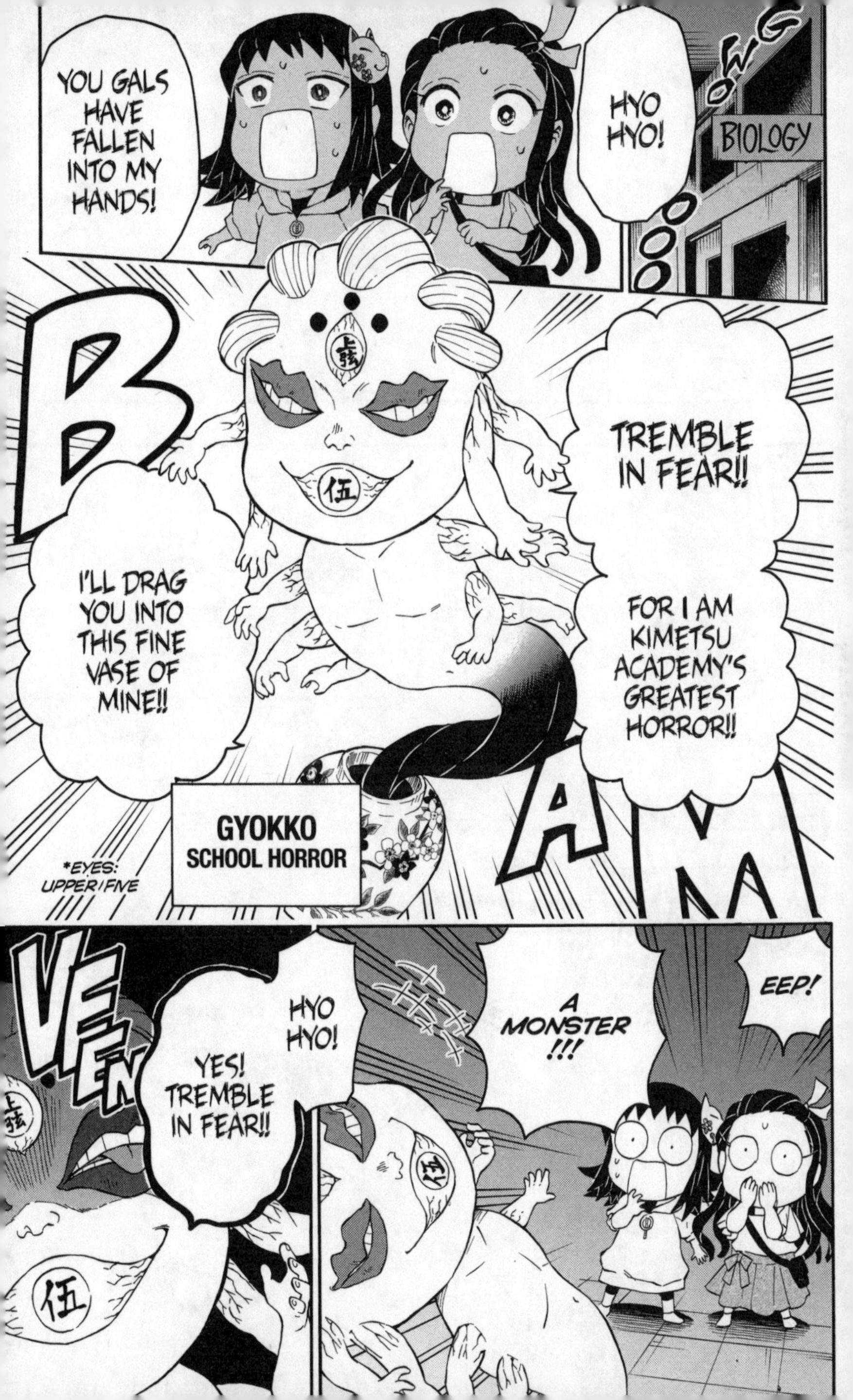

BIOLOGY
GOOOO
HYO HYO!
YOU GALS HAVE FALLEN INTO MY HANDS!
BAM
TREMBLE IN FEAR!!
FOR I AM KIMETSU ACADEMY'S GREATEST HORROR!!
I'LL DRAG YOU INTO THIS FINE VASE OF MINE!!
GYOKKO
SCHOOL HORROR
*EYES: UPPER/FIVE
EEP!
A MONSTER !!!
HYO HYO!
YES! TREMBLE IN FEAR!!
VEEN

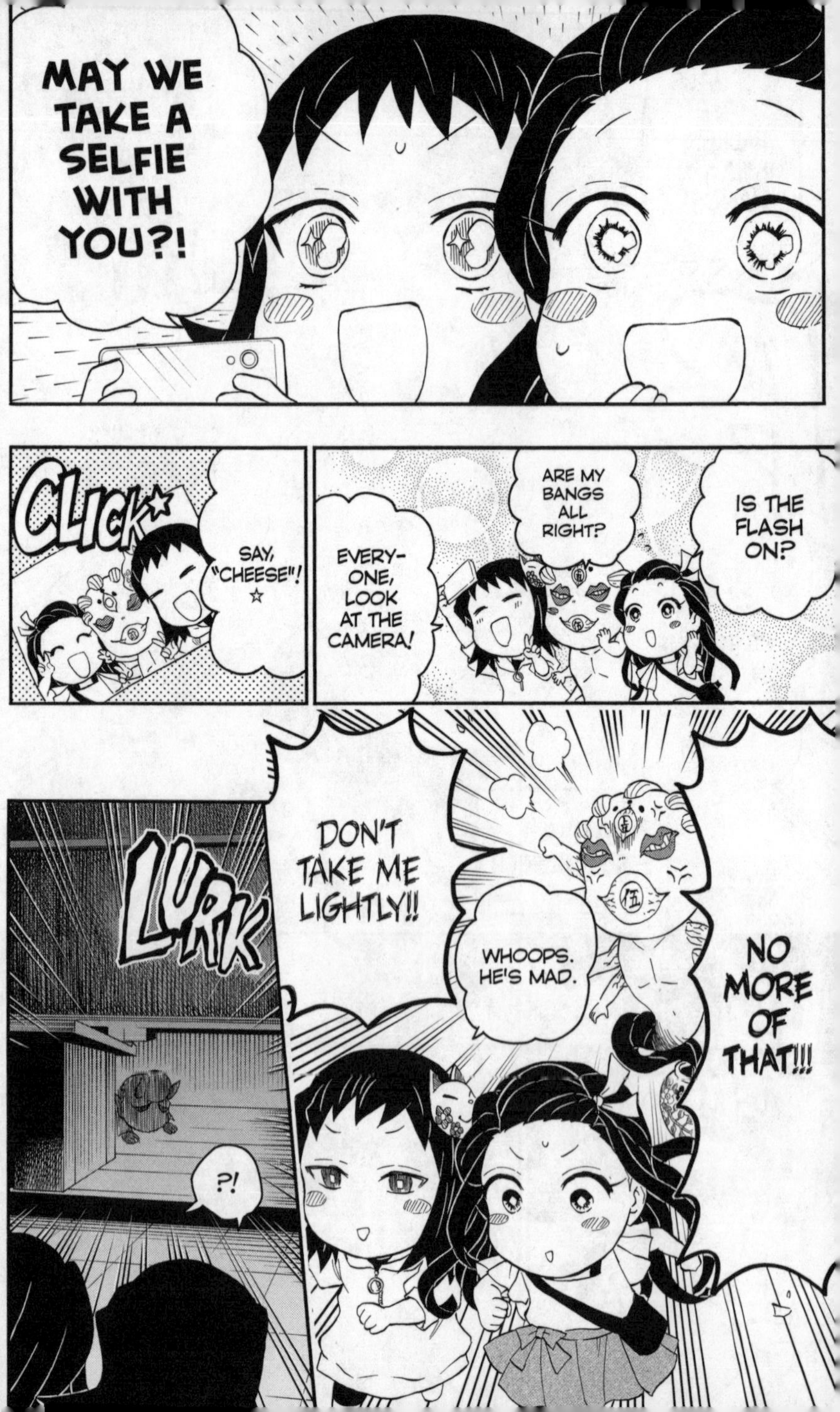
MAY WE TAKE A SELFIE WITH YOU?!
IS THE FLASH ON?
ARE MY BANGS ALL RIGHT?
EVERY-ONE, LOOK AT THE CAMERA!
CLICK☆
SAY, "CHEESE"! ☆
DON'T TAKE ME LIGHTLY!!
NO MORE OF THAT!!!
WHOOPS. HE'S MAD.
LURK
?!

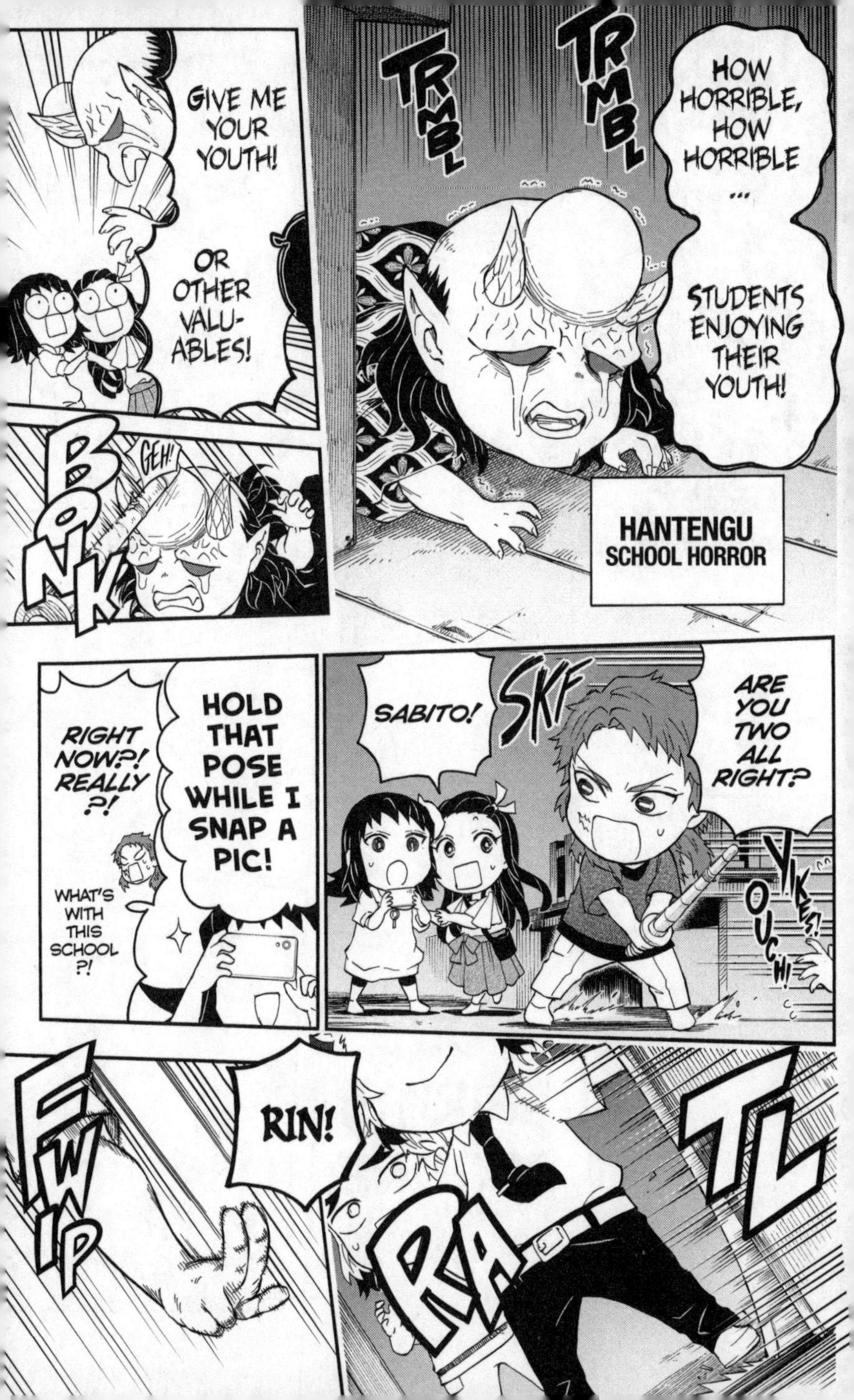
TRMBL
TRMBL
HOW HORRIBLE, HOW HORRIBLE...
STUDENTS ENJOYING THEIR YOUTH!
HANTENGU
SCHOOL HORROR
GIVE ME YOUR YOUTH!
OR OTHER VALU-ABLES!
GEH!
BONK
SKF
ARE YOU TWO ALL RIGHT?
SABITO!
YIKES!
OUCH!
HOLD THAT POSE WHILE I SNAP A PIC!
RIGHT NOW?! REALLY ?!
WHAT'S WITH THIS SCHOOL ?!
TL
PA
RIN!
FWIP

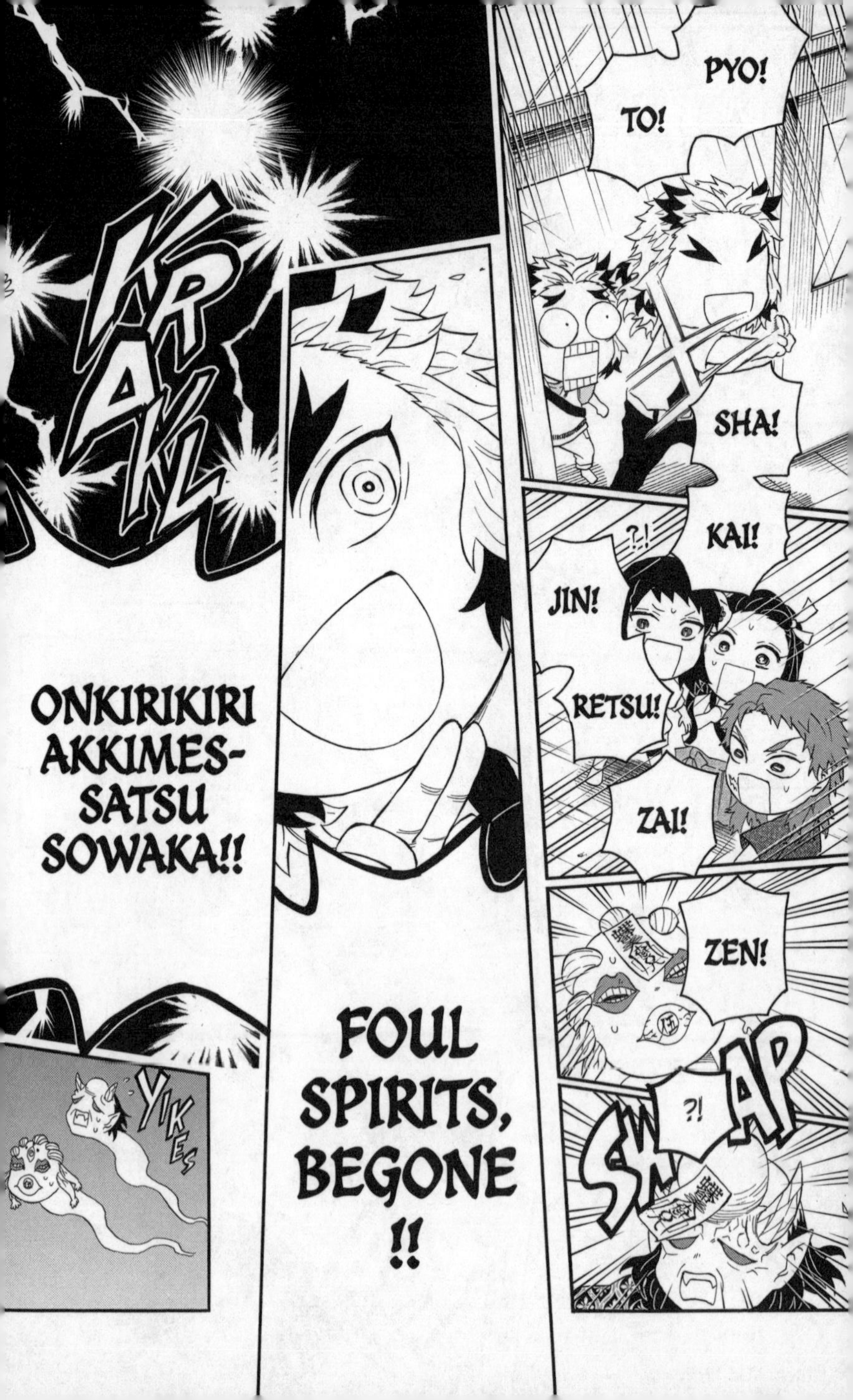
PYO!
TO!
SHA!
KAI!
?!
JIN!
RETSU!
ZAI!
ZEN!
SNAP
?!
FOUL SPIRITS, BEGONE !!
KRAKL
ONKIRIKIRI AKKIMES-SATSU SOWAKA!!
YIKES

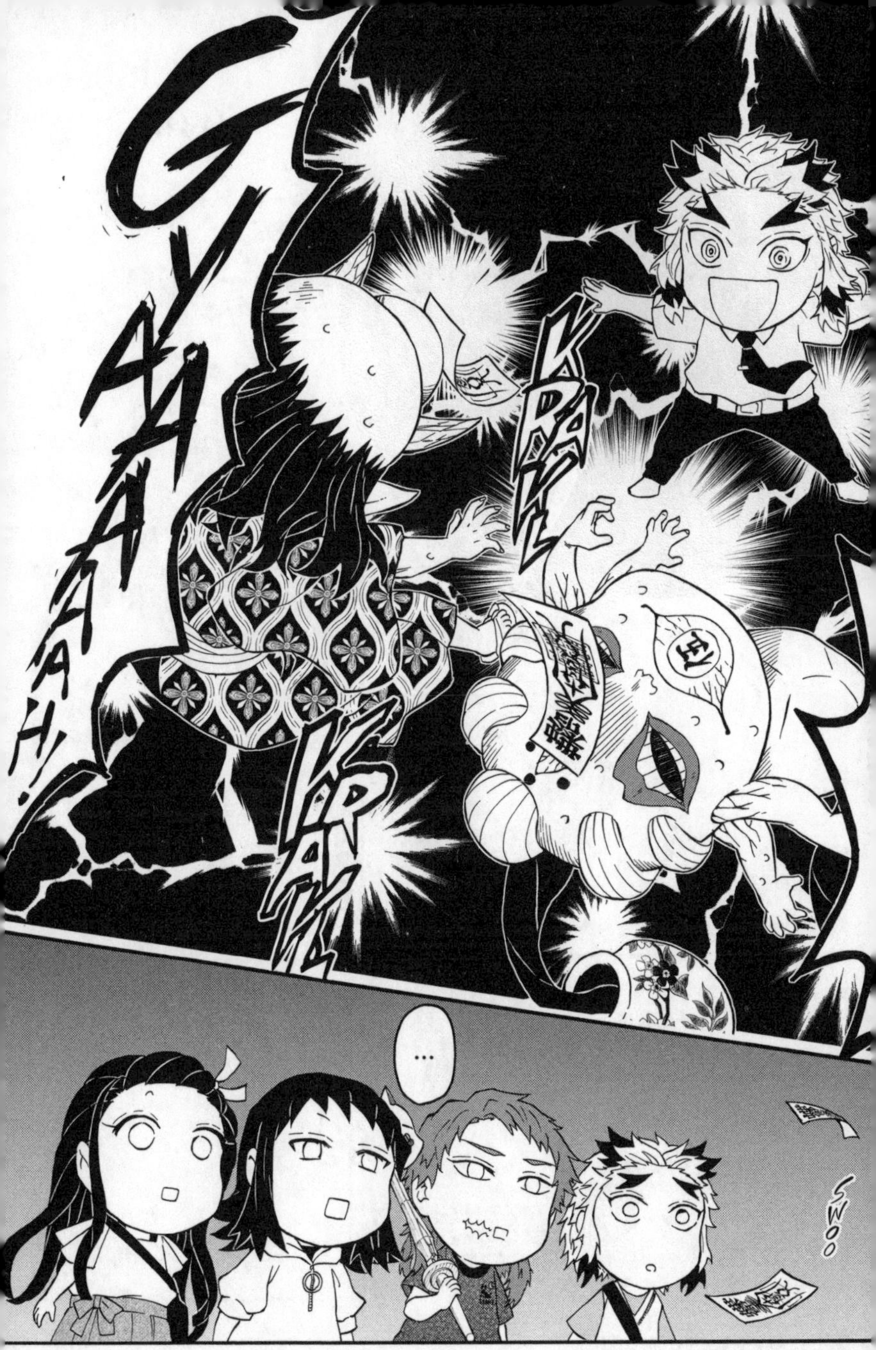
GYAAAAAH!!
...
SWOO

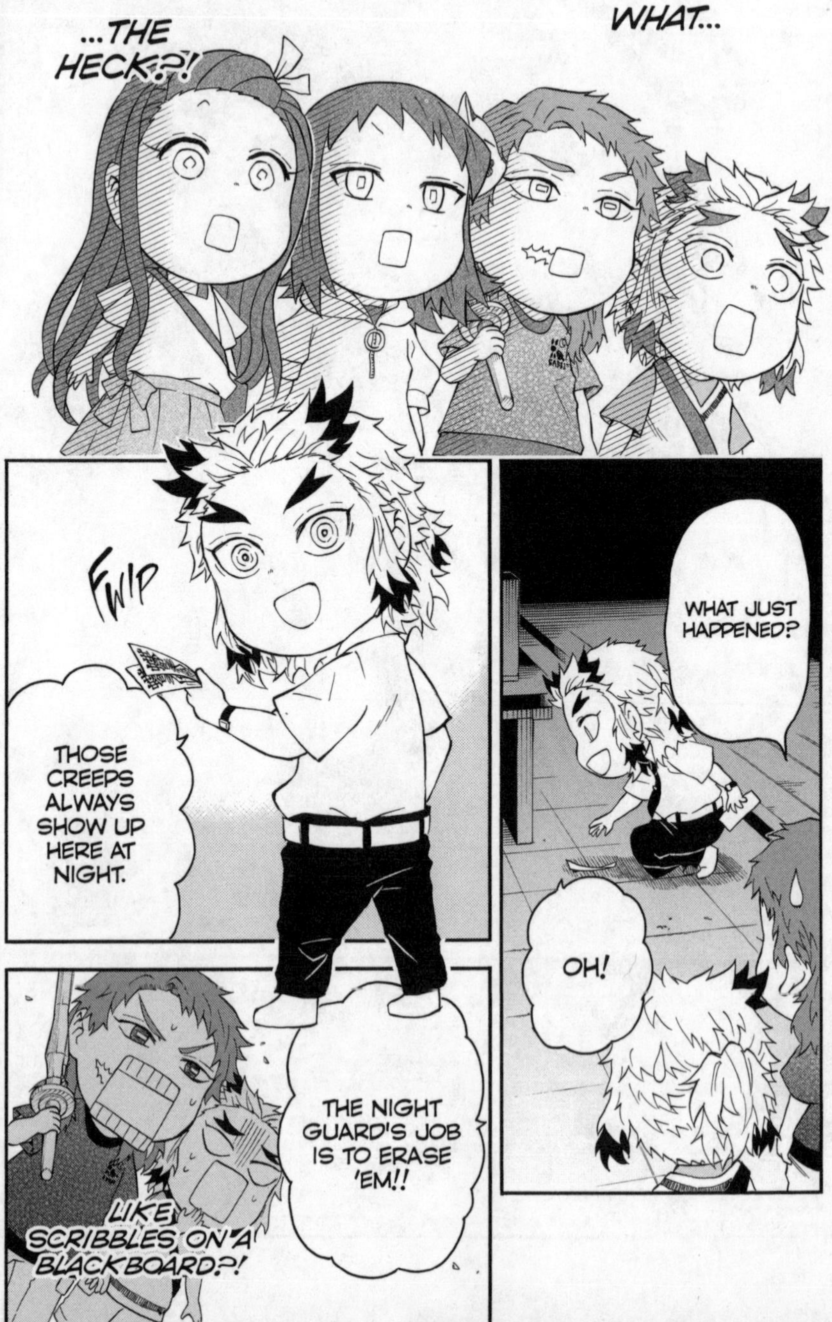
WHAT...
...THE HECK?!
WHAT JUST HAPPENED?
OH!
FWIP
THOSE CREEPS ALWAYS SHOW UP HERE AT NIGHT.
THE NIGHT GUARD'S JOB IS TO ERASE 'EM!!
LIKE SCRIBBLES ON A BLACKBOARD?!

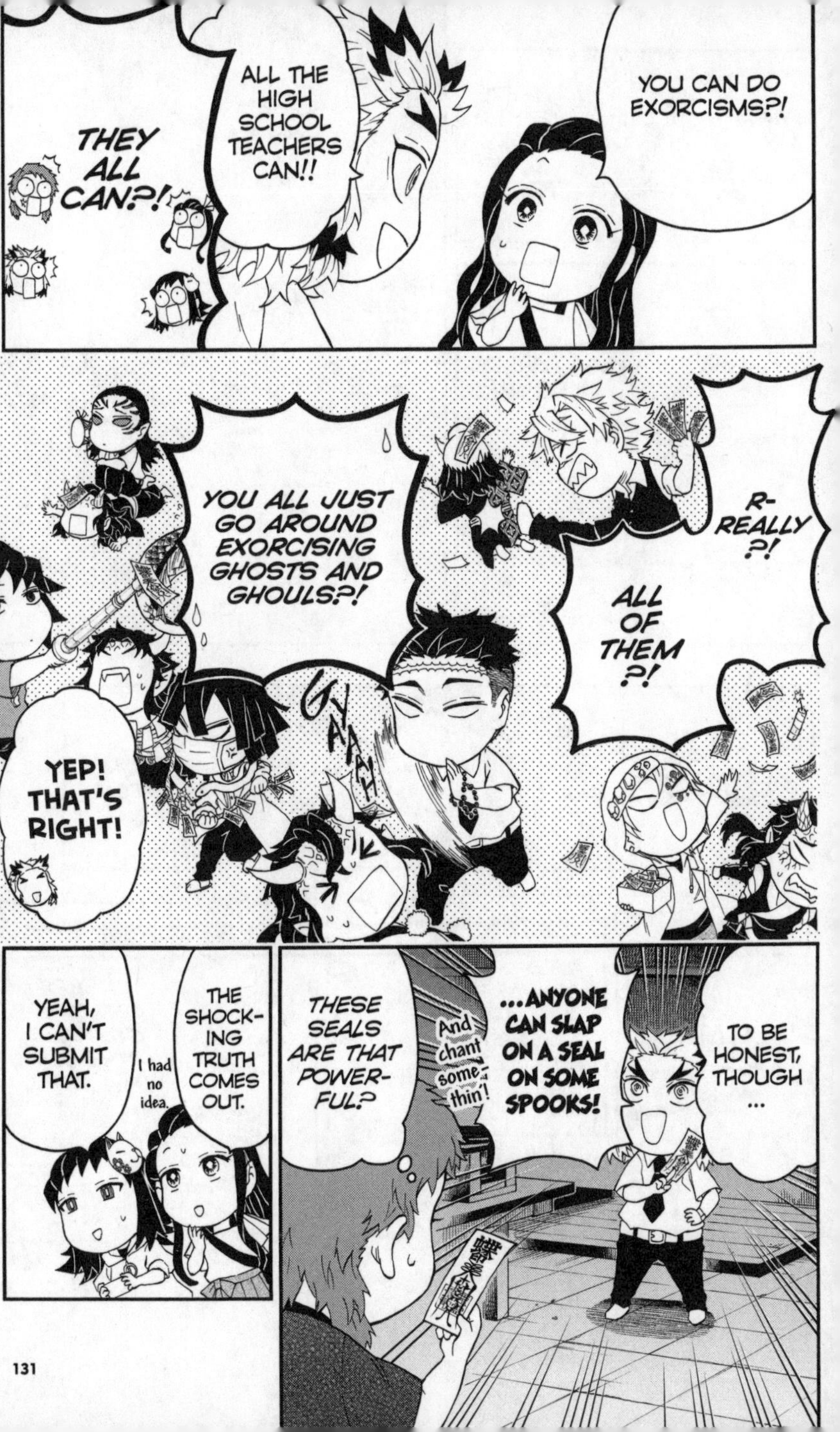
YOU CAN DO EXORCISMS?!
ALL THE HIGH SCHOOL TEACHERS CAN!!
THEY ALL CAN?!
R-REALLY?!
ALL OF THEM?!
YOU ALL JUST GO AROUND EXORCISING GHOSTS AND GHOULS?!
GYAAAH
YEP! THAT'S RIGHT!
TO BE HONEST, THOUGH...
...ANYONE CAN SLAP ON A SEAL ON SOME SPOOKS!
And chant somethin'!
THESE SEALS ARE THAT POWERFUL?
THE SHOCKING TRUTH COMES OUT.
I had no idea.
YEAH, I CAN'T SUBMIT THAT.

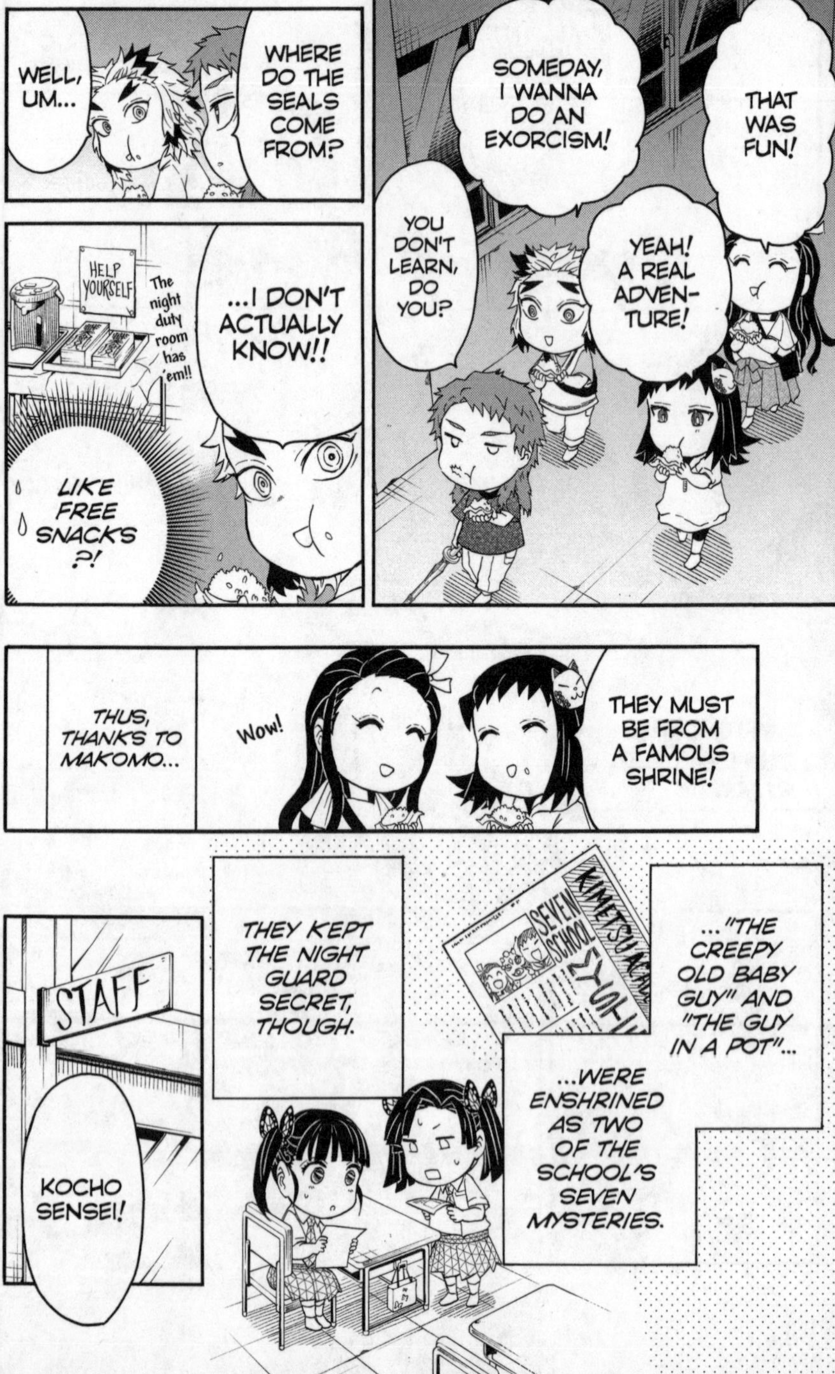
THAT WAS FUN!
SOMEDAY, I WANNA DO AN EXORCISM!
YEAH! A REAL ADVENTURE!
YOU DON'T LEARN, DO YOU?
WHERE DO THE SEALS COME FROM?
WELL, UM...
...I DON'T ACTUALLY KNOW!!
HELP YOURSELF
The night duty room has 'em!!
LIKE FREE SNACKS?!
THEY MUST BE FROM A FAMOUS SHRINE!
Wow!
THUS, THANKS TO MAKOMO...
..."THE CREEPY OLD BABY GUY" AND "THE GUY IN A POT"...
...WERE ENSHRINED AS TWO OF THE SCHOOL'S SEVEN MYSTERIES.
SEVEN SCHOOL
THEY KEPT THE NIGHT GUARD SECRET, THOUGH.
STAFF
KOCHO SENSEI!

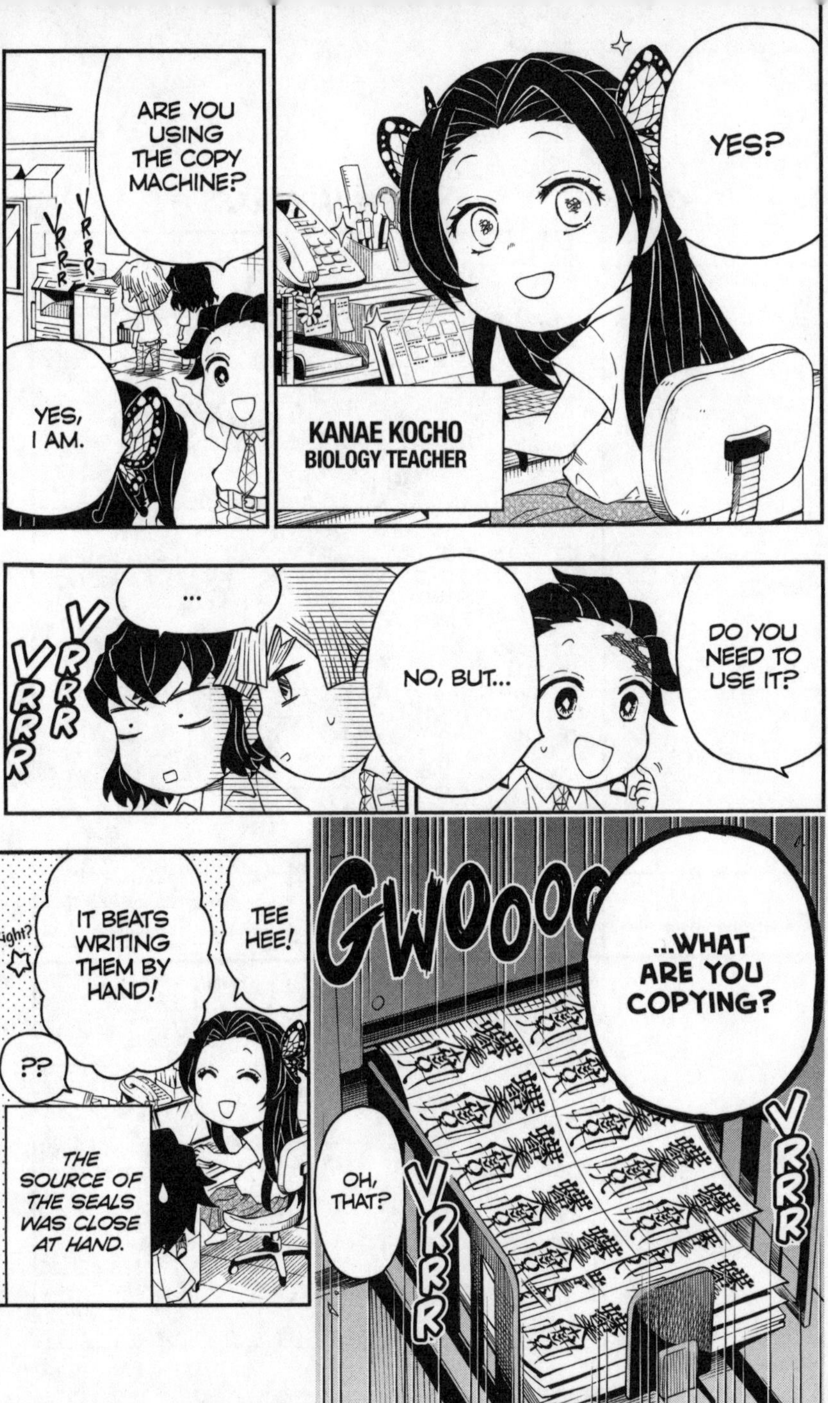
YES?
KANAE KOCHO
BIOLOGY TEACHER
ARE YOU USING THE COPY MACHINE?
VRRR
VRRR
YES, I AM.
DO YOU NEED TO USE IT?
NO, BUT...
...
VRRR
VRRR
GWOOOO
...WHAT ARE YOU COPYING?
VRRR
OH, THAT?
VRRR
TEE HEE!
IT BEATS WRITING THEM BY HAND!
Right?
??
THE SOURCE OF THE SEALS WAS CLOSE AT HAND.

LIFE IN TARO CLASS

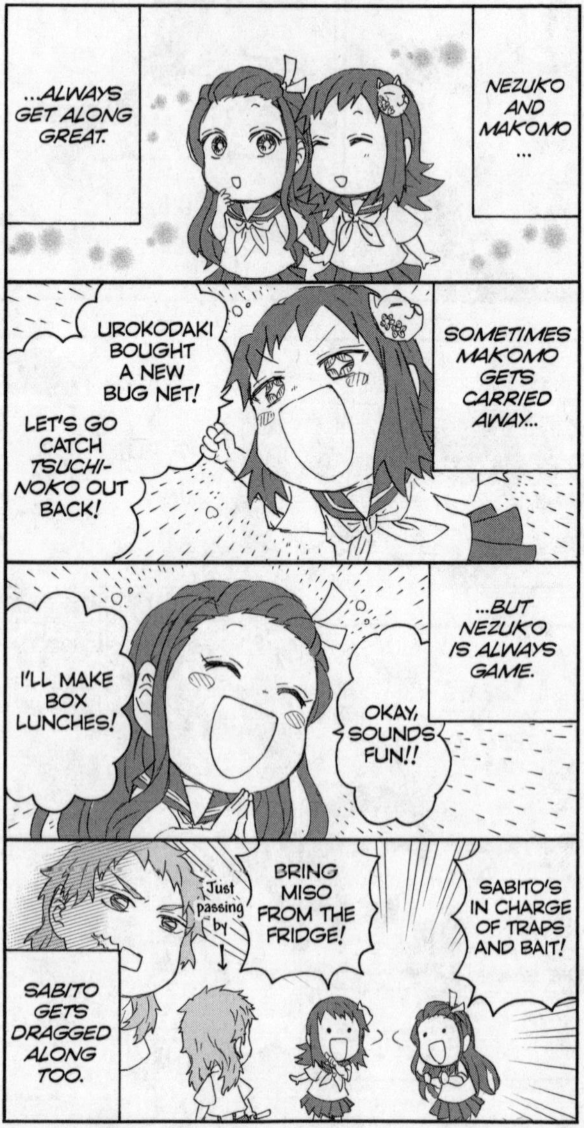
NEZUKO AND MAKOMO ...
...ALWAYS GET ALONG GREAT.
SOMETIMES MAKOMO GETS CARRIED AWAY...
UROKODAKI BOUGHT A NEW BUG NET!
LET'S GO CATCH *TSUCHI-NOKO* OUT BACK!
...BUT NEZUKO IS ALWAYS GAME.
OKAY, SOUNDS FUN!!
I'LL MAKE BOX LUNCHES!
SABITO'S IN CHARGE OF TRAPS AND BAIT!
BRING MISO FROM THE FRIDGE!
Just passing by
SABITO GETS DRAGGED ALONG TOO.

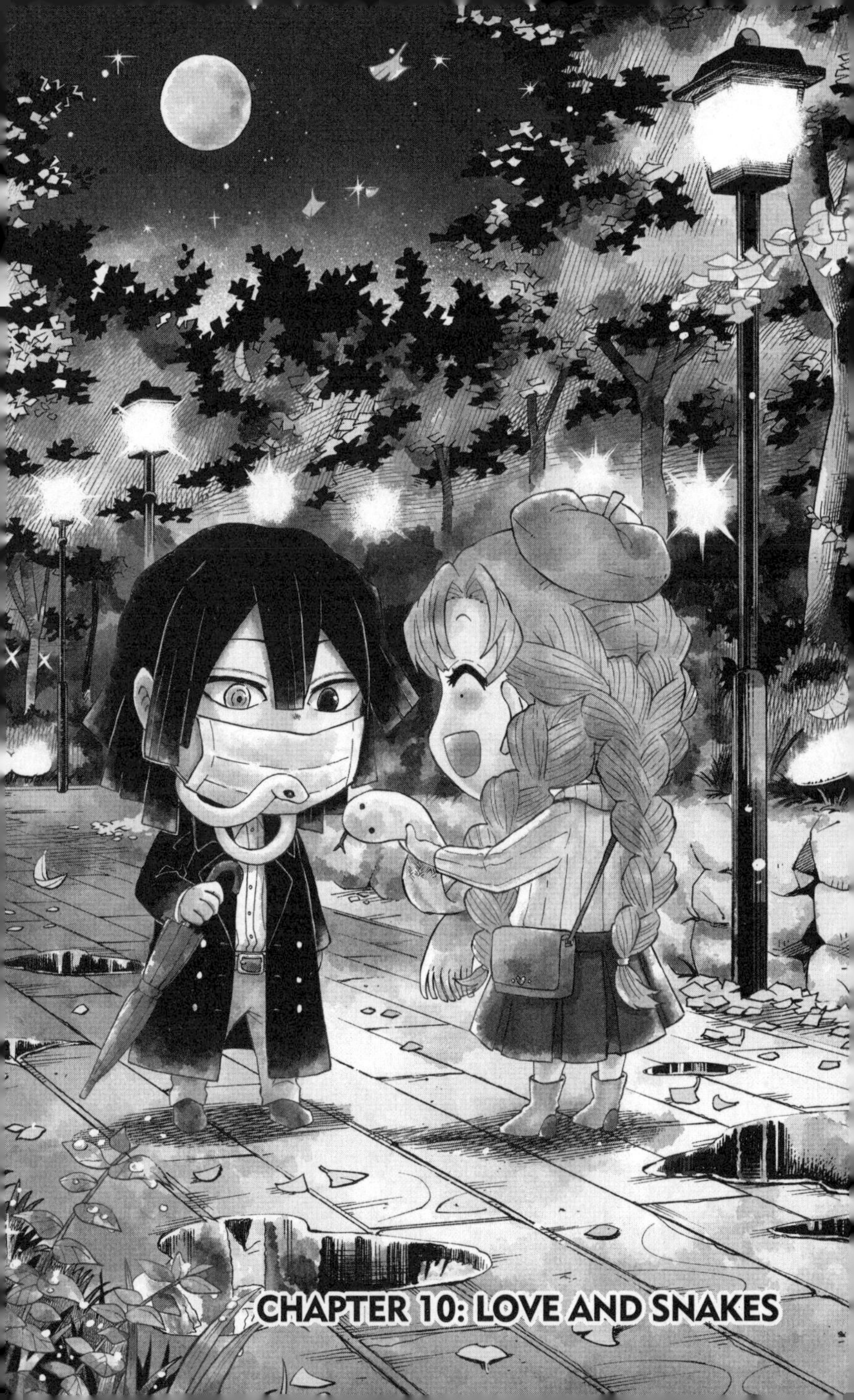

CHAPTER 10: LOVE AND SNAKES

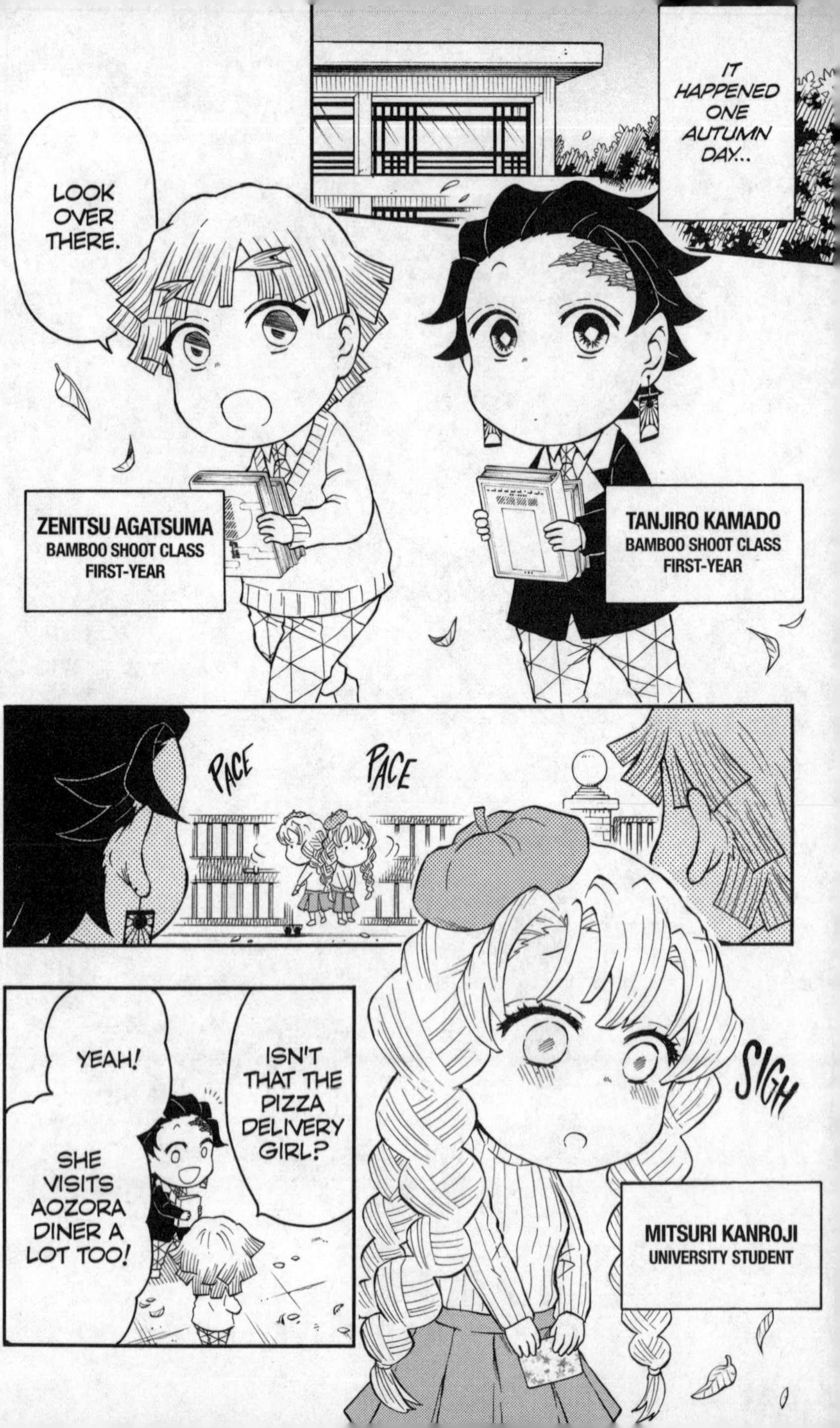

IT HAPPENED ONE AUTUMN DAY...
LOOK OVER THERE.
TANJIRO KAMADO
BAMBOO SHOOT CLASS
FIRST-YEAR
ZENITSU AGATSUMA
BAMBOO SHOOT CLASS
FIRST-YEAR
PACE
PACE
SIGH
MITSURI KANROJI
UNIVERSITY STUDENT
ISN'T THAT THE PIZZA DELIVERY GIRL?
YEAH!
SHE VISITS AOZORA DINER A LOT TOO!

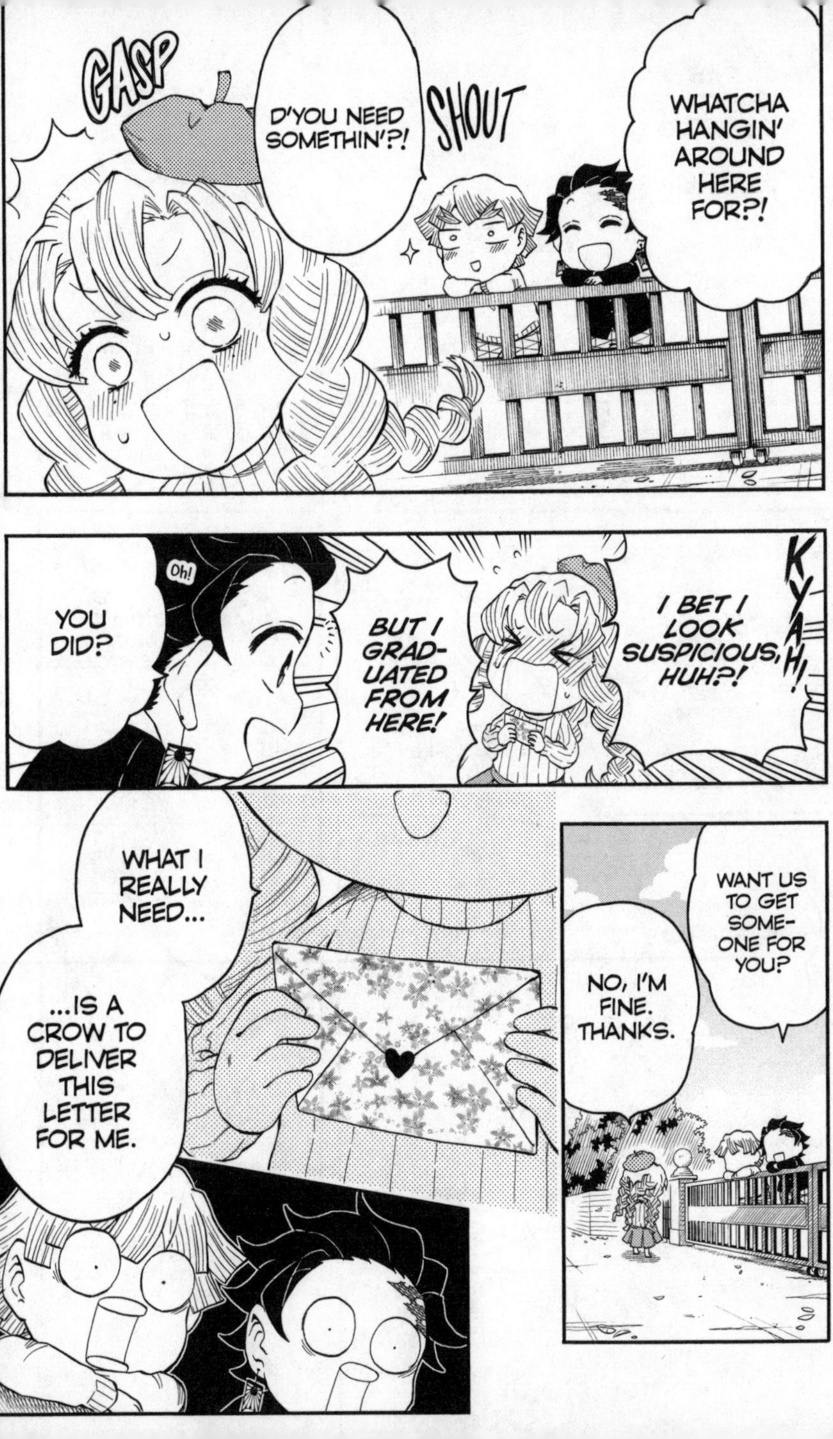
WHATCHA HANGIN' AROUND HERE FOR?!
SHOUT
D'YOU NEED SOMETHIN'?!
GASP
KYAH!
I BET I LOOK SUSPICIOUS, HUH?!
BUT I GRAD-UATED FROM HERE!
Oh!
YOU DID?
WANT US TO GET SOME-ONE FOR YOU?
NO, I'M FINE. THANKS.
WHAT I REALLY NEED...
...IS A CROW TO DELIVER THIS LETTER FOR ME.

IT'S FOR...

CHEMISTRY

...OBANAI IGURO?! OUR CHEMISTRY TEACHER?!

NO FREAKING WAY...

NAG NAG

Oh, you forgot your homework?

Then why even bother coming?!

NOT A CHANCE!

WELL, I GUESS HE'S POPULAR!

HE'S A GLOOMY AND ANNOYING SNAKE!!

ROMANCE ISN'T A COMPETITION! BE STRONG, ZENITSU!

HE BEAT ME!!

I CAN'T BELIEVE IT!!

FINE, WHATEVER. BUT...

AFTER ALL... HM? I BET SHE'LL DUMP HIM! ...THAT GUY AND KANROJI?

Mask

HE'LL PROBABLY FROTH AT THE MOUTH AND COLLAPSE!

Ward against women? Kaburamaru (snake)

WOMAN WOMAN ...HE'S BASICALLY ALLERGIC TO WOMEN!

HIS HEART POUNDS AND HE SWEATS BUCKETS!

WELL, IT'S NOT OUR DECISION. SO MAYBE IT'D BE BEST IF WE DIDN'T DELIVER THIS.

...

ANYWAY, UM...

OBANAI IGURO
CHEMISTRY TEACHER

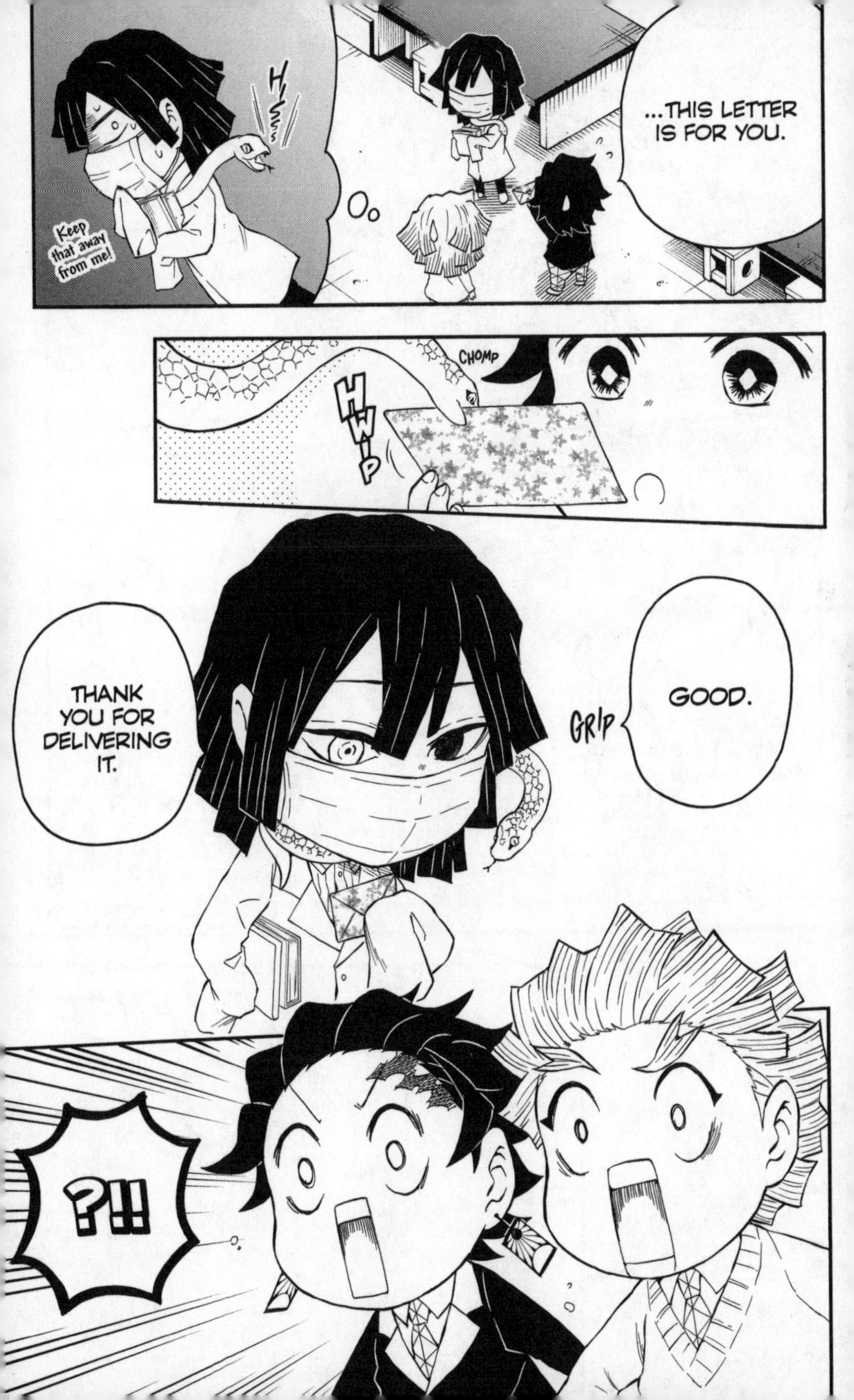
...THIS LETTER IS FOR YOU.
Oo
HISSS
Keep that away from me!
CHOMP
HWIP
GOOD.
GRIP
THANK YOU FOR DELIVERING IT.
?!!

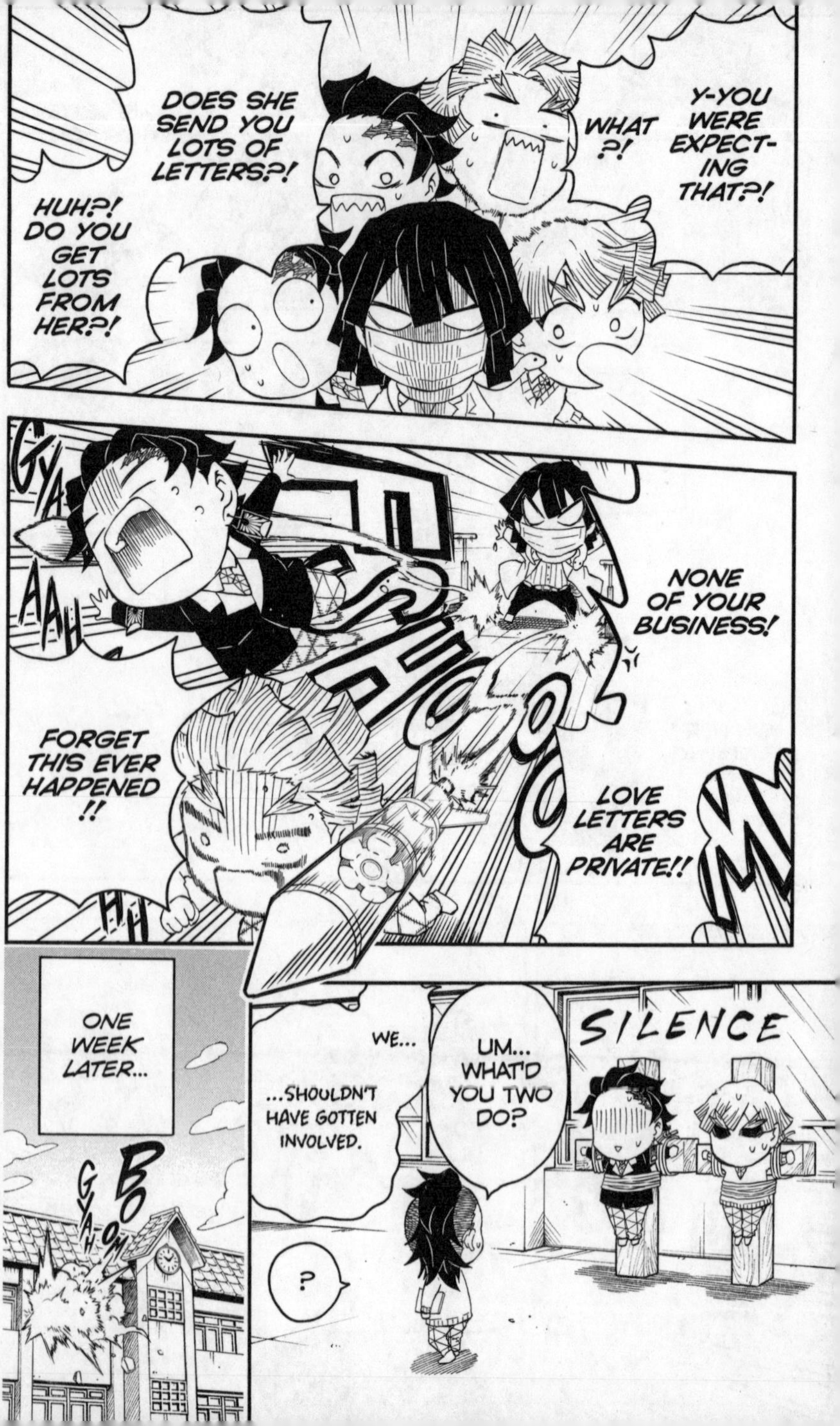
Y-YOU WERE EXPECTING THAT?!
WHAT ?!
DOES SHE SEND YOU LOTS OF LETTERS?!
HUH?! DO YOU GET LOTS FROM HER?!
NONE OF YOUR BUSINESS!
LOVE LETTERS ARE PRIVATE!!
FORGET THIS EVER HAPPENED!!
SILENCE
UM... WHAT'D YOU TWO DO?
WE...
...SHOULDN'T HAVE GOTTEN INVOLVED.
?
ONE WEEK LATER...
BOOM
GYAAH

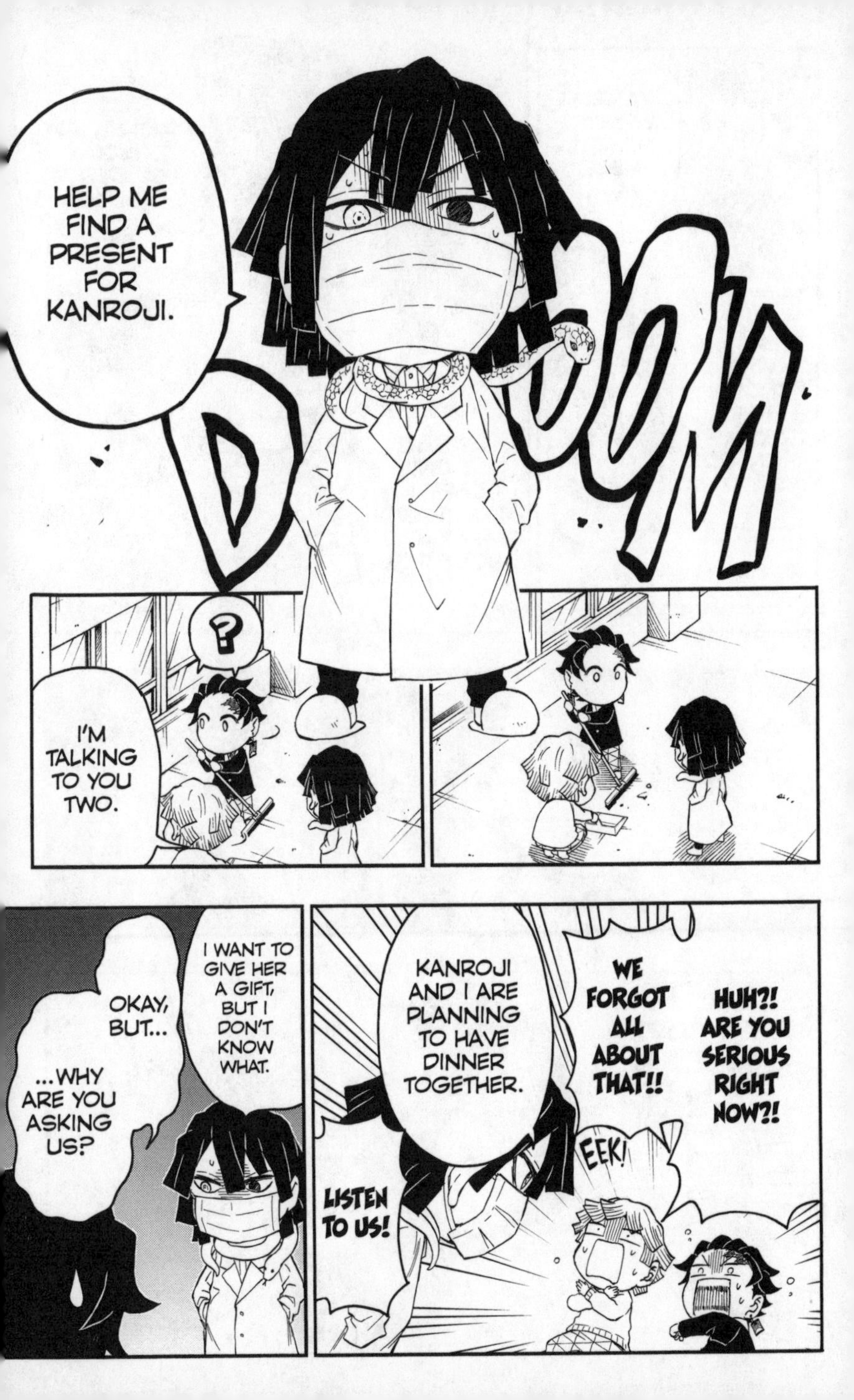
HELP ME FIND A PRESENT FOR KANROJI.
DOOM
?
I'M TALKING TO YOU TWO.
KANROJI AND I ARE PLANNING TO HAVE DINNER TOGETHER.
HUH?! ARE YOU SERIOUS RIGHT NOW?!
WE FORGOT ALL ABOUT THAT!!
EEK!
LISTEN TO US!
I WANT TO GIVE HER A GIFT, BUT I DON'T KNOW WHAT.
OKAY, BUT...
...WHY ARE YOU ASKING US?

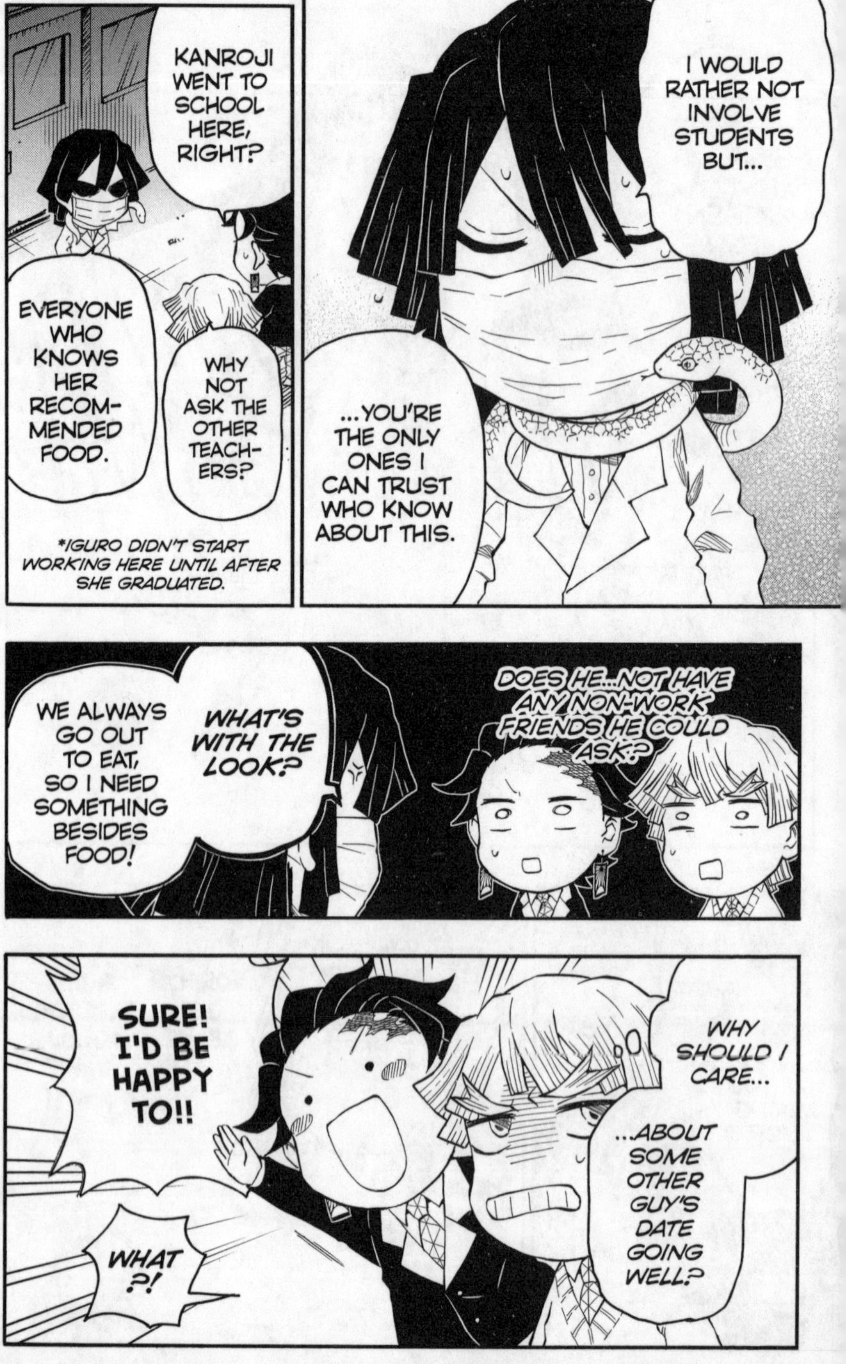
I WOULD RATHER NOT INVOLVE STUDENTS BUT...
...YOU'RE THE ONLY ONES I CAN TRUST WHO KNOW ABOUT THIS.
KANROJI WENT TO SCHOOL HERE, RIGHT?
WHY NOT ASK THE OTHER TEACHERS?
EVERYONE WHO KNOWS HER RECOMMENDED FOOD.
*IGURO DIDN'T START WORKING HERE UNTIL AFTER SHE GRADUATED.
DOES HE...NOT HAVE ANY NON-WORK FRIENDS HE COULD ASK?
WHAT'S WITH THE LOOK?
WE ALWAYS GO OUT TO EAT, SO I NEED SOMETHING BESIDES FOOD!
WHY SHOULD I CARE...
...ABOUT SOME OTHER GUY'S DATE GOING WELL?
SURE! I'D BE HAPPY TO!!
WHAT ?!

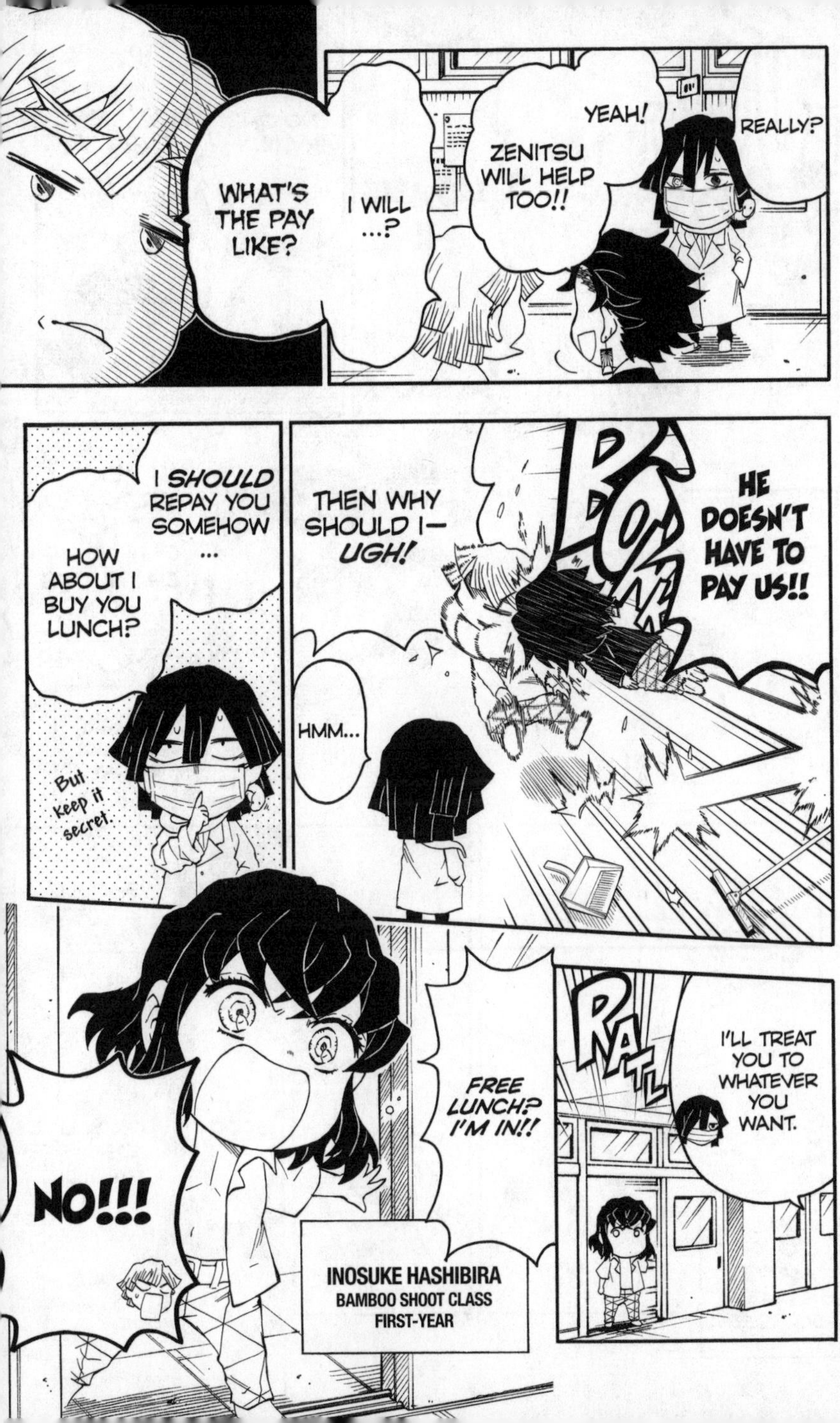
REALLY?
YEAH!
ZENITSU WILL HELP TOO!!
I WILL ...?
WHAT'S THE PAY LIKE?
HE DOESN'T HAVE TO PAY US!!
THEN WHY SHOULD I— *UGH!*
HMM...
I *SHOULD* REPAY YOU SOMEHOW ...
HOW ABOUT I BUY YOU LUNCH?
But keep it secret.
I'LL TREAT YOU TO WHATEVER YOU WANT.
FREE LUNCH? I'M IN!!
NO!!!
INOSUKE HASHIBIRA
BAMBOO SHOOT CLASS
FIRST-YEAR

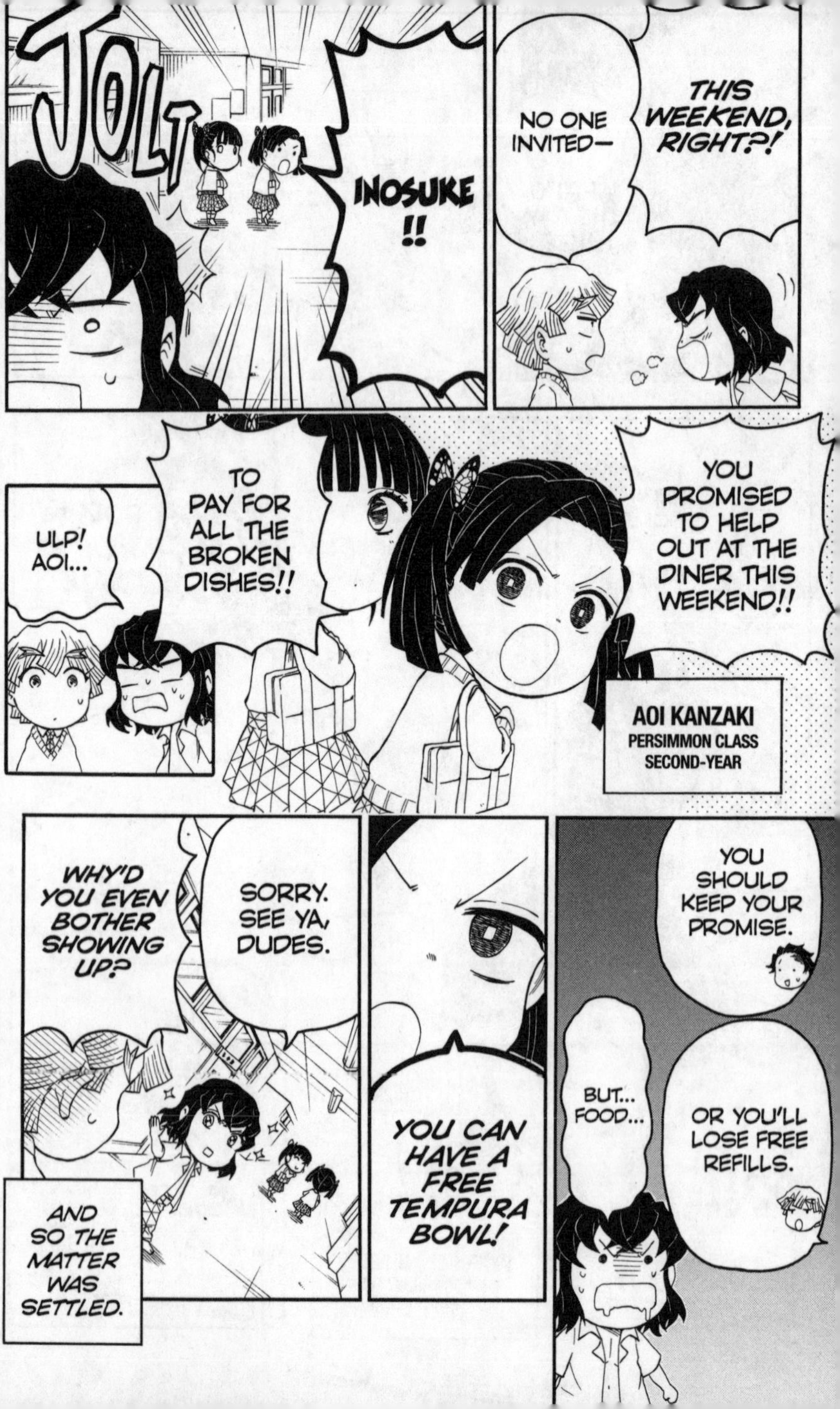
THIS WEEKEND, RIGHT?!
NO ONE INVITED—
JOLT
INOSUKE!!
YOU PROMISED TO HELP OUT AT THE DINER THIS WEEKEND!!
TO PAY FOR ALL THE BROKEN DISHES!!
AOI KANZAKI
PERSIMMON CLASS SECOND-YEAR
ULP! AOI...
YOU SHOULD KEEP YOUR PROMISE.
OR YOU'LL LOSE FREE REFILLS.
BUT... FOOD...
YOU CAN HAVE A FREE TEMPURA BOWL!
SORRY. SEE YA, DUDES.
WHY'D YOU EVEN BOTHER SHOWING UP?
AND SO THE MATTER WAS SETTLED.

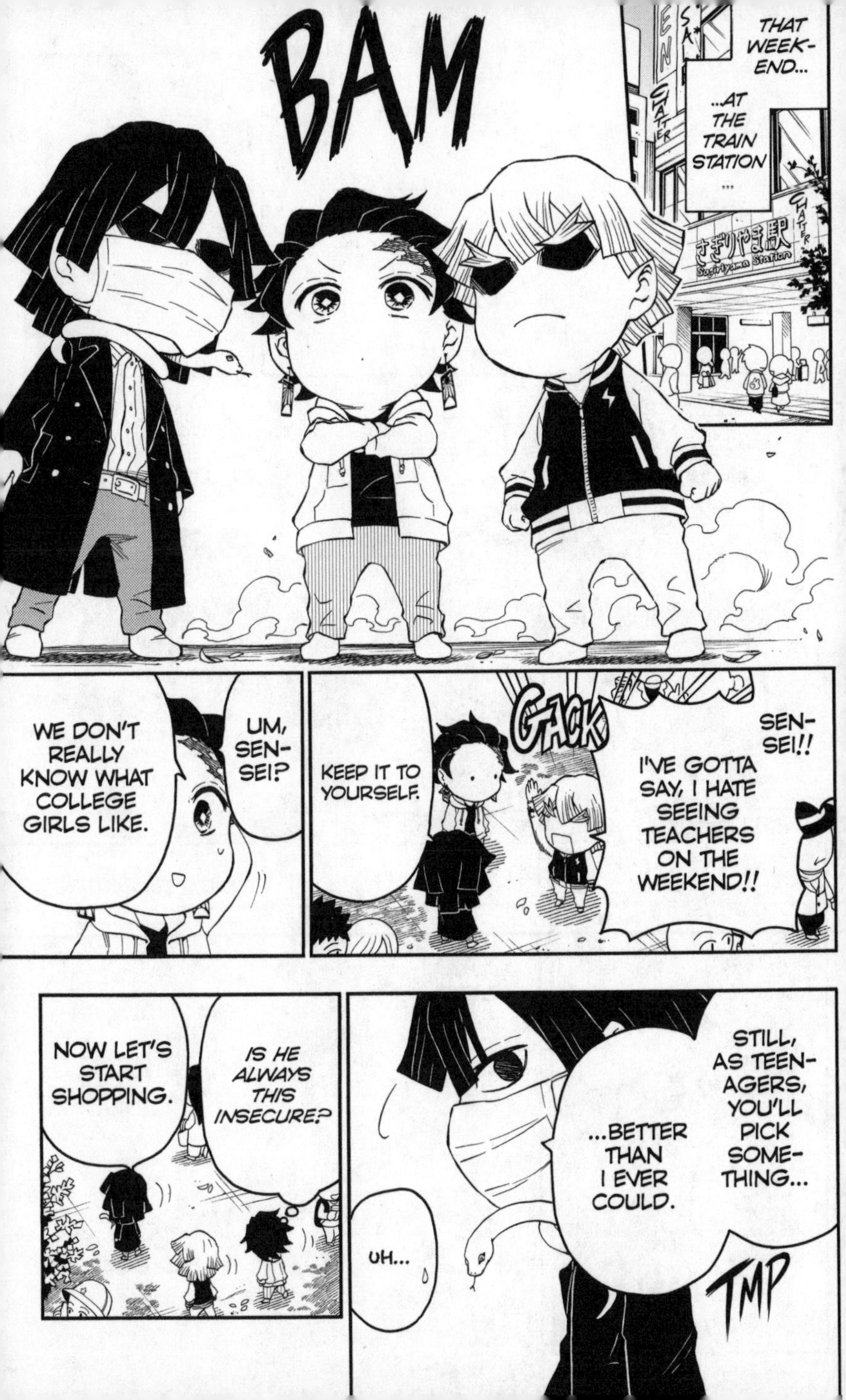
BAM
THAT WEEK-END...
...AT THE TRAIN STATION ...
さぎりやま駅
Sagiriyama Station
SEN-SEI!!
I'VE GOTTA SAY, I HATE SEEING TEACHERS ON THE WEEKEND!!
GACK
KEEP IT TO YOURSELF.
UM, SEN-SEI?
WE DON'T REALLY KNOW WHAT COLLEGE GIRLS LIKE.
STILL, AS TEEN-AGERS, YOU'LL PICK SOME-THING...
...BETTER THAN I EVER COULD.
UH...
TMP
IS HE ALWAYS THIS INSECURE?
NOW LET'S START SHOPPING.

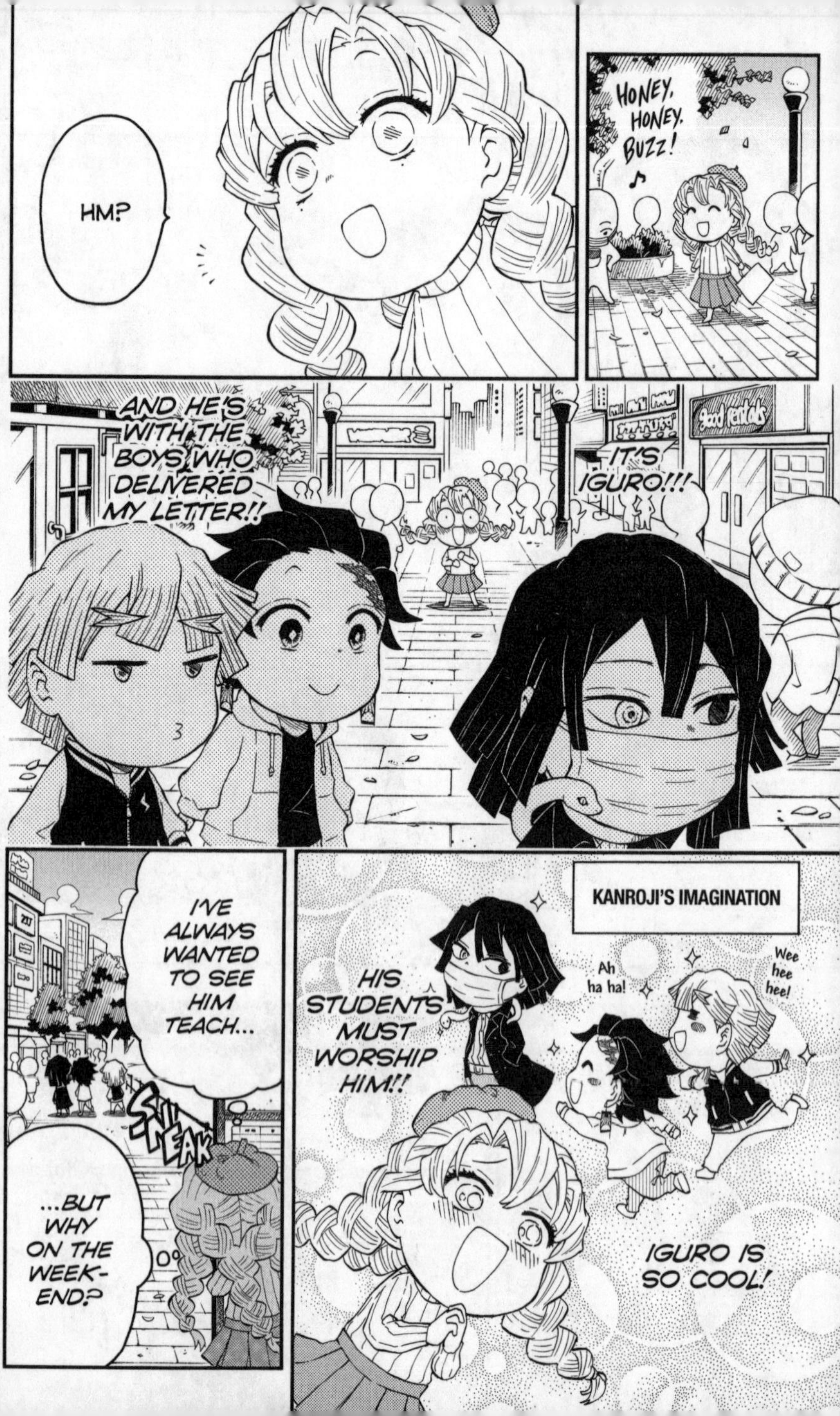
HONEY, HONEY, BUZZ!
HM?
IT'S IGURO!!!
AND HE'S WITH THE BOYS WHO DELIVERED MY LETTER!!
KANROJI'S IMAGINATION
Wee hee hee!
Ah ha ha!
HIS STUDENTS MUST WORSHIP HIM!!
IGURO IS SO COOL!
I'VE ALWAYS WANTED TO SEE HIM TEACH...
SNEAK
...BUT WHY ON THE WEEK-END?

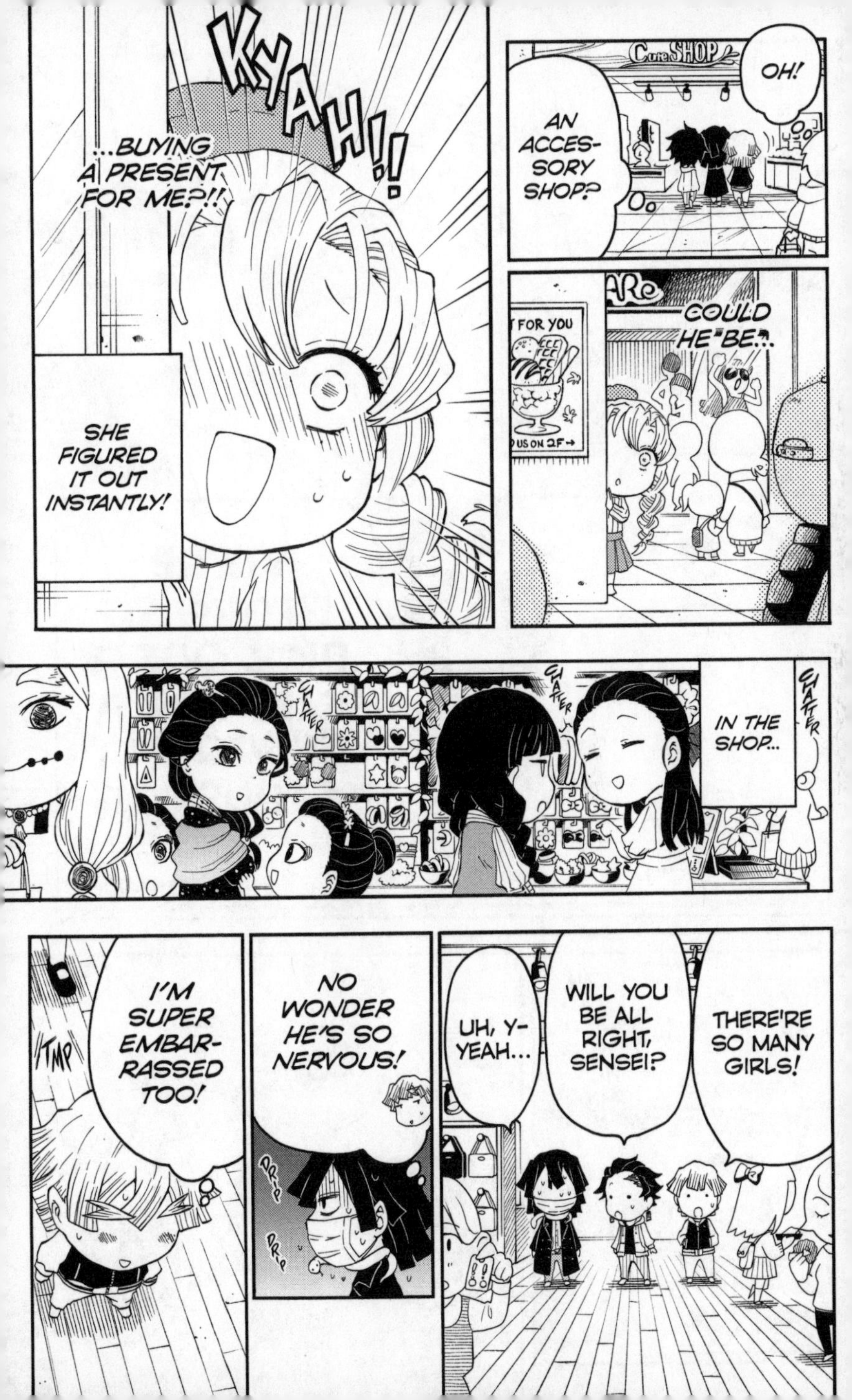
Cute SHOP
OH!
AN ACCES-SORY SHOP?
FOR YOU
US ON 2F →
COULD HE BE...?
KYAH!!
...BUYING A PRESENT FOR ME?!!
SHE FIGURED IT OUT INSTANTLY!
CHATTER
IN THE SHOP...
CHATTER
CHATTER
THERE'RE SO MANY GIRLS!
WILL YOU BE ALL RIGHT, SENSEI?
UH, Y-YEAH...
NO WONDER HE'S SO NERVOUS!
DRIP
DRIP
I'M SUPER EMBAR-RASSED TOO!
TMP

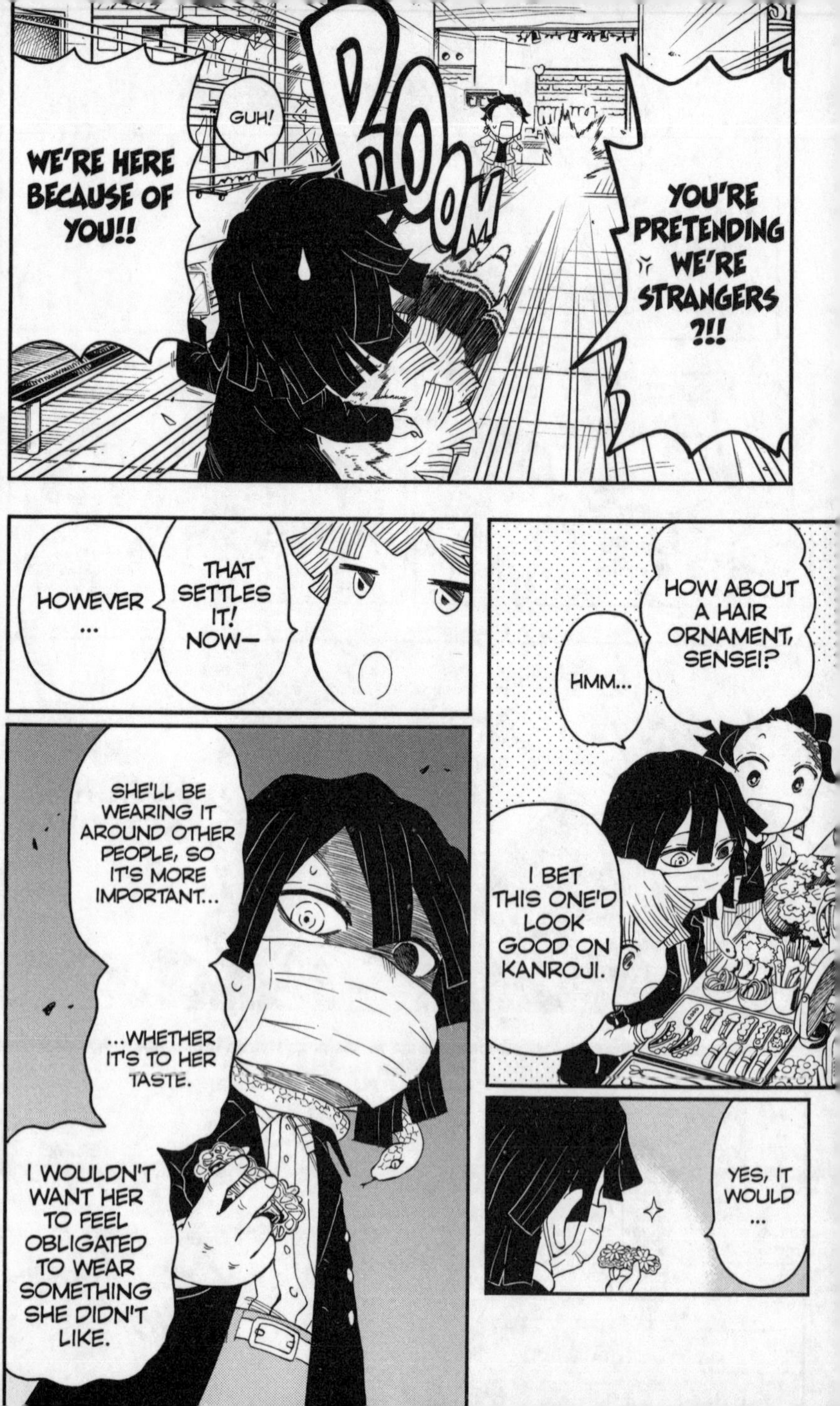
YOU'RE PRETENDING WE'RE STRANGERS ?!!
BOOM
GUH!
WE'RE HERE BECAUSE OF YOU!!
HOW ABOUT A HAIR ORNAMENT, SENSEI?
HMM...
I BET THIS ONE'D LOOK GOOD ON KANROJI.
YES, IT WOULD ...
THAT SETTLES IT! NOW—
HOWEVER ...
SHE'LL BE WEARING IT AROUND OTHER PEOPLE, SO IT'S MORE IMPORTANT...
...WHETHER IT'S TO HER TASTE.
I WOULDN'T WANT HER TO FEEL OBLIGATED TO WEAR SOMETHING SHE DIDN'T LIKE.

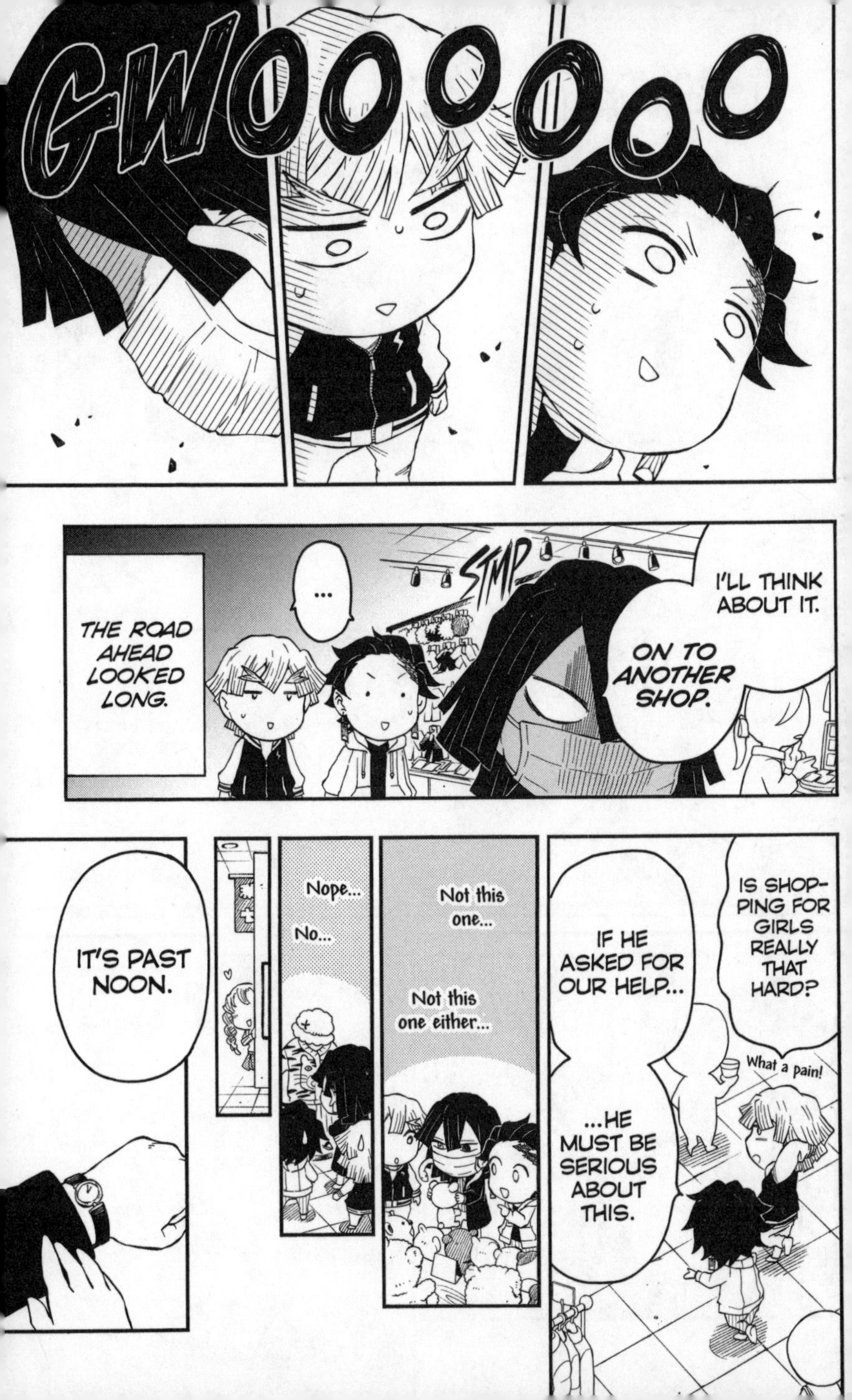
GWOOOOOOO
I'LL THINK ABOUT IT.
ON TO ANOTHER SHOP.
STMP
...
THE ROAD AHEAD LOOKED LONG.
IS SHOP-PING FOR GIRLS REALLY THAT HARD?
What a pain!
IF HE ASKED FOR OUR HELP...
...HE MUST BE SERIOUS ABOUT THIS.
Not this one...
Not this one either...
Nope...
No...
IT'S PAST NOON.

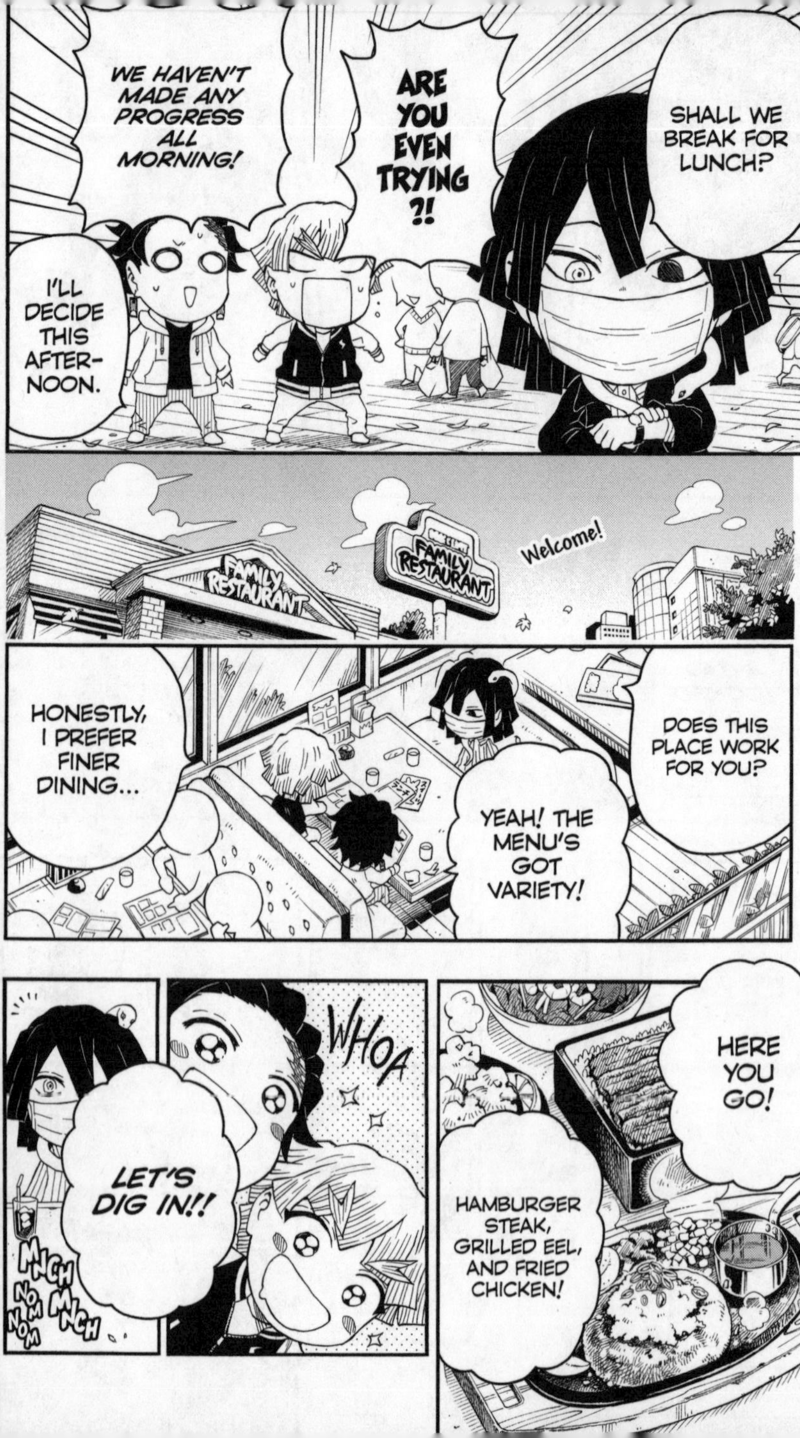
SHALL WE BREAK FOR LUNCH?
ARE YOU EVEN TRYING?!
WE HAVEN'T MADE ANY PROGRESS ALL MORNING!
I'LL DECIDE THIS AFTER-NOON.
FAMILY RESTAURANT
FAMILY RESTAURANT
Welcome!
DOES THIS PLACE WORK FOR YOU?
YEAH! THE MENU'S GOT VARIETY!
HONESTLY, I PREFER FINER DINING...
HERE YOU GO!
HAMBURGER STEAK, GRILLED EEL, AND FRIED CHICKEN!
WHOA
LET'S DIG IN!!
MNCH MNCH
NOM NOM

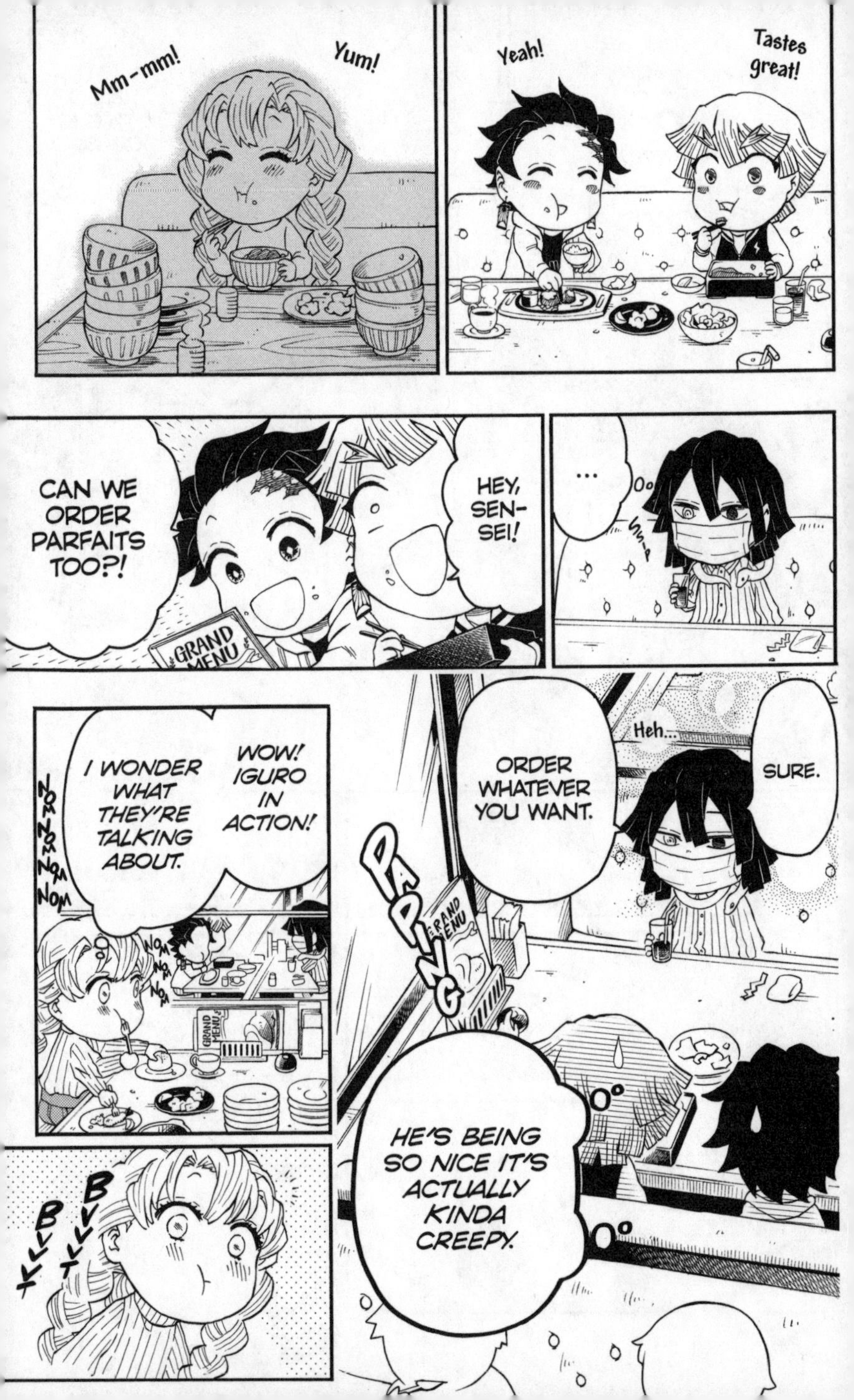
Tastes great!
Yeah!
Yum!
Mm-mm!
...
HEY, SEN-SEI!
CAN WE ORDER PARFAITS TOO?!
Heh...
SURE.
ORDER WHATEVER YOU WANT.
PAPING
WOW! IGURO IN ACTION!
I WONDER WHAT THEY'RE TALKING ABOUT.
NOM NOM NOM NOM NOM
NOM NOM NOM
HE'S BEING SO NICE IT'S ACTUALLY KINDA CREEPY.
BVVT BVVT

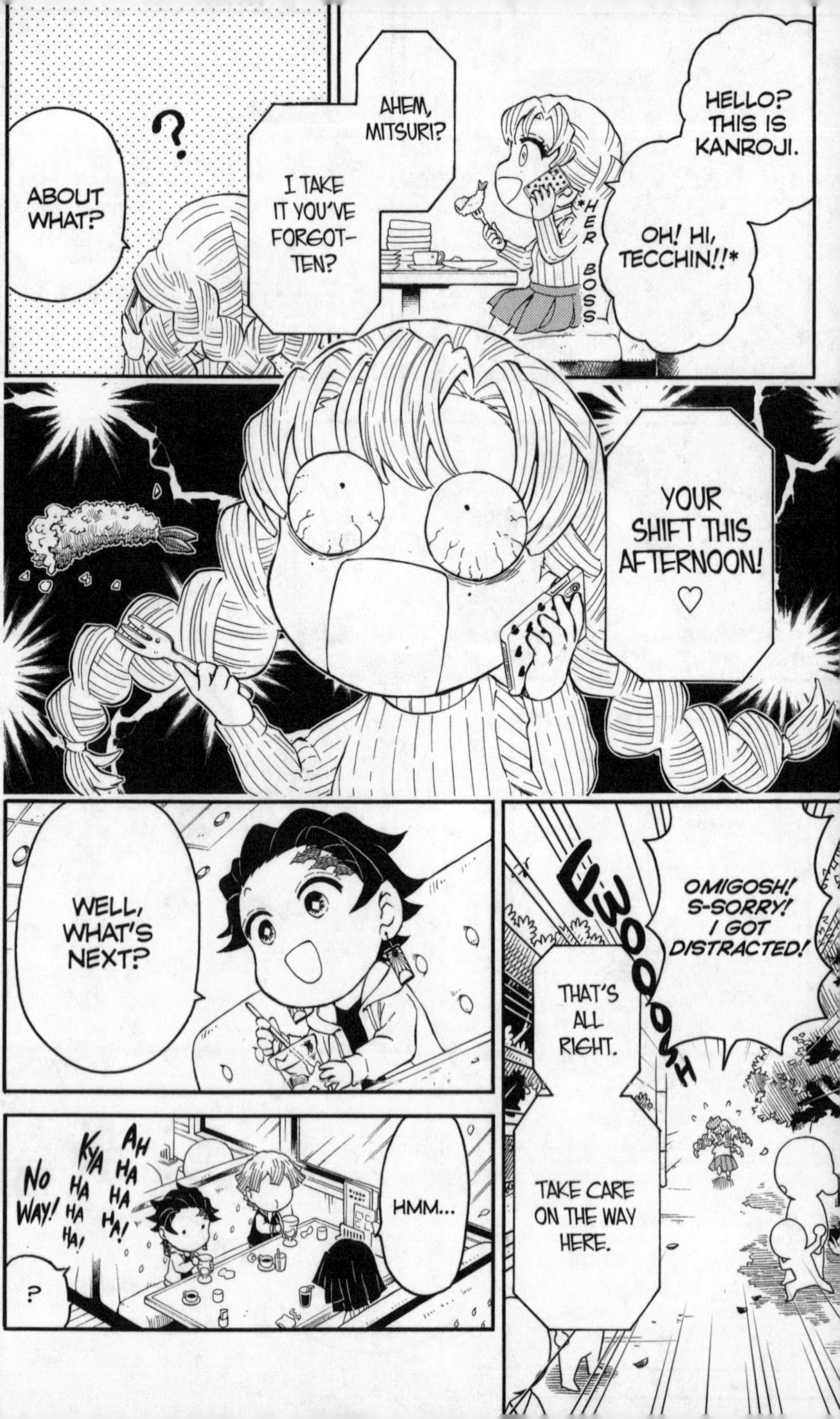
HELLO? THIS IS KANROJI.
OH! HI, TECCHIN!!*
*HER BOSS
AHEM, MITSURI?
I TAKE IT YOU'VE FORGOT-TEN?
?
ABOUT WHAT?
YOUR SHIFT THIS AFTERNOON! ♡
OMIGOSH! S-SORRY! I GOT DISTRACTED!
THAT'S ALL RIGHT.
FWOOOOSH
TAKE CARE ON THE WAY HERE.
WELL, WHAT'S NEXT?
HMM...
AH HA HA HA HA!
KYA HA HA HA HA!
NO WAY!
?

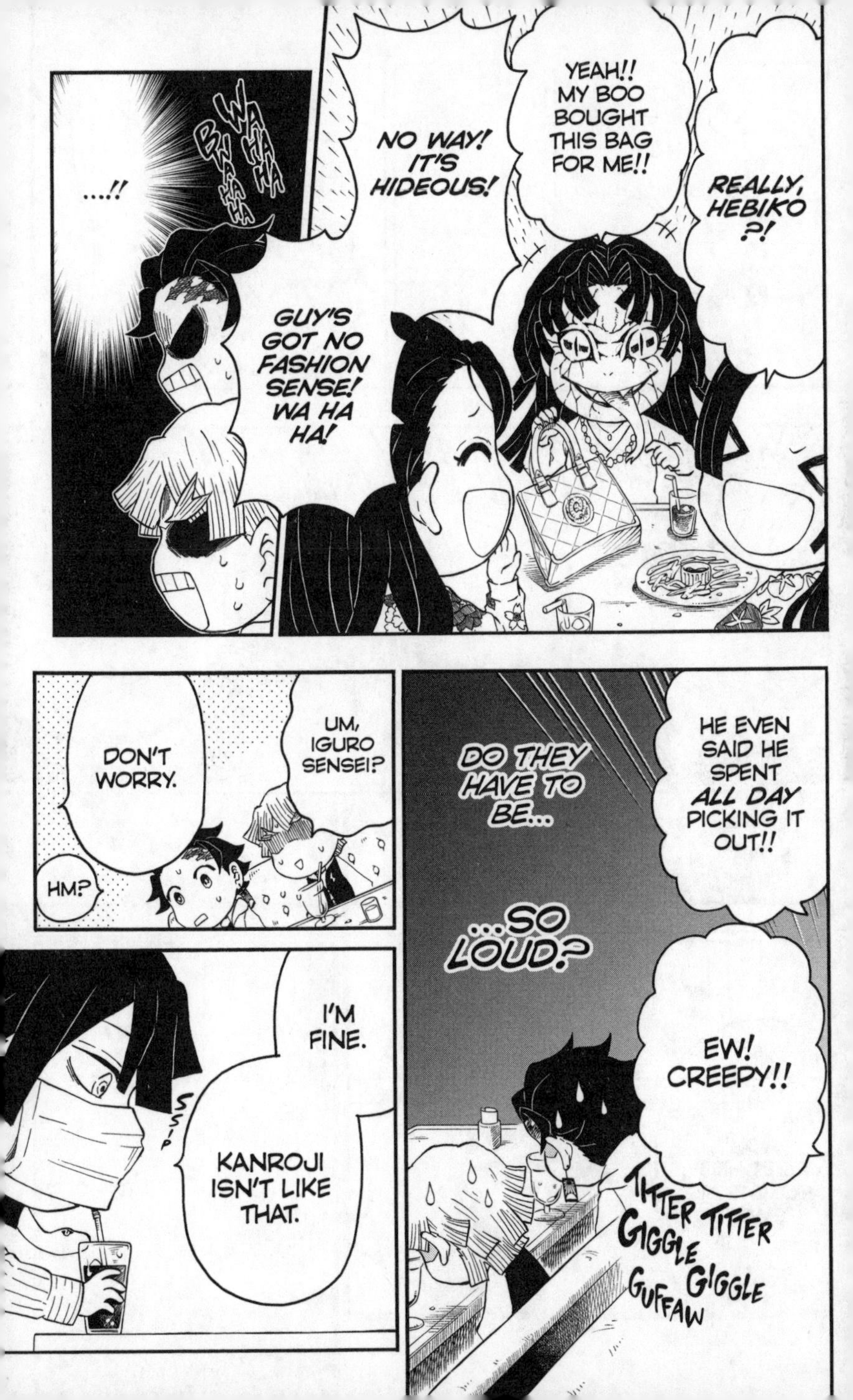
REALLY, HEBIKO?!
YEAH!! MY BOO BOUGHT THIS BAG FOR ME!!
NO WAY! IT'S HIDEOUS!
GUY'S GOT NO FASHION SENSE! WA HA HA!
WA HA HA BWA HA HA
...!!
HE EVEN SAID HE SPENT ALL DAY PICKING IT OUT!!
DO THEY HAVE TO BE...
...SO LOUD?
EW! CREEPY!!
TITTER TITTER GIGGLE GIGGLE GUFFAW
UM, IGURO SENSEI?
HM?
DON'T WORRY.
I'M FINE.
KANROJI ISN'T LIKE THAT.
SSIP

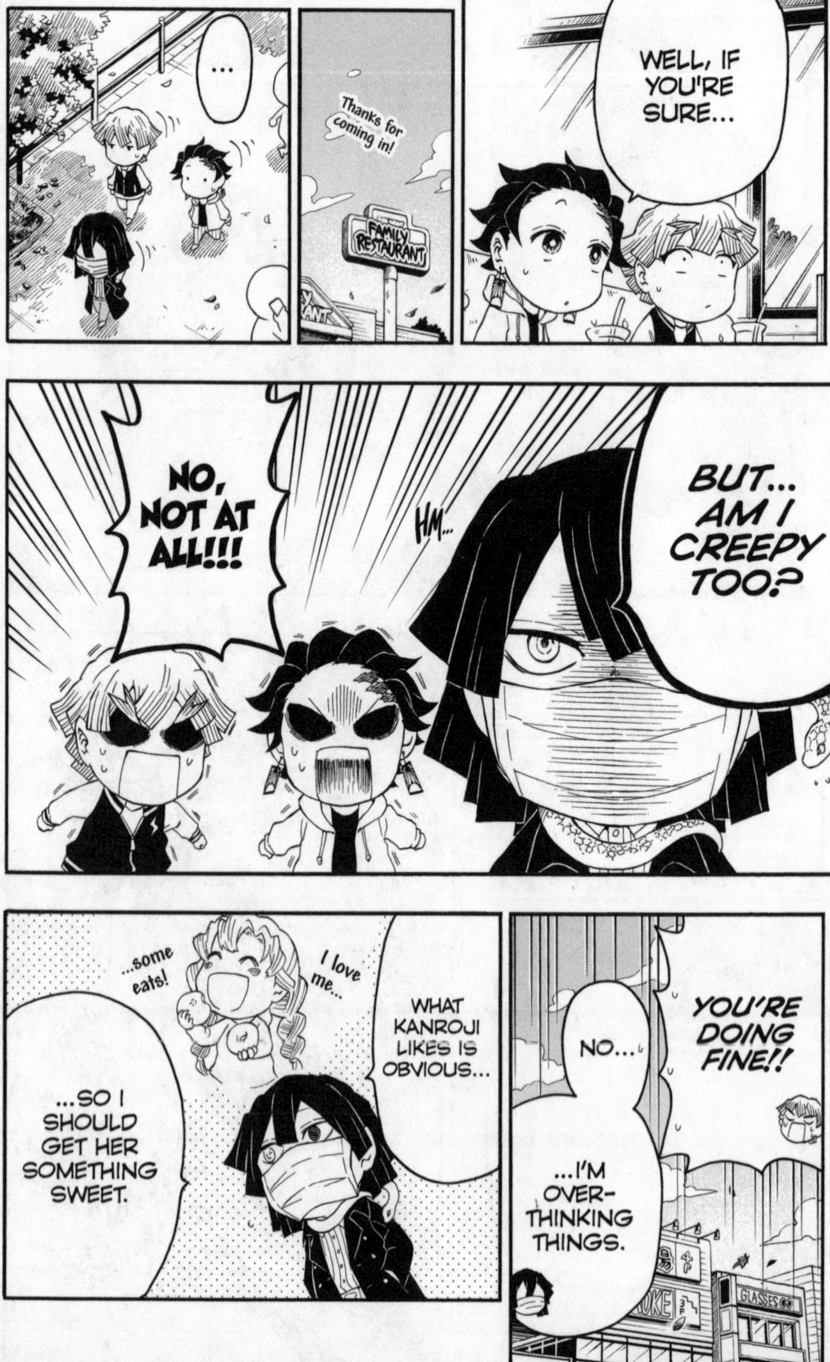
WELL, IF YOU'RE SURE...
Thanks for coming in!
FAMILY RESTAURANT
...
BUT... AM I CREEPY TOO?
HM...
NO, NOT AT ALL!!!
YOU'RE DOING FINE!!
NO...
...I'M OVER-THINKING THINGS.
I love me...
...some eats!
WHAT KANROJI LIKES IS OBVIOUS...
...SO I SHOULD GET HER SOMETHING SWEET.
GLASSES

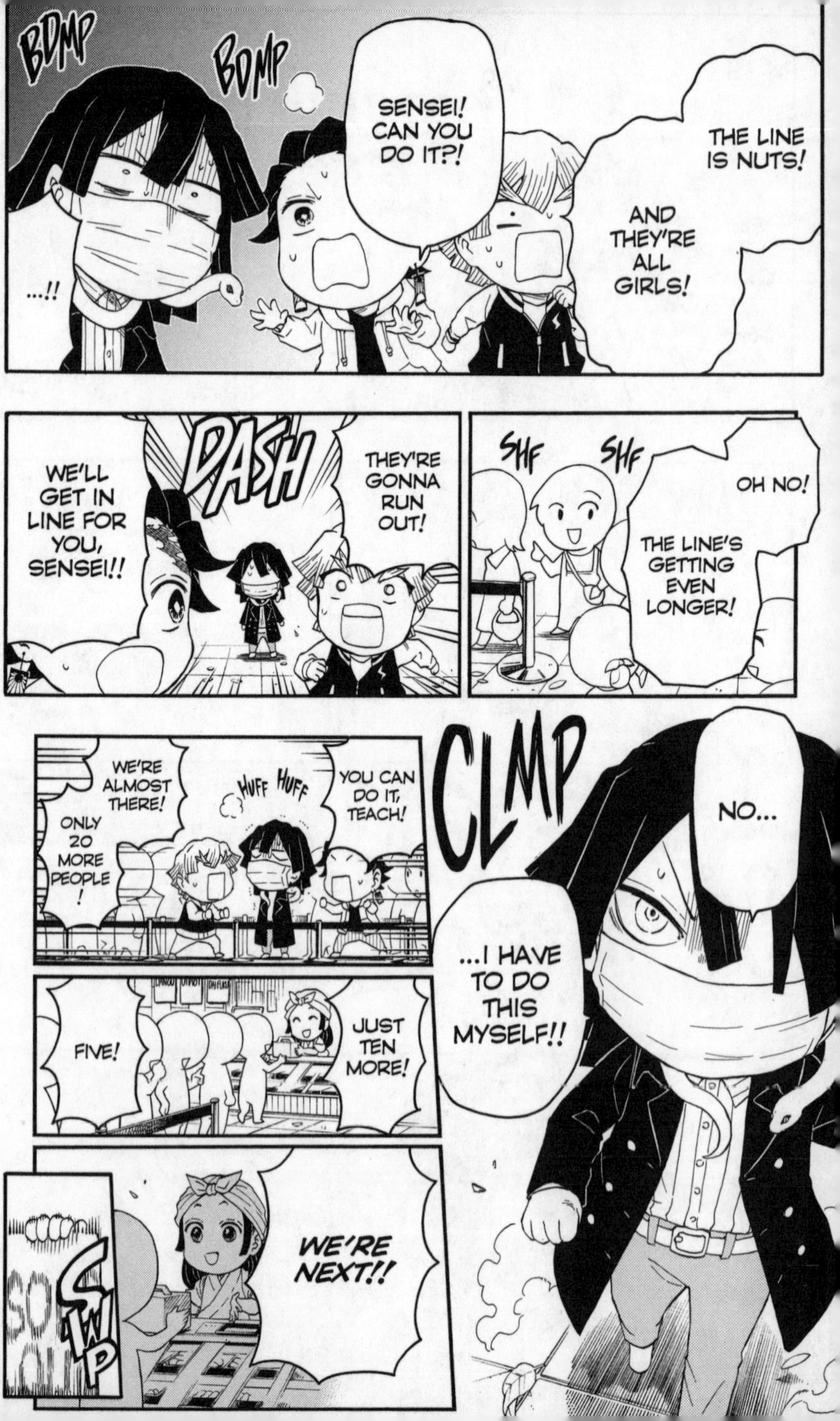
THE LINE IS NUTS!
AND THEY'RE ALL GIRLS!
SENSEI! CAN YOU DO IT?!
BOMP
BDMP
...!!
SHF
SHF
OH NO!
THE LINE'S GETTING EVEN LONGER!
THEY'RE GONNA RUN OUT!
DASH
WE'LL GET IN LINE FOR YOU, SENSEI!!
CLMP
NO...
...I HAVE TO DO THIS MYSELF!!
YOU CAN DO IT, TEACH!
HUFF HUFF
WE'RE ALMOST THERE!
ONLY 20 MORE PEOPLE!
JUST TEN MORE!
FIVE!
WE'RE NEXT!!
SWP

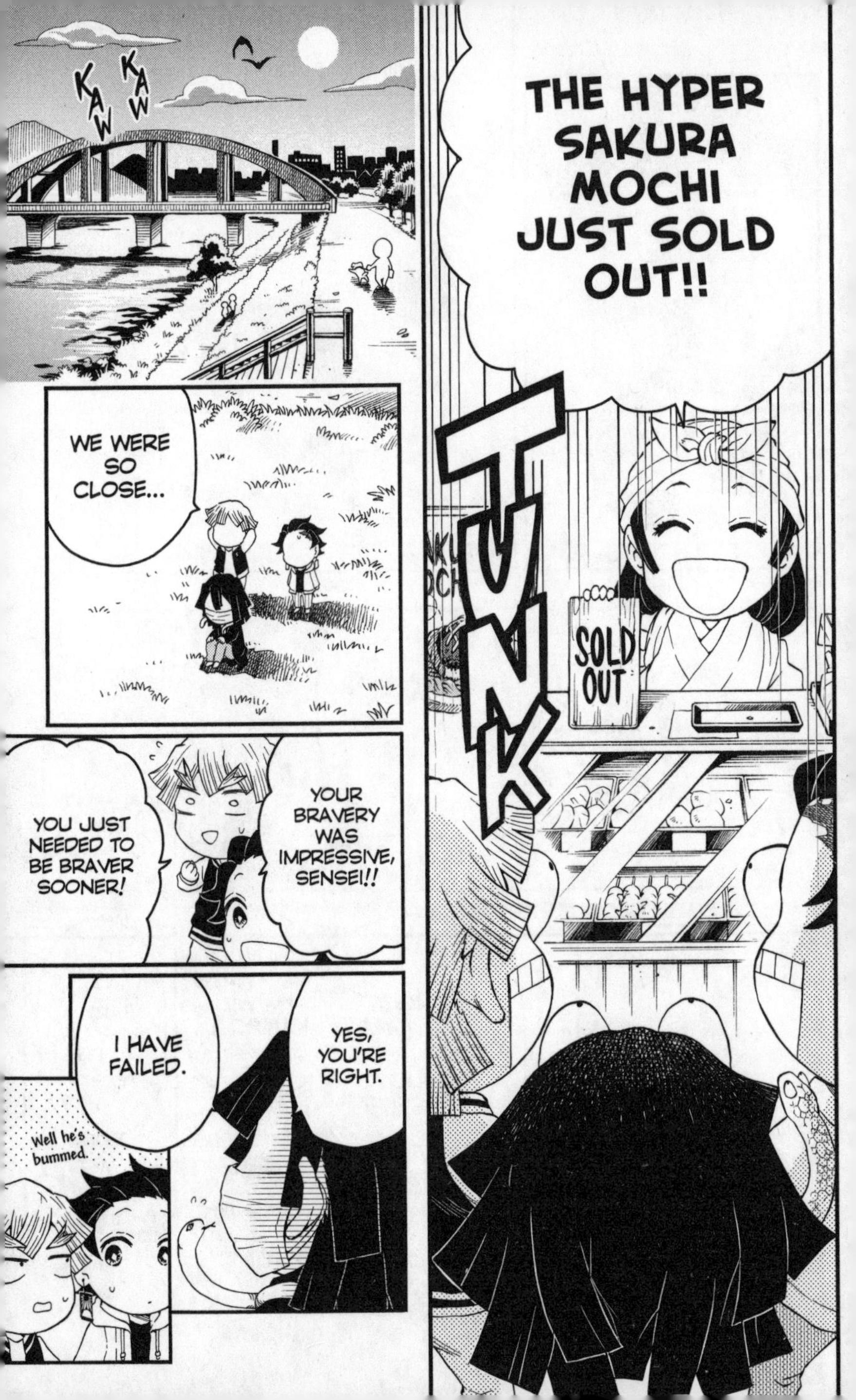
THE HYPER SAKURA MOCHI JUST SOLD OUT!!
TUNK
SOLD OUT
KAW
KAW
WE WERE SO CLOSE...
YOUR BRAVERY WAS IMPRESSIVE, SENSEI!!
YOU JUST NEEDED TO BE BRAVER SOONER!
YES, YOU'RE RIGHT.
I HAVE FAILED.
Well he's bummed.

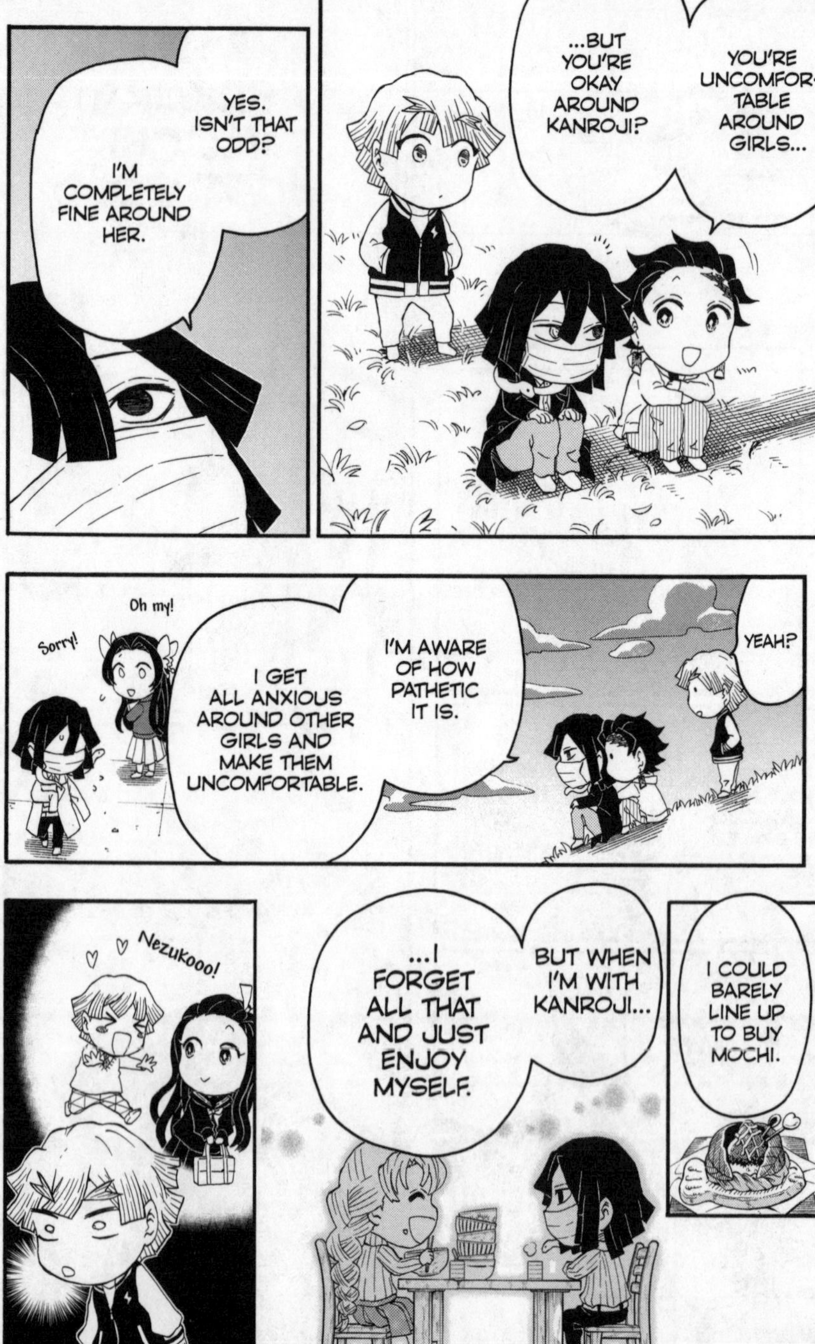
YOU'RE UNCOMFORTABLE AROUND GIRLS...
...BUT YOU'RE OKAY AROUND KANROJI?
YES. ISN'T THAT ODD?
I'M COMPLETELY FINE AROUND HER.
YEAH?
I'M AWARE OF HOW PATHETIC IT IS.
I GET ALL ANXIOUS AROUND OTHER GIRLS AND MAKE THEM UNCOMFORTABLE.
Oh my!
Sorry!
I COULD BARELY LINE UP TO BUY MOCHI.
BUT WHEN I'M WITH KANROJI...
...I FORGET ALL THAT AND JUST ENJOY MYSELF.
Nezukooo!

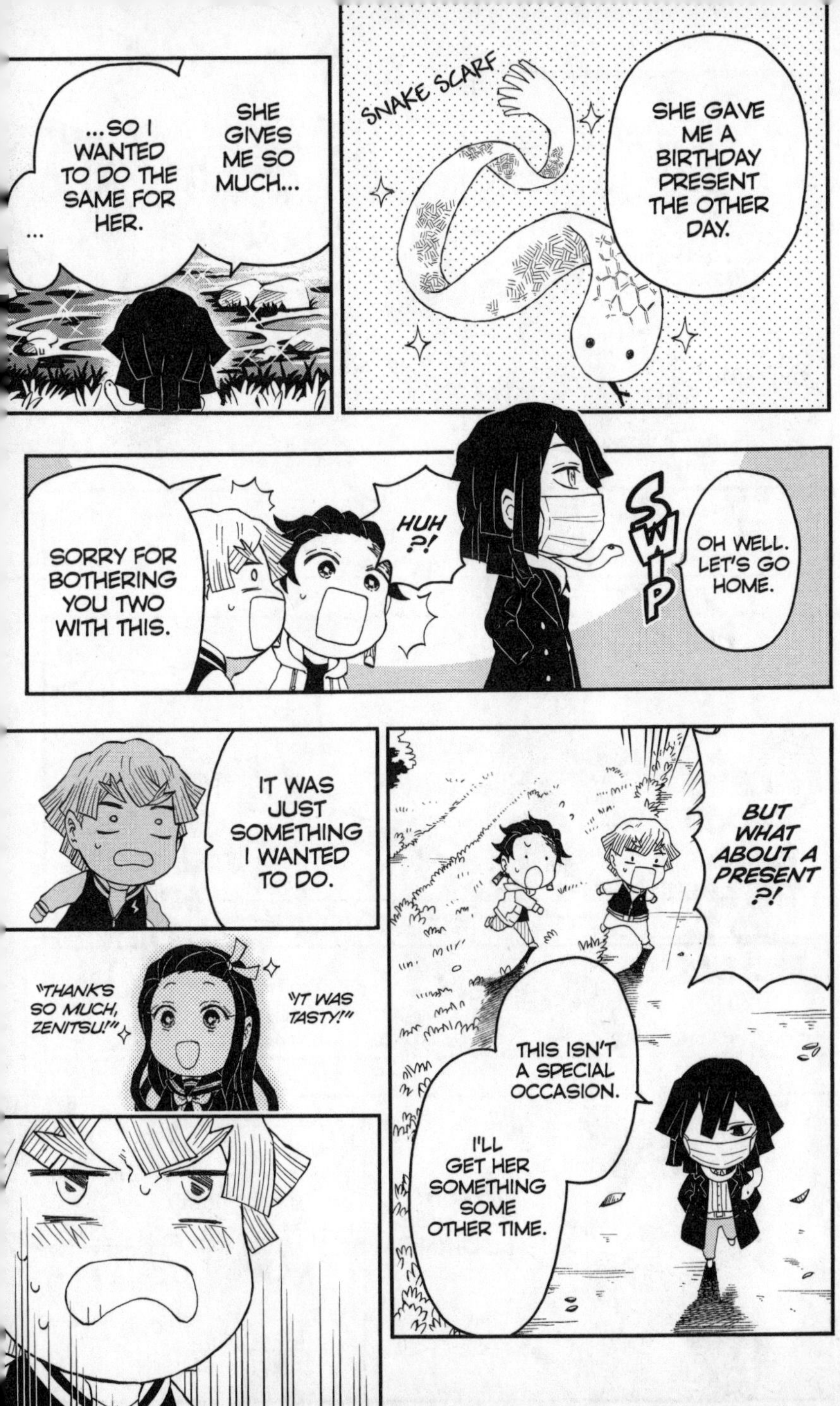
SNAKE SCARF
SHE GAVE ME A BIRTHDAY PRESENT THE OTHER DAY.
SHE GIVES ME SO MUCH...
...SO I WANTED TO DO THE SAME FOR HER.
...
OH WELL. LET'S GO HOME.
SWIP
HUH?!
SORRY FOR BOTHERING YOU TWO WITH THIS.
BUT WHAT ABOUT A PRESENT?!
THIS ISN'T A SPECIAL OCCASION.
I'LL GET HER SOMETHING SOME OTHER TIME.
IT WAS JUST SOMETHING I WANTED TO DO.
"IT WAS TASTY!"
"THANKS SO MUCH, ZENITSU!"

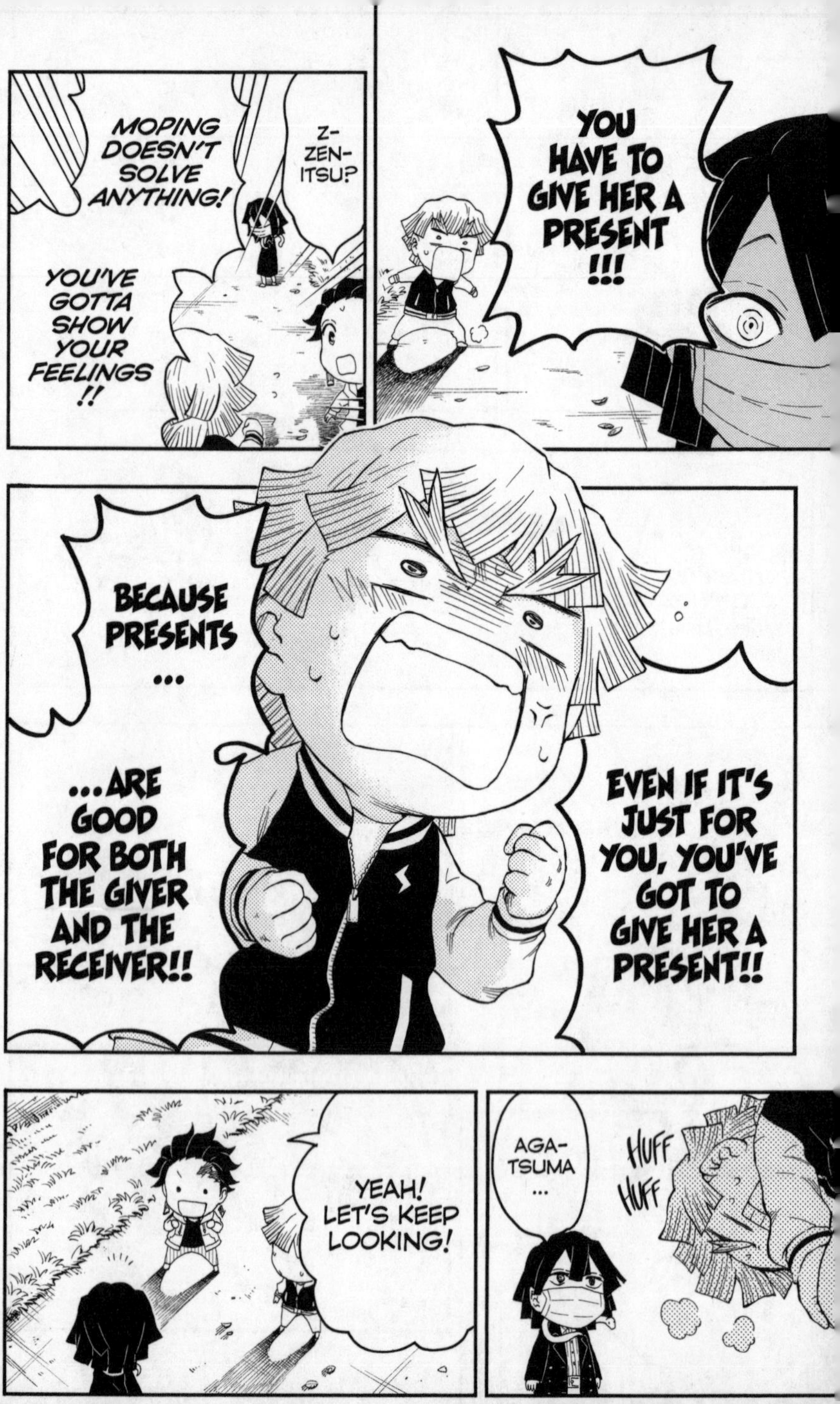
YOU HAVE TO GIVE HER A PRESENT !!!
Z-ZEN-ITSU?
MOPING DOESN'T SOLVE ANYTHING!
YOU'VE GOTTA SHOW YOUR FEELINGS !!
EVEN IF IT'S JUST FOR YOU, YOU'VE GOT TO GIVE HER A PRESENT!!
BECAUSE PRESENTS ...
...ARE GOOD FOR BOTH THE GIVER AND THE RECEIVER!!
AGA-TSUMA ...
HUFF HUFF
YEAH! LET'S KEEP LOOKING!

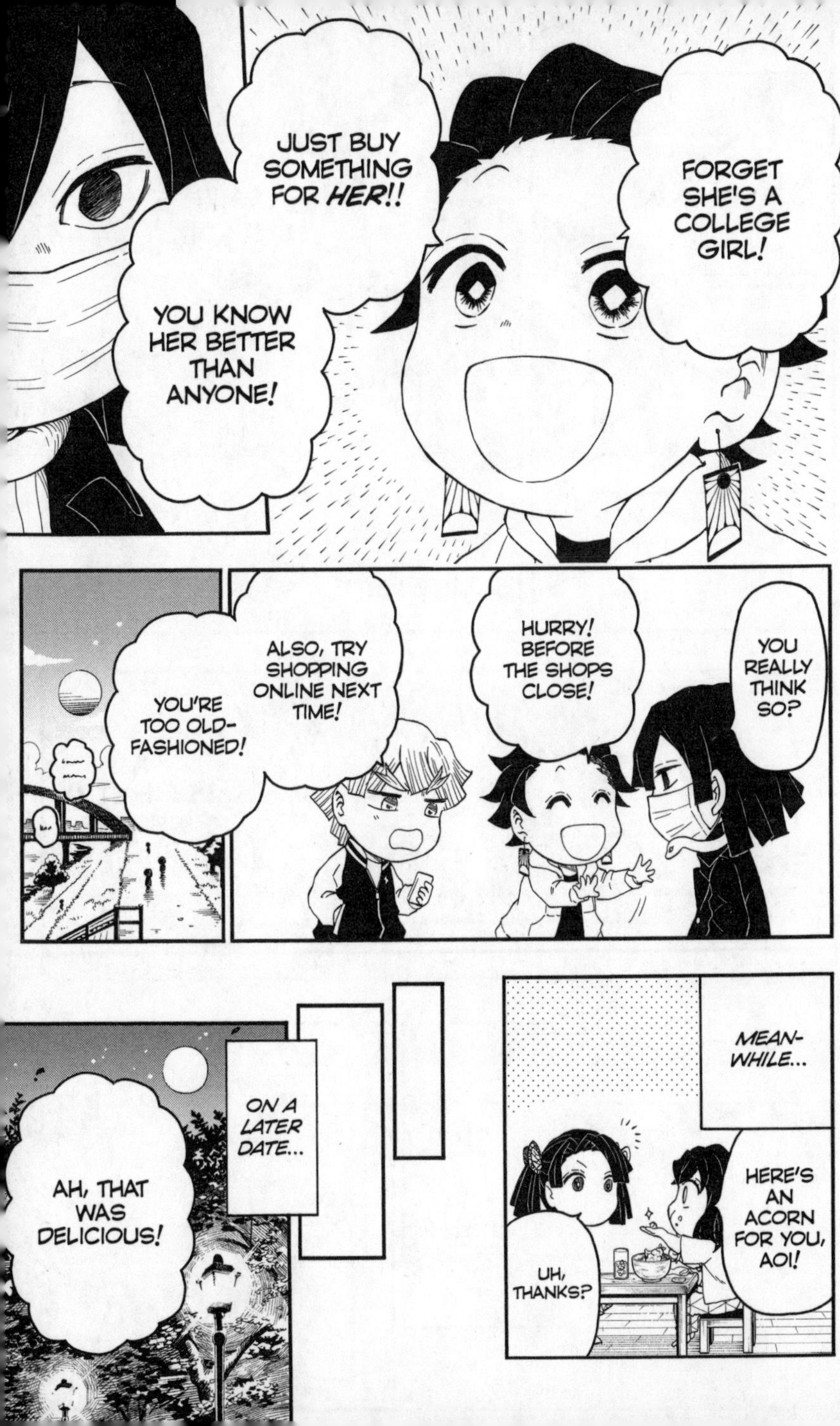
FORGET SHE'S A COLLEGE GIRL!
JUST BUY SOMETHING FOR HER!!
YOU KNOW HER BETTER THAN ANYONE!
YOU REALLY THINK SO?
HURRY! BEFORE THE SHOPS CLOSE!
ALSO, TRY SHOPPING ONLINE NEXT TIME!
YOU'RE TOO OLD-FASHIONED!
MEAN-WHILE...
HERE'S AN ACORN FOR YOU, AOI!
UH, THANKS?
ON A LATER DATE...
AH, THAT WAS DELICIOUS!

BY THE WAY...

...I BROUGHT SOMETHING FOR YOU.

RUSTL

OH?

I LOVE HAVING DINNER WITH YOU!!

OPEN IT UP.

I HAD NO IDEA!

A PRESENT?! WHAT A SURPRISE!!

OOH! WHAT CUTE SOCKS!

I HAD TO GO TO WORK...

...SO I HAVE NO IDEA WHAT IT IS!

TEE HEE HEE!

B DMP

B DMP

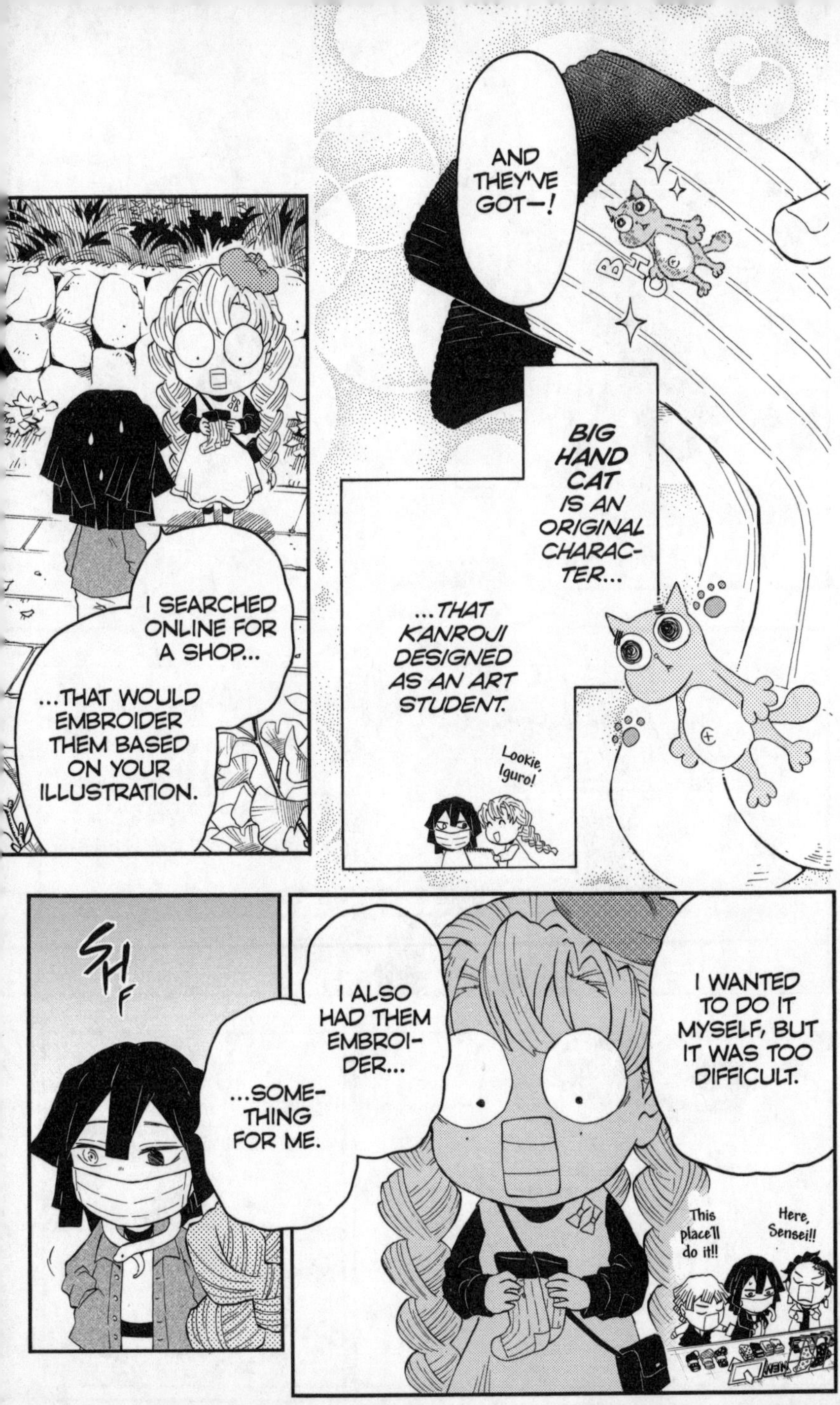
AND THEY'VE GOT—!
BIG HAND CAT IS AN ORIGINAL CHARACTER...
...THAT KANROJI DESIGNED AS AN ART STUDENT.
Lookie, Iguro!
I SEARCHED ONLINE FOR A SHOP...
...THAT WOULD EMBROIDER THEM BASED ON YOUR ILLUSTRATION.
I WANTED TO DO IT MYSELF, BUT IT WAS TOO DIFFICULT.
I ALSO HAD THEM EMBROIDER...
...SOMETHING FOR ME.
Here, Sensei!!
This place'll do it!!
SHF

...

...TO MATCH YOUR SOCKS.

FWIP

A HANDKER-CHIEF...

?!

PLIP

...
BUT
...

IT'S STRANGE.

I WANT MY ART TO MAKE THE WORLD HAPPY...

IGURO... I, UM...

K...

KAN-ROJI?

...RIGHT NOW...

...IT'S MAKING ME THE HAPPIEST OF ALL!

OH...

THAT'S GOOD.

IGURO...

...WOULD GO ON TO BE MUCH KINDER TO TANJIRO AND ZENITSU.

I'M GLAD.

...THEY CAN'T HELP BUT SMILE.

...A CROW CARRYING A LOVE LETTER...

BUT NOW WHEN THEY SEE...

JUST KIDDING!

NO NAP-PING IN CLASS!

CHAPTER 10 DELETED SCENES
USELESS TEACHERS

Kanroji in high school

Q. WHAT WOULD MAKE A GOOD PRESENT FOR KANROJI?

I NEED HELP

HIMEJIMA SENSEI SUGGESTED THE OBVIOUS.

...SO MAYBE FOOD?

SHE ONCE BROUGHT A WHOLE STACK OF BOX LUNCHES...

FOR KANROJI?

That made an impression!

SHINAZUGAWA SENSEI GAVE IT MINIMAL THOUGHT.

MAYBE JUST ONE BIG BOX LUNCH INSTEAD?

KOCHO SENSEI'S IDEA WAS ROMANTIC (BUT UNREALISTIC.)

YOU COULD GROW FLOWERS THERE! HOW ROMANTIC!

BUY HER A FRUIT FIELD! SHE'D LOVE THAT!

UZUI WENT FOR STEREOTYPES.

SO TREAT HER TO A FINE MEAL!!

COLLEGE KIDS ARE POOR!!

HAGANEZUKA SENSEI RECOMMENDED THINGS HE WANTS.

A GRINDSTONE.

GOTO PLAYED IT CASUAL.

SHE'LL LIKE ANYTHING YOU GET HER.

KYOGAI SENSEI WAS THOUGHTFUL.

...SO STUFF HER WITH FOOD.

SHE CAN'T BUY FROM THE SCHOOL KIOSK ANYMORE...

DESPITE BEING HER FORMER TEACHER, RENGOKU WAS STILL RENGOKU.

HOW ABOUT A BAG OF RICE?!

HE DIDN'T BOTHER ASKING TOMIOKA SENSEI.

THAT EXPLAINS IT.

...

WHICH ONLY LEFT...

VOLUME 2 (END)

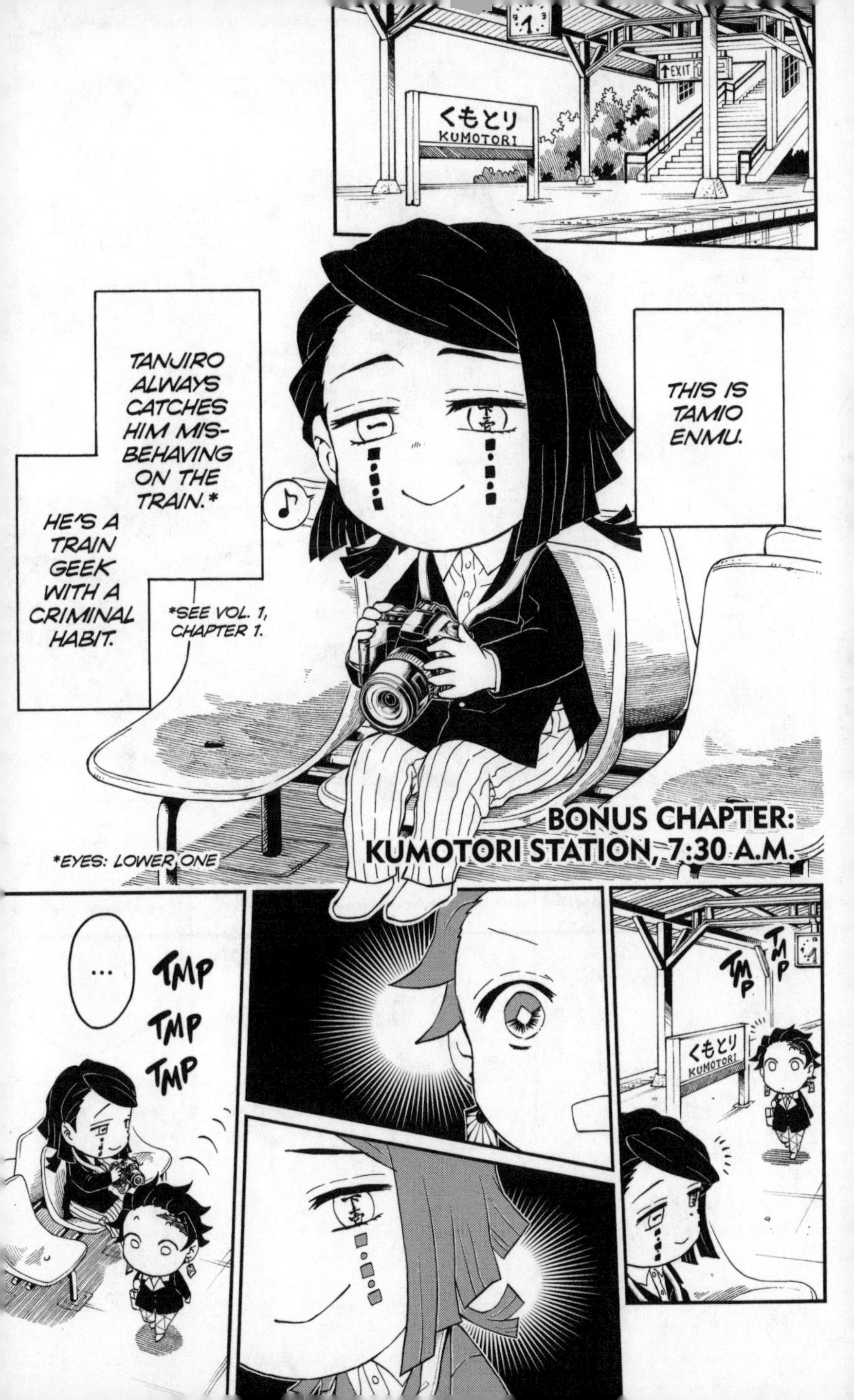

くもとり
KUMOTORI
EXIT
THIS IS TAMIO ENMU.
TANJIRO ALWAYS CATCHES HIM MIS-BEHAVING ON THE TRAIN.*
HE'S A TRAIN GEEK WITH A CRIMINAL HABIT.
*SEE VOL. 1, CHAPTER 1.
♪
BONUS CHAPTER: KUMOTORI STATION, 7:30 A.M.
*EYES: LOWER ONE
TMP
TMP
くもとり
KUMOTORI
...
TMP
TMP
TMP

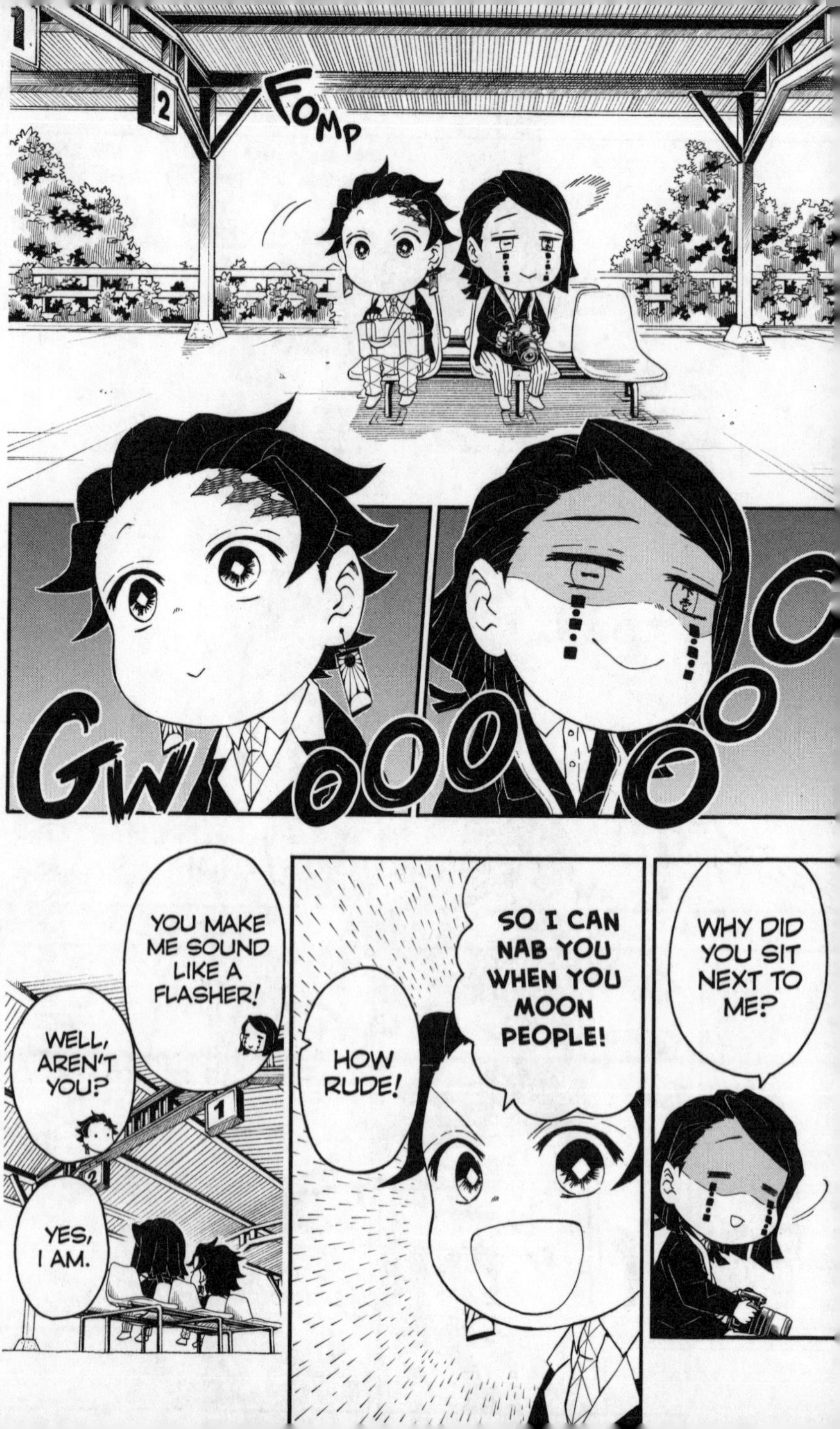
FOMP
GWOOOOOOOO
WHY DID YOU SIT NEXT TO ME?
SO I CAN NAB YOU WHEN YOU MOON PEOPLE!
HOW RUDE!
YOU MAKE ME SOUND LIKE A FLASHER!
WELL, AREN'T YOU?
YES, I AM.

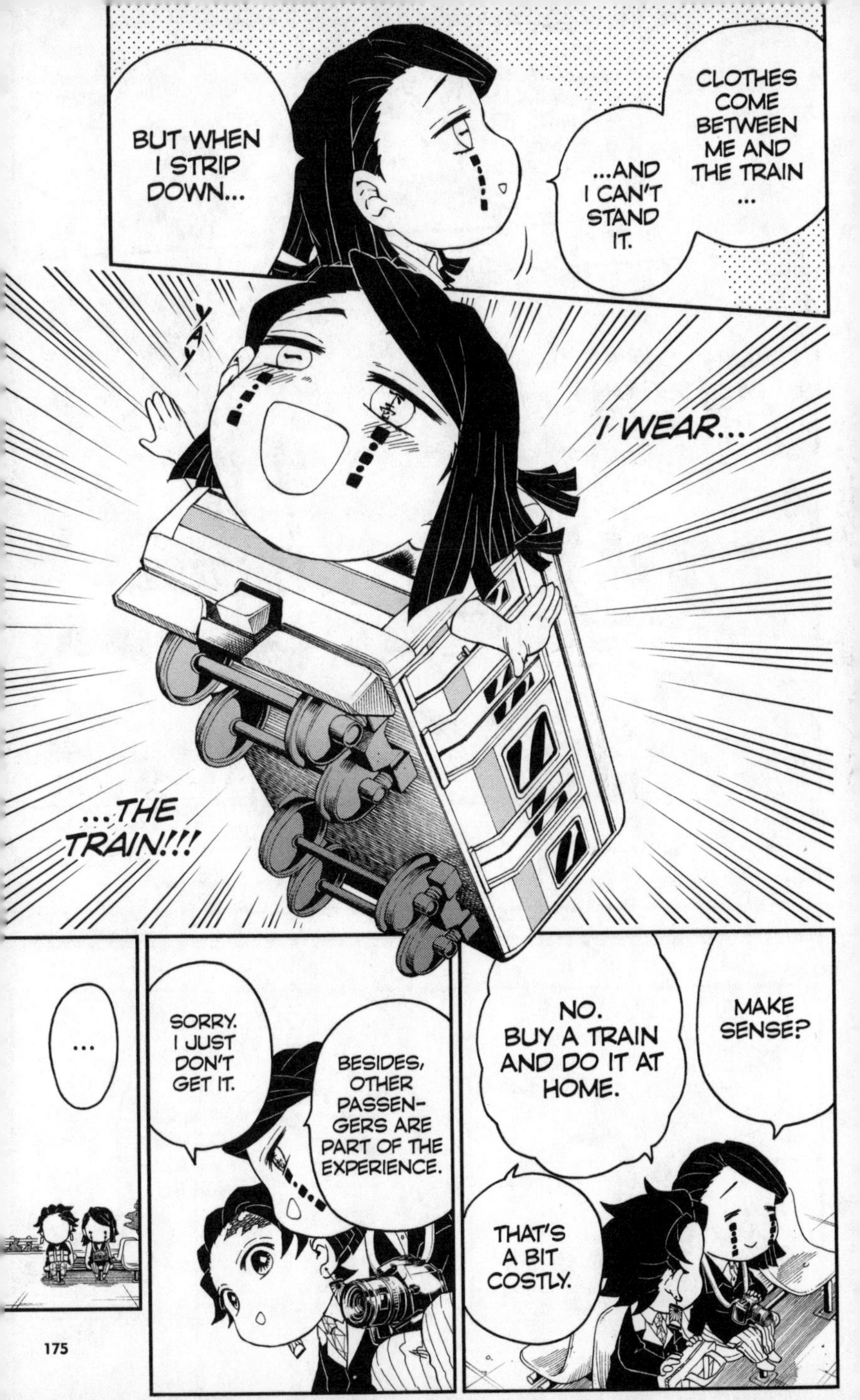
CLOTHES COME BETWEEN ME AND THE TRAIN...
...AND I CAN'T STAND IT.
BUT WHEN I STRIP DOWN...
YAY
I WEAR...
...THE TRAIN!!!
MAKE SENSE?
NO. BUY A TRAIN AND DO IT AT HOME.
THAT'S A BIT COSTLY.
BESIDES, OTHER PASSEN-GERS ARE PART OF THE EXPERIENCE.
SORRY. I JUST DON'T GET IT.
...

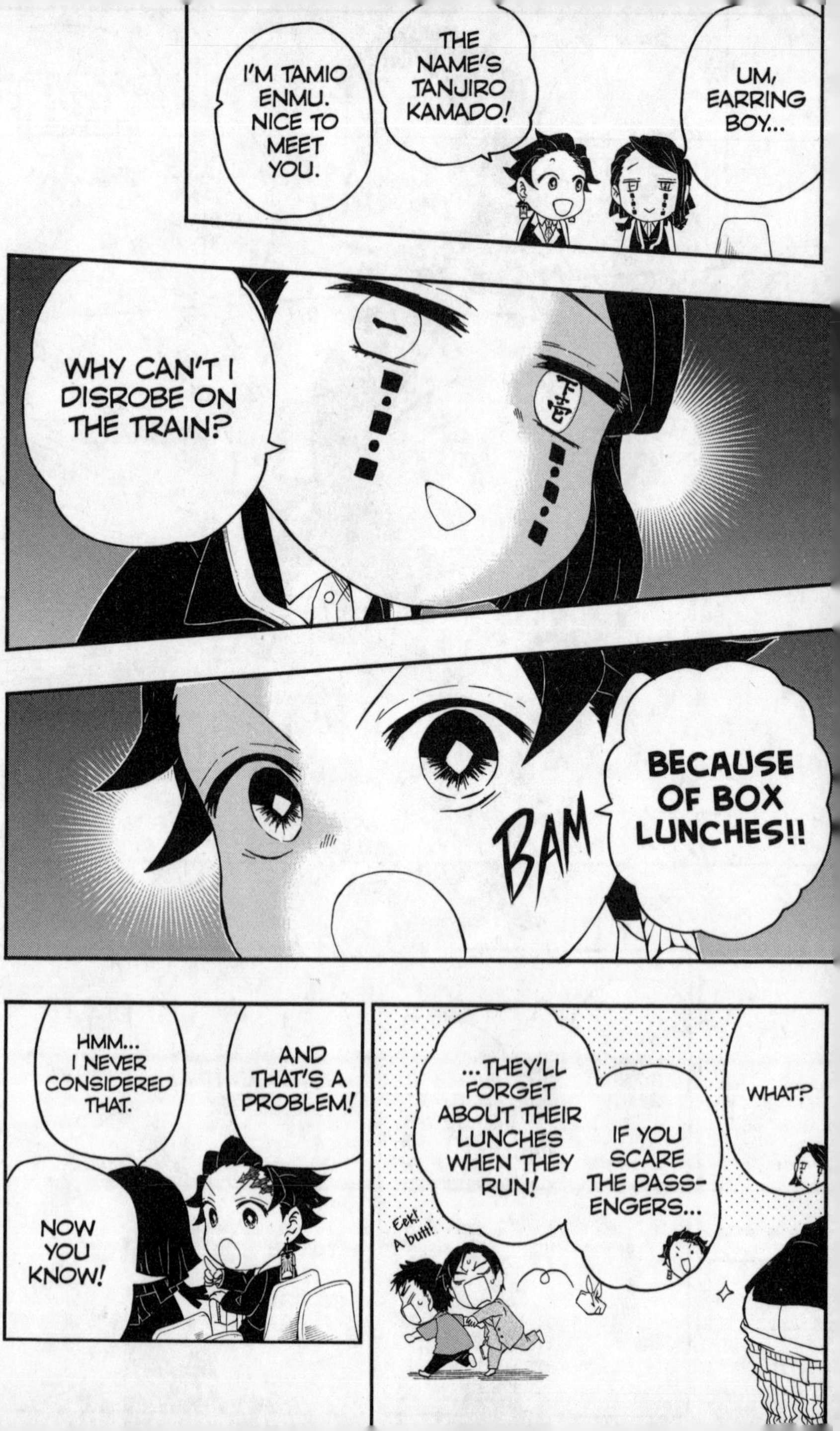
UM, EARRING BOY...
THE NAME'S TANJIRO KAMADO!
I'M TAMIO ENMU. NICE TO MEET YOU.
WHY CAN'T I DISROBE ON THE TRAIN?
BAM
BECAUSE OF BOX LUNCHES!!
WHAT?
IF YOU SCARE THE PASS-ENGERS...
...THEY'LL FORGET ABOUT THEIR LUNCHES WHEN THEY RUN!
Eek! A butt!
AND THAT'S A PROBLEM!
HMM... I NEVER CONSIDERED THAT.
NOW YOU KNOW!

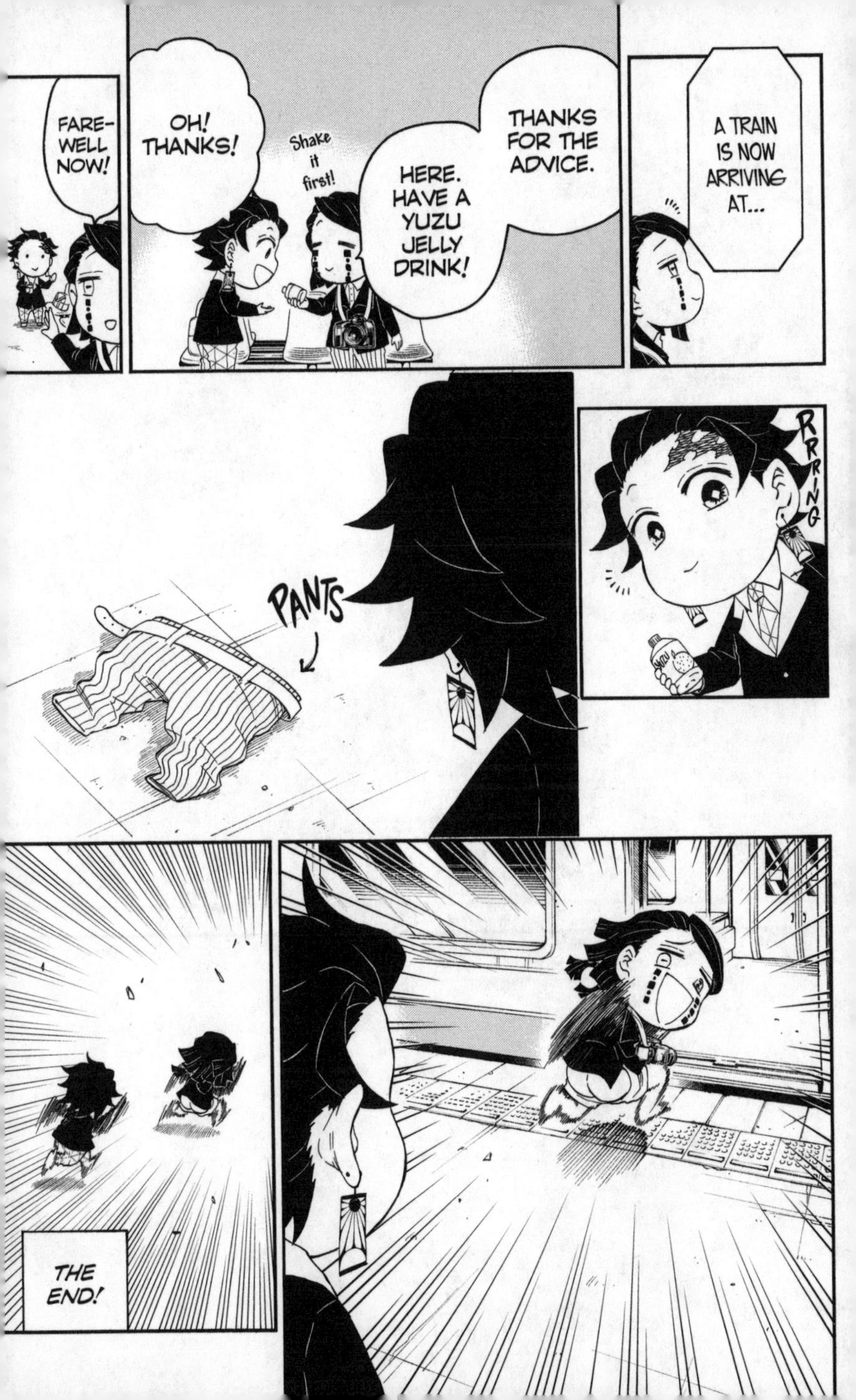
A TRAIN IS NOW ARRIVING AT...
THANKS FOR THE ADVICE.
HERE. HAVE A YUZU JELLY DRINK!
Shake it first!
OH! THANKS!
FARE-WELL NOW!
RRRING
PANTS
THE END!

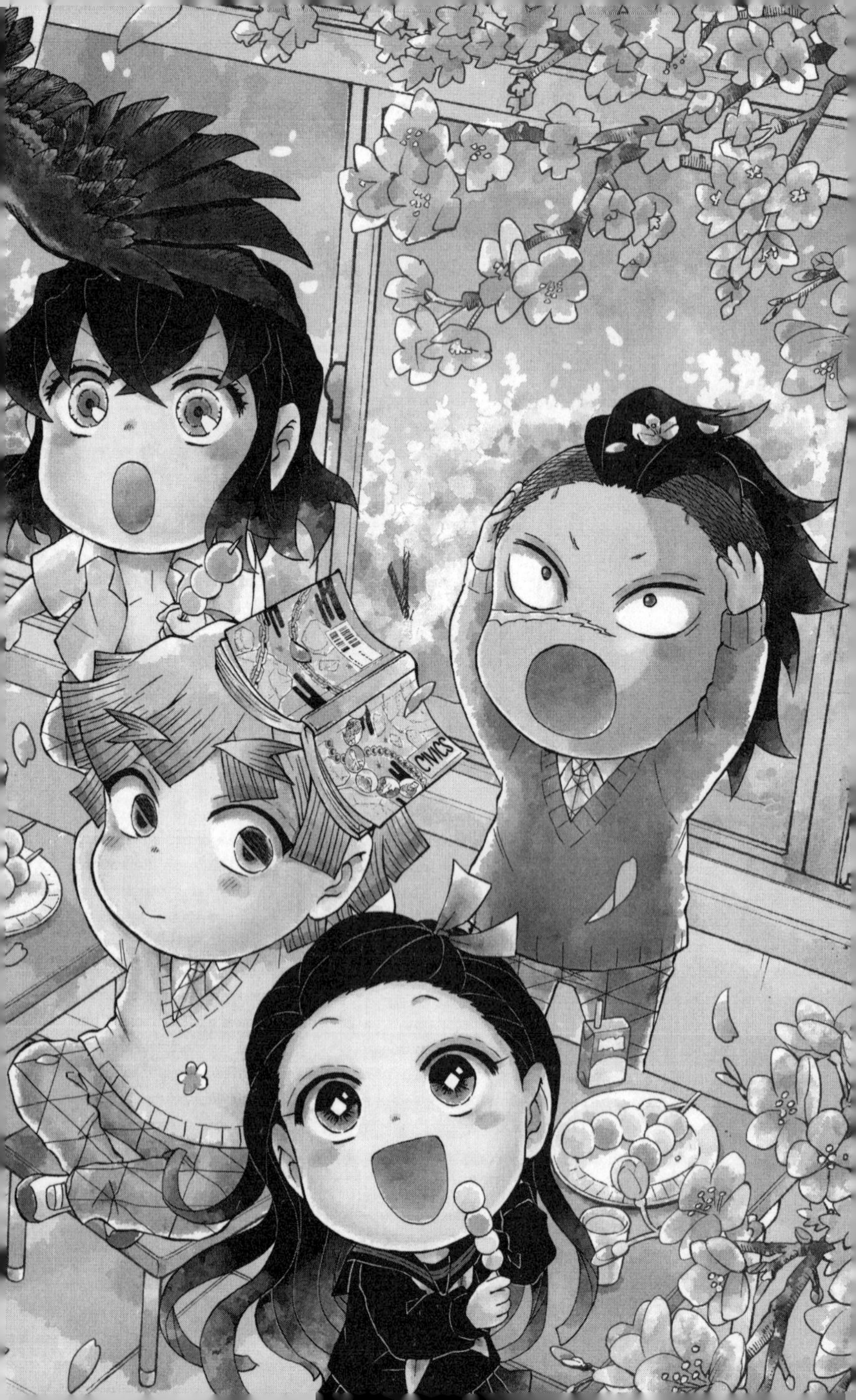
CIVICS

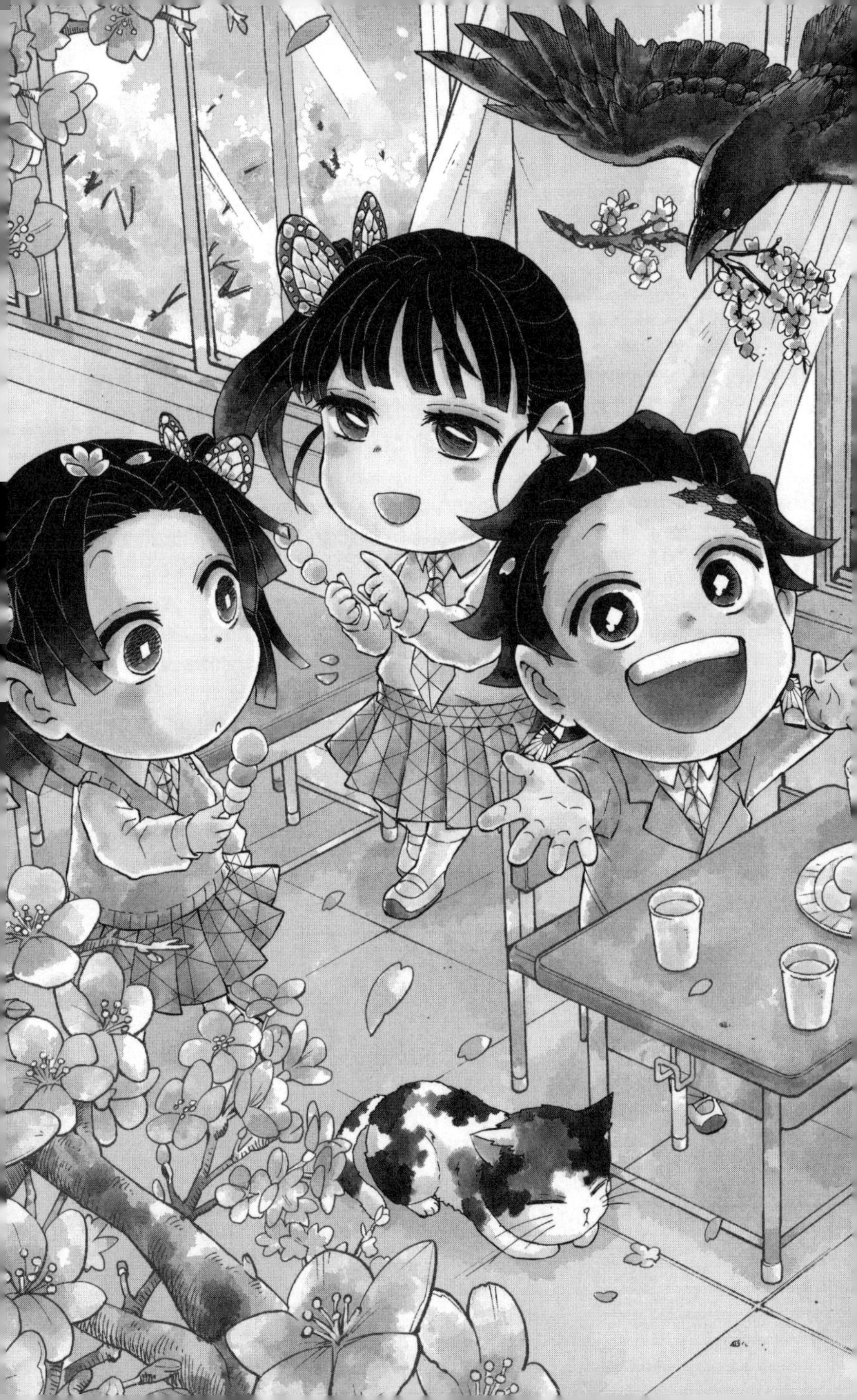

AFTERWORD

Welcome to volume 2! Thanks for reading! Just like with volume 1, this was only possible through the efforts of a lot of people, so thank you all very much. I'll be counting on you in the future too.

This volume goes on sale in July, and the story takes place from early summer to autumn, so I'm thrilled to see how the seasons have synced up. What a happy coincidence!

The serialized releases never match the actual season, so I drew the preceding two-page spread to match with the real world. Without any connection to the story, the sakura trees are in full bloom! I have to say, I like that illustration, but I was never satisfied with the color illustration of Makomo and the others for chapter 9, so I put them on the back cover of this volume.

I suspect volume 3 will take place from autumn to winter. Nothing is slated yet, though, so here's hoping it gets the green light!

STAFF

REGULARS
Nagashima
Kantaro Kumano
Keisuke Futta

HELPERS
Kojiro
Tachi Biwa

SPECIAL THANKS
Saikyo Jump editor: Toide-san
The *Demon Slayer: Kimetsu no Yaiba* original manga team
Graphic novel editor: Abe-san
Designers: Deguchi-san, Abe-san
Original creator: Koyoharu Gotouge
All the readers!

Natsuki Hokami

帆上夏希.

Good work! This is Gotouge! Volume 2 of *Kimetsu Academy* is on sale! Here's a big thanks to Hokami Sensei, the editors, assistants, and readers! The number of characters playing a role is ramping up, making these pages more boisterous than ever!

As the fun continues to take off, I hope you'll come along for the ride!!

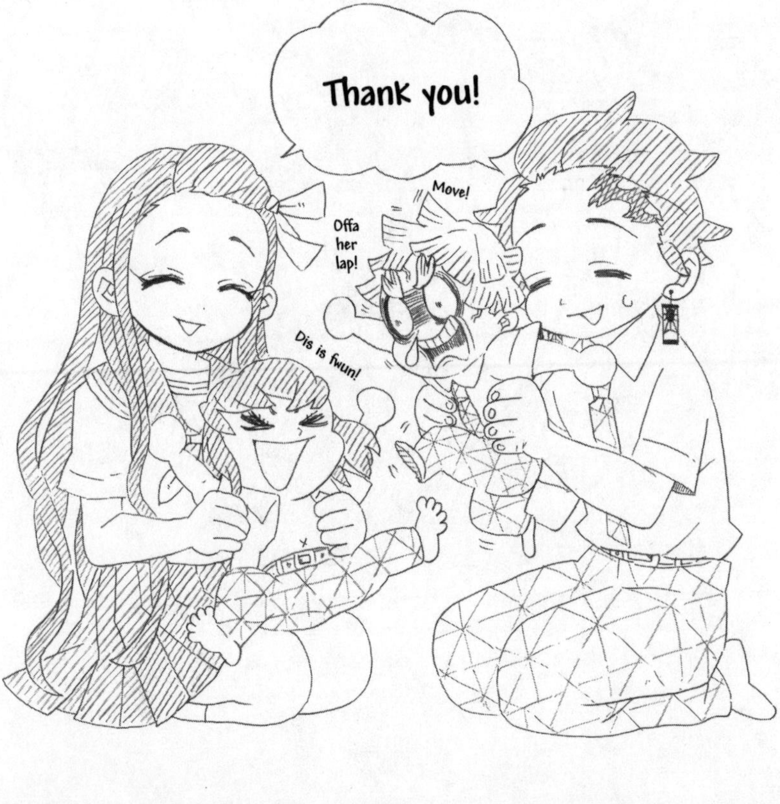
Thank you!
Move!
Offa her lap!
Dis is fwun!

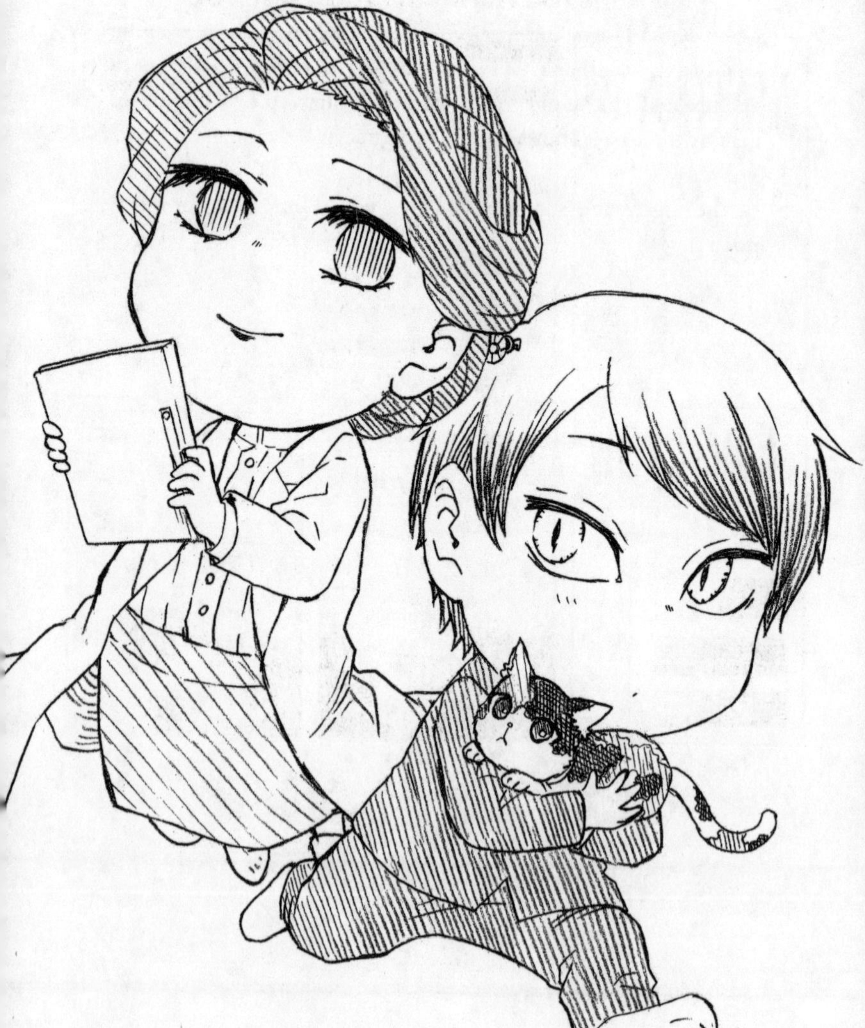

FIRST-YEAR TEXTBOOK DESIGNS FOR KIMETSU ACADEMY HIGH SCHOOL

CIVICS
CHEMISTRY
MATH A
BIOLOGY
HISTORY
ENGLISH
I

For a while, I only had a rough idea for these,
but I asked my staff and they came up with proper designs.
The other grades basically look the same.

You're reading the wrong way!

In keeping with the original Japanese comic format, *Demon Slayer: Kimetsu Academy* reads from right to left, meaning that action, sound effects, and word-balloon order are completely reversed from English order.

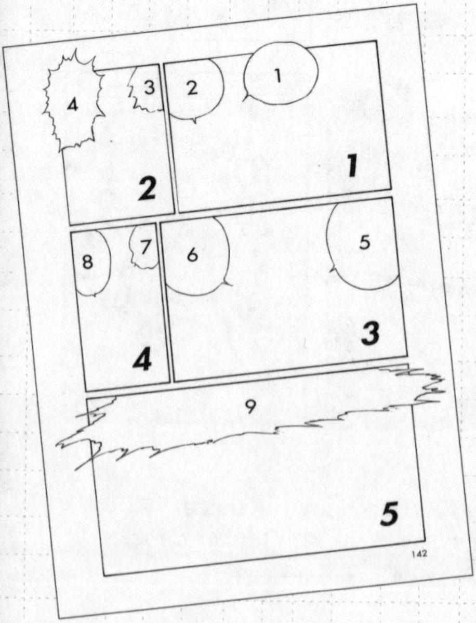
1
2
1
3
4
2
5
6
3
7
8
4
9
5
142

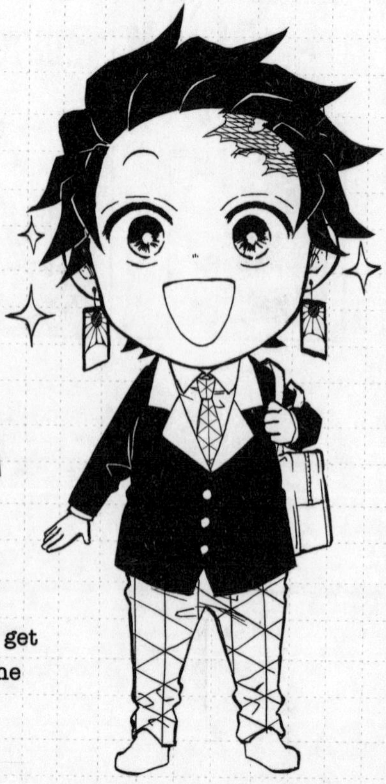

Check out the diagram shown here to get the hang of things, and then turn to the other side of the book to get started!